IMPOTENT FATHERS

The Marlborough Family, 1778, by Sir Joshua Reynolds, The Red Drawing Room, Blenheim Palace, Oxon. Reproduced by kind permission of His Grace the Duke of Marlborough.

IMPOTENT FATHERS

Patriarchy and Demographic Crisis in the Eighteenth-Century Novel

Brian McCrea

DELAWARE

Newark: University of Delaware Press
London: Associated University Presses

Associated University Presses
440 Forsgate Drive
Cranbury, NJ 08512

Associated University Presses
16 Barter Street
London WC1A 2AH, England

Associated University Presses
P.O. Box 338, Port Credit
Mississauga, Ontario
Canada L5G 4L8

The paper used in this publication meets the requirements
of the American National Standard for Permanence of Paper
for Printed Library Materials Z39.48–1984.

Library of Congress Cataloging-in-Publication Data

McCrea, Brian.
    Impotent fathers : patriarchy and demographic crisis in the eighteenth-century British novel / Brian McCrea.
        p.   cm.
    Includes bibliographical references and index.
    ISBN 0–87413–656–3 (alk. paper)
    1. English fiction—18th century—History and criticism. 2. Patriarchy in literature. 3. Literature and society—England—History—18th century.
4. Demographic transition—England—History—18th century. 5. Inheritance and succession in literature. 6. Power (Social sciences) in literature.
7. Property in literature. 8. Kinship in literature. 9. Family in literature.
I. Title.
PR858.P34M37   1998
823'.509355—DC21   97–24000
                                                                    CIP

PRINTED IN THE UNITED STATES OF AMERICA

For Sara (once more),
Joanne, and Abbey

Contents

Acknowledgments

Alistair Duckworth read what purported to be a complete first draft of this book and pointed out, with characteristic but kind rigor, that it was much less than that. His comments guided and helped me during several years of adding to and revising the manuscript. Paul Hunter read a later draft and helped me to recast the introduction and chapter 4; Dana Peterson and Elizabeth Langland read an early version of chapter 6. Their criticisms were bracing (to understate the case a bit) and helped me to make my argument both more pointed and less tendentious.

Portions of this book have appeared in articles in the *Indiana Journal of Hispanic Literature*, the *Journal of Narrative Technique*, *Studies in the Novel*, and *Eighteenth-Century Fiction*. I am grateful to the editors of those journals, particularly to Elaine Riehm, for the encouragement they gave me.

The Division of Sponsored Research at the University of Florida supported me with a research grant in the summer of 1995. I have also had the good fortune to participate in two summer institutes and a summer seminar sponsored by the National Endowment for the Humanities. I take great pleasure in recalling the superb hospitality with which my family and I were treated by Edward H. Friedman during our 1989 visit to Arizona State University, by Hans Aarsleff during our 1990 visit to Princeton University, and by Peter Medine during our 1992 visit to the University of Arizona.

Sir Joshua Reynolds's portrait of the Marlborough family is reproduced by kind permission of His Grace the Duke of Marlborough.

The dedication acknowledges my three wonderful but sometimes startlingly different daughters. From them I have learned to treat with suspicion all theorizing about the father-daughter bond and to be wary of generalizations about patriarchal power.

The Frontispiece

Sir Joshua Reynolds worked on this portrait of George, 4th Duke of Marlborough, and his family during the late 1770s, altering it even after its showing at the Royal Academy in 1778. The duke is not at the center of the portrait, that place being given to his wife, Caroline. She, while subject to our gaze, stands outside the line of vision of the duke, the lines of vision of her children, even as her right hand links the duke and the Marquess of Blandford to the rest of the family.

There was no 2d Duke of Marlborough The only son of John Churchill died of smallpox on 20 February 1702–3, before his father was to become the hero of Blenheim and Ramillies and then 1st Duke of Marlborough. Upon Marlborough's death in 1722, he was succeeded by his eldest daughter, Henrietta; upon her death in 1733, the title was assumed by Charles Spencer, 5th Earl of Sunderland, the third son of Marlborough's second daughter, Anne. To become the 3d Duke of Marlborough, Spencer not only had to have his older brothers predecease him, he also had to give his Sunderland properties to his younger brother, per his parents' wedding agreement. This meant that until the death of the duchess dowager, Marlborough's famous Sarah, in 1744, Spencer could not occupy Blenheim Palace and actually had less income than his brother. Spencer's son, the duke we see here, assumed the title upon his father's death in 1758. He would outlive everyone in the picture, apart from the marquess and the youngest child, Lady Anne, who shrinks in fright at an ugly mask thrust at her by her sister, Lady Charlotte.

At what, I wonder, is everyone in this portrait looking? And what is happening at the portrait's center, the section that, I like to think, Reynolds kept reworking? The left side of the portrait is easy reading, particularly for anyone who has been in a depart-

11

ment of English during the past twenty years. Father and son are privileged by patriarchal power. Between them the family jewels pass (in a morocco case held by the marquess), and with them both political and aesthetic authority reside (in his left hand, the duke holds a cameo portrait of the emperor Augustus). The subjects on the right side look away from the patriarch and suggest the entertaining but also frightening possibility of masking, of pretending to be someone not marked by the father.

In the chapters that follow, I do not interpret or explain the enigmatic figure at the center of Reynolds's portrait. Instead, I suggest her affinity with characters at the center of novels by men and women alike. As the patriarch becomes a decentered, even marginalized figure, women in eighteenth-century novels have great but uncertain power. Reynolds, apparently, could balance the two sides of his portrait only by having his subjects avoid looking at each other and by centering it on the duchess, whom he had painted as a young woman, a young mother, and a peeress. In novels of the period, however, characters come to see the cost of representing masculine authority through the female line; the passions, needs, and rights of the women who stand at the center of succession, as the duchess stands at the center of this portrait, become both impossible to dismiss and difficult to speak.

IMPOTENT FATHERS

Introduction:

The Orphan Heiress: Demography, Law, and Patriarchy in the Eighteenth-Century Novel

Because the impediment is removed by death.

—James Ley, Earl of Marlborough,
A Learned Treatise Concerning Wards and Liveries (1642)

Literary women, readers and writers alike, have long been confused and intimidated by the patriarchal etiology that defines a solitary Father God as the only creator of all things.

—Sandra M. Gilbert (1979)

Nancy Armstrong has described fiction, particularly eighteenth- and nineteenth-century British fiction, "both as the document and as the agency of cultural history."[1] This book will study how writers in eighteenth-century Britain at once recorded and helped to define "a major demographic crisis among the English landed elite," a "demographic slump"[2] that lasted from 1650 to 1740. We only can speculate about the causes of the "slump"—the most convincing speculation being that of E. Leroy Ladurie, who argues that a "microbial unification of the world" took place early in the seventeenth century, with explorers and traders bringing to Europe diseases for which immunity systems were not prepared.[3] But the effects of the crisis, as documented by Lawrence and Jeanne C. Fawtier Stone, are clear. In England during the period 1650–1740, "about a half of all landowners failed to produce an adult male heir to succeed them. Moreover . . . less than half of those fathers who did produce an adult male heir lived to see them [*sic*] married" (Stones, 76). This "failure to reproduce" was both widespread and new; amongst the "cohort of owners" the

15

Stones study, the proportion of fathers "who died leaving no sons to succeed them rose from 26 per cent [the figure for the last half of the seventeenth century] to the extraordinary figure of 52 per cent" (101).

The demographic crisis of 1650–1740 greatly complicated "the descent of property and seats from generation to generation" (101). Even in those cases in which fathers left sons to survive them, the odds were against the father's living to see the son marry. "This meant that many more oldest sons were left free to choose their own brides without interference from their fathers" (103)—the case of Samuel Richardson's Mr. B. and of Miss Sidney Biddulph's brother, Sir George. In those cases in which "a failure in the male line" threatened patrilinear descent, families developed ingenious "strategies of indirect inheritance . . . to save the principle of family continuity" (104). Basic to all these strategies, as the Stones catalog them, is their reliance upon "fictive kin." Whether in the early and relatively easy practice of giving "the son and heir of an heiress his mother's surname as a first name" or in the "more radical" practice (seen in Tobias Smollett's Matthew Bramble and in Lord M.'s plans for the "child" of Lovelace and Clarissa) of changing the surname of a husband or relative "who . . . abandoned his own name" (128, 129), a family might preserve its "ancient and venerated surname . . . by a series of pious fictions" (127). A third practice—modification of the surname "by tacking on by hyphenation the name of the benefactor" (135)—also becomes popular during this period, as "many blocks of real estate and family seats were passing . . . through heiresses of ancient families as the male lines failed" (136).

While work on the demographic crisis has not as yet played an important role in studies of the novel, historians have incorporated it into a basic reunderstanding of kinship and property in the seventeenth and eighteenth centuries—a reunderstanding that is relevant to the novel, insofar as marriage and family are both its great theme and its central scene. In a series of essays published in the 1940s and 1950s,[4] Sir John Habakkuk accounted for the "Rise of Great Estates" in the seventeenth and eighteenth centuries by suggesting that English families used "strict settlements" to achieve that end (and thus to empower themselves). In Habakkuk's account, a strict settlement allowed families to limit the power of heirs to alter the "entail," that is, to alter the course of an estate's descent. Both Habakkuk and his recent critics agree upon the typical marriage settlement used by English families in this period: a life interest in the patrimony would be secured in the groom, with the property entailed to the oldest living son produced by the marriage. "Habakkuk argued that if resettlement took place upon the son's marriage, before the death of the life-tenant [the father] and the son accepted a life estate while relinquishing his remainder, this had the potential of making entail permanent."[5] In other words, a son of marriageable age had to decide if he wanted to give up his right to break the entail in order to receive property and/or income "up front." If the son waited for his father to die, he entered his patrimony as a "tenant," free to entail it as he pleased. Habakkuk's account of the strict settlement, then, assumed that fathers lived to see their sons marry; indeed, it assumed that sons might calculate that their fathers would live well past their marriages.

Using evidence taken from T. H. Hollingsworth's "Demography of the British Peerage," as well as his own research into the marriage settlements of landed families in Kent and Northamptonshire, Lloyd Bonfield has discredited Habakkuk's influential thesis.[6] Like the Stones' data, Hollingsworth's indicates that "between the mid-seventeenth and mid-eighteenth century only about 48 per cent of fathers survived" to their sons' marriages, that is, lived to seek the "resettlement" that is central to Habakkuk's argument (Smith, 55). Bonfield adds that insofar as the figure of 48 percent assumes that all men would have had male successors, it overstates the possibilities for strict settlement. R. M. Smith summarizes the Habakkuk-Bonfield encounter:

> The effects of the "demographic lottery" are important, for . . . if the likelihood of heiresses is taken into account the proportion of fathers who produced a surviving male child and also lived to that child's marriage hovered in the late seventeenth and early eighteenth centuries at under one third of all cases. Bonfield consequently drew the convincing conclusion that resettlement in the manner described by Habakkuk was the exception rather than the rule. (55)

If Bonfield is correct in his assessment of Habakkuk's work, we still are left to account for the "rise" of "Great Estates." Historians are rightly chary of taking literature as evidence, but Richardson shows very clearly that "Great Estates" awaited attractive (Lovelace) or scheming (Harlowe Jr.) young men who could lay claim to "extinct" titles. The effects of the demographic crisis were so powerful that estates were combined and enlarged without the intervention of strict settlements.[7]

For all the breadth of Bonfield's research into marriage settlements, the key to his overturning Habakkuk's work is a simple question: "Do fathers during the period actually survive to the marriage of their eldest son?" (Bonfield, 485). If we change this question slightly, we can see the relevance of his work and the work of the major historians of population—the Stones, Hollingsworth, E. A. Wrigley, and R. S. Schofield—to the novel: "Do propertyholders have sons?" In eighteenth-century novels, as in eighteenth-century life, they tend not to. And from their impotence arise both confusion and opportunity (at least for female heirs). Sandra Gilbert's description of a "patriarchal etiology" and the various "waves" of feminist criticism that have followed *The Madwoman in the Attic*, all premise a specifically male, paternal authority that "confines," marginalizes, and suppresses the female. But any attempt to locate that "etiology" in the period 1650–1740 may be challenged by study of the "demographic climate" as powerfully as Habakkuk's account of the strict settlement has been. "Failure in the male line" is at the center of eighteenth-century fiction by men and women alike. Written amidst a "demographic lottery," novels by Burney and Lennox, as well as by Fielding and Smollett, begin in the absence rather than the presence of paternal authority. Death removes "impediments," even as it creates uncertainty for virtuous heiresses.[8]

Consider the "etiology" of the anonymously authored *The Orphan Heiress of Sir Gregory* (1799), a book that presents itself as *An Historical Fragment of the Last Century*. Although *The Orphan Heiress* is not a fragment and speaks as much to events in 1799 as in 1649,[9] it does adumbrate the historical novels of Scott (it predates *Waverley* by fifteen years) by giving a central role to social and political change in the shaping of its protagonist's life. Spanning fourteen years—from the aftermath of Cromwell's victory over the Royalists at Edgehill (1642) to the last days of his Lord Protectorship, when rumors of "restoration of monarchy" (98, 143) are furtively heard—*The Orphan Heiress* refers repeatedly to Cromwell as "the Usurper" (93, 108) and presents him as a man driven in equal parts by fear and greed: "The image of the murdered king was always before him" (103). He trusts no one, sleeps in his armor, and always "carries . . . about him" an "Italian fusion too subtle and potent for any art to master" (228). This poison will claim the life of the orphan heiress Margaret. In both her life and death, the Civil War stands as a definitive event: her father, Sir Gregory, dies fighting Commonwealth soldiers who have invaded his house, the battle so intense that blood floods the stairs; Cromwell engineers her displacement from her estate to give it to his "adherent"; Italian poison cankers her Stuart white rose, turning a sweetmeat in that shape into the means of her murder. Published in the same year as the 18th Brumaire and Napoleon's "election" as First Consul, the story of Margaret's victimization in the seventeenth century had powerful resonance for British readers at the end of the eighteenth.

While the ghastly violence of its opening scene and its demonization of Cromwell are striking features of *The Orphan Heiress*, its situating of Margaret offers an understated but powerful version of the "demographic climate" described by Bonfield and others. In advance of the Civil War, Margaret's family has been affected by the "demographic lottery." As the chaplain who narrates the story puts the case, Sir Gregory's happy and virtuous life included

> those visitations of Providence, which, however afflictive, are kindly meant to remind us of our mortality. Of these Sir Gregory suffered many in the death of his children; one out of eight, only surviving. It was my dearest joy to baptize them; it was my sad fate to bury them; till the tender Margaret alone was left. (7)

Sir Gregory exemplifies aristocratic virtue and taste. He has the physical courage and strength to defend his house in hand-to-hand combat—"Here Rebellion found what it was to contend with the Valour of Loyalty" (14). And, anticipating that the rebels might seize his land, he has the financial acumen to convert as much of his "yearly income" as possible to "pounds in specie" (50). He protects this portion of his fortune by devising "secret sliders" in the wainscotting of his dining room. But for all his virtue and intelligence, Sir Gregory fails—and this is in advance of the Civil War—to sustain patrilinear succession. In the absence of a surviving male heir, it falls to Margaret to represent her father. With the line of male succession broken, villains like Cromwell can propose other versions of kinship.

Sir Gregory has a clear sense of how the succession should go; his will refers to Margaret as "my dear and only remaining child, to whom, *of course*, will descend my lands and possessions, in case the issue of the brooding contest [the Civil War] shall not prove subversive of the laws" (49, my italics). Cromwell, however, in order to award the property to one of his adherents, casts upon a young man, Ephraim Hacket, because Hacket, while "of an obscure family," had a grandfather who "was distantly related to the grandfather of the lady Judith [Sir Gregory's wife]." The chaplain, who is also Margaret's guardian, summarizes Cromwell's course of action:

> As young Hacket had particularly distinguished himself in some dark transactions of that arch-hypocrite, it was thought fit to make enquiries respecting his family, and to see whether he had pretensions to the property of any of the King's friends; and this small grain of affinity to the lady Judith was thought sufficient, in the balance of Rebellion, to weigh down the ponderous claim of the only daughter. (84)

Two points about Cromwell's villainy are particularly relevant to the topics of property and gender in the eighteenth-century novel. First, Cromwell can traduce both the will of Sir Gregory and legal precedent only because Margaret is alone; the estate is a particularly tempting prize because "in the event of Margaret's death, Sir Gregory's family would be extinct" (84). Second, Cromwell turns to a version of succession that will be common in both eighteenth-century life and literature: he invents an heir for a vacant estate from a male in the female line, "distantly related to . . . the lady Judith." With rumors of a Restoration about, Hacket poisons Margaret to remove her rival claim to the property, for all characters in *The Orphan Heiress* assume that the "restoration of monarchy . . . would also be a restoration of private property" (98). Margaret is victimized in the absence of her father, and the means to her victimization is a fictionalization of kinship authored by Cromwell.

Both her biological father and her figurative father believe that the law is on Margaret's side. Hers is a "ponderous claim" to the estate, one that should outweigh "the small grain of affinity" Hacket can claim. In the "etiology" that operates here, Cromwell stands against and outside the law (he becomes an accessory to murder). This elaboration of Margaret's legal standing redacts a great principle of seventeenth-century English jurisprudence, that is, the right to property based upon the "representation" of the father, a right that operated, it is important to note, apart from sex. A central if now largely neglected text in this regard is Matthew Hale's *De Successionibus apud Anglos: The Law of Hereditary Descents*. One of seventeenth-century England's most respected jurists, Hale was a centrist who moved from working under the Commonwealth to working under Charles II. One of his twentieth-century editors argues that "his acceptability to both the Protector and the restored king is evidence of his neutrality in politics rather than of the maneuvers . . . of a truly political figure. He was . . . perceived from all quarters as a professional whose first allegiance went to the law itself."[10] Hale's *The History of the Common Law in England* became a standard eighteenth-century law textbook.[11] It was first published in 1713 from a manuscript that Hale left at his death in 1676. *De Successionibus* is the ninth chapter of Hale's manuscript, and it was published in three different editions in 1699 and 1700. This proliferation of editions strongly suggests how "hot" succession law was becoming in the "demographic climate" of this era.

Hale is an important, if now "largely unstudied major figure"[12] in legal writing because his approach is historical and, thus, relative. *De Successionibus* opens by tracing the principles of succession in Greek, Roman, and Hebrew writing, and then in English law. Hale values "Customs" and traces how they can effect variation in "the Rules" of Law.[13] This prefatory history portrays primogeniture as one custom among several, rather than as a divine or natural law. Hale notes that Roman law did not grant "preference to the Male" (19), that in England, "It seems . . . until the Conquest, the Descent of Lands was, at least to the Sons alike, and, for aught appears also, to all the Daughters, and that there was no difference in Hereditary Transmission of Lands and Goods . . . in reference to the Children" (36). Primogeniture came into prominence, in Hale's account, only because of its social utility: "This equal division of Inheritances among the Children was found to be very inconvenient. . . . Inheritances were so crumbled, that there were very few persons of able Estates, left to undergo publick Charges or Offices" (37–38). Thus, from the time of William the Conqueror onward, but only "little by little," did "the Generality of Descents or Successions . . . [go] to the eldest Son." And exceptions, most notably in Kent, remained (45).

This emphasis upon the provisionality of primogeniture governs Hale's account of how the law operates in his day. While his writing may appear wedded to a patriarchal vocabulary designed to "confuse" and "intimidate" women, in fact for Hale death complicates succession, and "Representation" empowers females. Hale does, indeed, believe that, "in all Descents immediately the Male is preferred before the Female" (72); Hale does, indeed, write, "The Male line . . . is more worthy than the Female line" (95). But once the father's authority stops working "immediately" and must instead be "represented," differences in sex lose their importance. Central to Hale's understanding of how the common law operates in matters of inheritance is his claim "that all the Descendants from such a Person, as . . . might have been Heir to another hold the same right by *Representation* as that Common Root, from which they are descended" (76, my italics). This means for Hale "that the Son or Grand-child, whether the Son or Daughter of the eldest Son, succeeds before the Youngest Son" (77). This point is so basic for Hale that he returns to it in an even more telling summary: "[The offspring] of the eldest Brother, whether it be Son or Daughter, shall be preferred before the youngest Brother, because though the Female be less worthy than the Male, yet she stands in right of Representation of the eldest Brother, who was more worthy than the youngest" (78–79). For Hale, then, "Representation" outweighs "sex" as a determinant of "worth," as so, in *The Orphan Heiress*, Margaret's "patrimonial rights" (74) should outweigh Hacket's "discovered" (75) claim to the estate.

If "right by Representation" is central to Hale's legal writings, it assumes that place because "the impediment" that patrilinear succession otherwise imposes upon women "is removed by death." Hale concludes *De Successionibus* with eight examples of complicated successions—successions requiring legal opinion (94–105). The first, third, fourth, fifth, and sixth turn upon the phrase "died without issue"; the eighth addresses a question created by "Default of Heirs." Of course, any writing about succession will refer to death: inheritance requires death. But Hale's phrase "without issue" points to the particular intensity that underlies his referencing of mortality. Hale's mentor was Sir William Noye, attorney general to Charles I. Thirty years older than Hale, Noye "treated him almost like a son," and Hale, when he began his legal career, was known as "young Noye."[14] Noye's textbook, *The Compleat Lawyer*, was first published in 1651, seventeen years after his death in 1634. Including *A Treatise Concerning Tenures and Estates in Lands of Inheritance for Life,. and other Hereditaments*, Noye's text is both a predecessor and a counterpart of Hale's *History*. But while Noye shares a topic—"Inheritance"—with Hale and a vocabulary—"Fee-Simple," "Fee-Tayl," "intail"—his writing is not affected by the anxiety about succession that drives Hale's.

The Compleat Lawyer consists of questions that Noye answers confidently and briefly: "*What is a Fee-Simple Conditional?* When Lands are given to me and to my Heirs for ever upon condition I do such or such a thing, etc."[15] As part of this rapid-fire guide to the law, Noye briefly contemplates the problem of extinction in a family line but quickly resolves it: "*How is Tenant in tail after possibility of issue extinct?* When Lands are given to a man and his wife . . . if the man or wife dye without issue between them, the Survivor is Tenant in tail after possibility, etc." (3). Noye favors "etc.," assuming that answers to questions at law are self-evident. Hale works through Noye's elisions, determining what happens when the "Survivor" dies. Contrast the complexity of this typical passage from Hale with Noye's "etc.": "*A*. hath issue two sons, *B*. and *C*. *B*. hath Issue a Son and a Daughter, *D*. and *E*. *D*. the Son hath Issue a Daughter, *F*. and *E*. the Daughter hath Issue a Son, *G*. *C*. nor any of his Descendants shall not inherit so long as there are Descendants from *D*. and *E*. and *E*. the Daughter, nor none of her Descendants shall inherit, so long as there are Descendants from *D*. the Son, *whether they be Male or Female*" (89–90, my italics). Noye, although he seeks to make a "Compleat Lawyer," does not, in the 1630s, touch upon the "right of Representation" that is central to Hale's work.

Because they are not empowered by the "right of Representation," women in Noye's work are accorded roughly the same legal status as "ideots" and "felons." A "Woman . . . without the consent of her Husband . . . cannot by Law make a Will" (99) because a woman, like an "ideot," is a ward, a dependent. In the case of a woman whose husband dies without issue, the widow "shall have her free bench [the use of a portion of her husband's property]" (28) during her lifetime. But Noye describes no other power accruing to her. Noye confidently assumes that primogeniture and custom are enough to resolve disputes about succession, but Hale writes in different "demographic climate" and tries to locate in complicated lineages (*A. B. C. D. E. F. G.*) where the "right of Representation" lies. Frequently, he discovers a woman to be the best representative of the male line.

Of course, even if they were "Orphan Heiresses," women faced legal and educational handicaps, particularly once they married and their property passed to the control of their husbands. However, as the life of Miss Sidney Biddulph attests, and recent work by Susan Staves and John Zomchick confirms, "jointure" and "free bench" were legal rights that women from propertied families held beyond and apart from a husband's or a father's power.[16] If men had property (and, frequently, the mortgages that came with it), women had money. As B. A. Holderness puts the case, "The most prominent function of the widow in English rural society between 1500 and 1900 was money lending."[17] Margaret's suitor, Sir Charles Sedley, hesitates to propose to her "whilst she was in possession of a fortune so much superior to my own . . . lest it should be thought my principal object was the emancipation of my own estates" (95). With Hacket's usurpation of the landed property, Sedley not only proves his love by proposing; unaware that Margaret still has the 15,000 pounds in specie, he also unwittingly gains the use of that money, apart from her jointure, to rescue his mortgaged properties.

If we attend to Hale's version of "Representation," particularly as it applies in a case like Margaret's or in the legal defeat suffered by Sidney Biddulph's husband, Mr. Arnold,[18] we can see an important anticipation of postmodern notions of gender. We can note of Hale, as Jill Campbell has noted of Fielding, that while he "does not use the term gender except to talk about grammatical instances or errors," his legal writing, like Fielding's fiction, suggests that "male and female identity might be . . . conventional, acquired, or historically determined."[19] In a period of demographic crisis, patriarchal power could not operate directly (as Noye assumed) but only via representation—representation that privileged daughters over younger sons. Study of *De Successionibus* does not disallow Gilbert's "patriarchical etiology," but it does suggest that etiologies may vary, particularly in relation to "demographic climate." By reading back from *The Orphan Heiress* to Hale, I do not accuse anyone of "cognitive atheism," nor do I hope (or even want) to stem the tide of gynocriticism. Instead, I hope to bring the demographic crisis and the fictionalization of kinship to which it led into a dialectical relation with some of the most influential recent work on the novel.

Of course, talk of dialectical criticism has abounded of late, most notably in Michael McKeon's *The Origins of the English Novel 1600–1740*. McKeon specifically calls for a "dialectical theory of genre" (20) and, in a fine sentence, asserts that "it is not that history happens to form, but that form happens in history" (6). McKeon rightly argues that the novel has its "origins" in "categorical instability" (20), that novels help individuals and societies both to record and to engage changes in our understandings of virtue and truth. But McKeon finally fails to achieve the "amalgam" for which he calls. *De Successionibus* and *The Orphan*

Heiress can help us chart two narrownesses that have befallen recent criticism of fiction, one specific to McKeon, one more generally associated with the varieties of feminist criticism.

McKeon's narrowness is the unfortunate counterpart of one of his scholarly virtues: his thoroughness. In reconstituting the various precedents for novels in philosophical, religious, and political writing, he overlooks the novels themselves. Readers must work through 357 pages before they get to relatively uninspired commentaries upon *Pamela* and *Joseph Andrews*. McKeon thus typifies critics who narrow the novel to a social referent. In a review essay of books by Armstrong, McKeon, Leopold Damrosch Jr., Terry Castle, Robert A. Erickson, and John Bender, Alistair Duckworth argues that these writers emphasize sociohistorical trends rather than "'internal' analysis of stylistic developments." The group "refuses to grant much—if anything—in the way of aesthetic autonomy" (55). While some might accuse Duckworth of incipient (or retrograde) belletrism,[20] his summary of the boundaries inhabited by these critics (some of the most influential working today) is both inclusive and incisive:

> While "Foucauldians" (like Bender and Armstrong) and "Bakhtinians" (like Castle) seem to agree that the eighteenth century witnessed the marginalization of popular culture and the emergence of bourgeois discourses and practices, the role of the novel in this process is very much in dispute. Is the genre a reflection, an interpretation, or an agent of historical change? Does it register, oppose, or enable, the exercise of social power? Foucauldians tend to see the novel as an accomplice of state policy, while Bakhtinians seek to honour the novel for its powers of resistance to oppressive rule. (54)

Foucauldians and Bakhtinians struggle energetically, learnedly but, finally, narrowly with the question of how much social bad faith they are to attribute to the novel, dismissing the "heroic role" (66) that a critic like Lionel Trilling once could attribute to the genre: "Its greatness and practical usefulness [lie] in its unremitting work of involving the reader himself in the moral life, inviting him to put his own motives under examination, suggesting that reality is not as his conventional education has led him to see it."[21] If seventeenth- and eighteenth-century families used fictions to change identities, if Matthew Hale could see the "right of Representation" giving women the legal standing of men, might we wish to reconsider Trilling's claim, to wonder at least about the power of fiction to alter that which it represents?

The feminist narrowness, like the Foucauldian, is owing to a virtue: the frequently astonishing synchronicity that Sandra M. Gilbert and Susan Gubar achieved in *The Madwoman in the Attic*.[22] No one writing after Northrop Frye's *Anatomy of Criticism* has achieved the range and perspicuity of reference that Gilbert and Gubar do; in a single sentence, sometimes a single phrase, we move from Anne Bradstreet to Anne Sexton, from the countess of Winchilsea to Sylvia Plath. But as Gilbert and Gubar argue that the struggle against "confinement," both physical and literary, is unique to a "feminine" aesthetic, they must make exclusions that are untenable. For one small example, they claim, "The distinction between male and female images of imprisonment is—and *always* has been—a distinction between . . . that which is metaphysical and metaphorical [the male] and . . . that which is social and actual [the female]" (86). Where this leaves Charles Dickens, haunted by his father's imprisonment for debt and his own "confinement" to work in a blacking factory, is hard enough to say that we might choose instead to scrap the distinction.

Of course, feminist criticism has undergone many permutations since Gilbert and Gubar's landmark study, but "patriarchal etiology" has remained basic to most versions of it, no doubt because that etiology explains so much about literature and life so well. But that etiology tells us more about the eighteenth-century novel if it stands in dialectical relationship to another. When the etiology of patriarchal presence strives against the etiology of patriarchal absence, we begin to understand why the lives of Clarissa Harlowe and Cecelia Beverley become both complicated and full of danger. A helpful example here comes from the recent surge of work on Frances Burney. In her fine book *The Iron Pen*, Julia Epstein connects crucial events in Burney's life—her appointment at court (where she was not allowed to sneeze), her mastectomy, her near drowning in a seaside cave—to her novels; she locates in Burney an "anger" that earlier critics overlooked. For Epstein, the etiology of that anger is obvious. Burney inevitably rages against "a dominant patriarchy that does not recognize its own social ideologies as anything but the 'obvious' and inevitable way the world is organized."[23]

However, as Epstein herself allows, writing was a source of power for Burney (23, 32, 37, 40, 50, 73), a way to manage trauma, a way to assert herself. In 1812, Burney gave a signed copy of *Evelina* to a French magistrate in order that he would allow her family to return to England. In 1801–2, Napoleon gave Burney's husband special treatment "for the sake of the novelist who had given him pleasure." With the income from her writing, Burney leased "Camilla Cottage," the small home in which she and her husband spent their happiest years.[24] Burney loved her father, her husband, and her son, but all three of them, her father in particular, failed her—failed to protect her from want and illness (and high tides), from the rigors of life at court, from the confusions of the Napoleonic era. To a remarkable degree, the three most important men in Burney's life shared a fecklessness, a penchant for not being there when they might have helped her.[25] Can these failings explain her anger, or must her father's only partially successful attempts to manage her career be its only source?

In the opening pages of *The Origins of the English Novel*, McKeon, as he criticizes two classic studies of fiction, adumbrates the dialectic I seek. In McKeon's view, a major failing of Ian Watt's *The Rise of the Novel* is Watt's overlooking that "'romance' continues to suffuse the period" of the novel's purported "rise" (McKeon, 3); a major failing of Northrop Frye's *Anatomy of Criticism* is that it "freezes history into immobile 'literary structure'" (8). Watt recognizes social imperatives, Frye structural. Watt argues that the additions of leisured women and members of the middle class to the reading public spurred literary innovation. I am adding "demographic crisis" to his etiology. However, Watt's emphasis upon "the enduring connections between the distinctive literary qualities of the novel and those of the society in which it began and flourished"[26] needs to be tempered by Frye's emphasis upon the "constructive principles of storytelling" that "remain constant" through changes of "social context."[27] As families dealt with the "demographic lottery" in seventeenth- and eighteenth-century England, they turned to several well-established fictions; however distant the relation that they found, they found a relation. And authors, as they represented families in crisis, turned to one of the oldest of storytelling's "constructive principles," the birth-mystery plot, even as they varied it to suit their different social backgrounds and agendas. As I work between Watt and Frye, I will make a number of assumptions, but one is crucial, even (for me anyway) liberating: novels may change the social conditions that they describe—or at least change the attitudes of readers toward those conditions. The novel may claim to offer more than a dialectic circumscribed by the prison and the carnival, by the repressive father and the silenced daughter.

Recalling McKeon's fine insight that "it is not that history happens to form, but that form happens in history," and recalling as well the nearly simultaneous and great achievements of Watt and Frye, the opening chapters will argue that Cervantes' *Don Quixote* and Milton's *Paradise Lost* are crucial precursors for eighteenth-century fiction because they both celebrate, even as they warn against, the ability of men and women to invent "kin" and thus to transform their identities. After the chapters on Cervantes and Milton, the book will center upon readings of demographic crisis and fictive kin in Defoe (with particular reference to *Moll Flanders* and *Roxana*), Fielding (whose birth-mystery plots and Cervantick "night scenes" reveal a shifting attitude toward patriarchy), and Smollett (whose anamnestic fictions, *Roderick Random* and *Humphry Clinker*, I will contrast with Fielding's mimetic fictions). Then come two longer chapters: one on the treatment of patriarchy in Richardson's *Clarissa*; one on the versions of fictive kinship, including the option of incest, that Burney, Inchbald, and Lennox offer in the second half of the eighteenth century. In tracing the manifestations of demographic crisis in Richardson and in novels by female writers, I will depart most directly from the "patriarchal etiology" that underlies much recent feminist criticism. Rather than portraying the patriarch as a powerful figure who either silences or violates the female spirit, Richardson, Lennox, Inchbald, and Burney offer us patriarchs who are absent, impaired, or dead. This weakened patriarch creates difficulties for female characters, but difficulties that have less to do with oppression than with the uncertainty created in families by the absence of a commanding father. Clarissa would gladly be sent to her attic (although she would prefer to be exiled to her dairy house), but she cannot bring her father to act in her case and instead falls victim to the schemes of her brother and of Robert Lovelace, both of them young men who are dangerous precisely because demographic crisis has freed them from traditional patriarchal constraints.

The conclusion looks at birth mysteries in nineteenth-century fictions and is particularly indebted to Peter Brooks's *Reading for the Plot*. As Brooks describes characters like Dickens's Pip and Stendhal's Julien Sorel imagining fathers for themselves, writing their own birth mysteries, he highlights how far nineteenth-century fiction stands apart from eighteenth-century, despite formal similarities. The birth mystery in Dickens and Stendhal operates much like Freud's family romance. Eighteenth-century

characters—be they Fielding's Tom Jones, Smollett's Roderick
Random, or Inchbald's Miss Milner—do not imagine new parents
for themselves. In nineteenth-century fiction, the birth mystery
serves personal agendas rather than social, responds to individual
psychological needs rather than to demographic crises within the
society as a whole.

The Orphan Heiress, although it treats with remarkable clarity
the failure of patrilinear succession and subsequent turn to
"Representation," ends where the novels I will be discussing
begin. *The Orphan Heiress* is narrated by a man; not only that, it is
narrated by an obtuse and complacent man. Sir Gregory's chaplain represents patriarchal power. He believes that "the traitor to
his King is generally an apostate to his God" (170). He accepts
with remarkable equanimity all manner of carnage because he
attributes all events to "Providence" (7, 20, 83). The editor who
presents the "fragment" describes the chaplain as a "man of
strong prejudices," and his seemingly imperturbable "Anglican
Rationalism"[28] diminishes his interest and value for critics writing
after Gilbert and Gubar.

The chaplain's equipoise depends in large measure upon his
impercipience, a connection that Henry James has outlined: "The
fixed constituents of almost any reproducible action are the fools
who minister, at a particular crisis, to the intensity of the free spirit
engaged with them."[29] Without attributing a Jamesian sophistication to *The Orphan Heiress*, we can note that the chaplain's character is defined by what he does not see, by what he cannot admit.
At Sir Gregory's funeral, he keeps the coffin "screwed down;
because his countenance . . . was disfigured, and rather excited an
emotion of terror, than the endearment of recollection" (40).
During the burial rite, the chaplain's "feelings were indescribable
and poignant in the extreme" (p, 42), but he says no more about
them. His great goal is to organize losses: "The coffins of the seven
children of Sir Gregory were arranged under the center arch. I
directed those of their parents to be placed on each side of them"
(43). These responses may seem appropriate for a priest, but the
cost of the chaplain's foolishness begins to register when he
cannot understand why Hacket accepts so calmly the news that
Margaret plans to marry Sedley (143) and, subsequent to her
murder, dismisses the servants who report seeing her "spirit": "I
discouraged every idea of vision" (205). Only when Margaret's
ghost stands before him for the third time and points "with the
finger of her right hand to the [white] rose, on which I now

discerned some drops of blood" (209) does the chaplain finally *get it*, finally understand "the obvious interpretation" (211) of the events of Margaret's murder. But this understanding—which most readers will have guessed at as early as the detailed description of the white rose sweetmeat—only comes to him "once my philosophy was put to flight" (210).

While the chaplain may seem empowered by his position as narrator, the story, finally, is about the inability of his "philosophy," however calming and consolatory in his case, to help him see. A pallid anticipation of Conrad's Marlowe, the chaplain would "screw down" and "arrange" the "terror" brought to Sir Gregory's family by "demographic lottery" and then by civil war. His own "fortunes [having] failed" while he was a student at Oxford, the chaplain need not learn from his ruin because he finds a benefactor in Sir Gregory and a "sanctuary of happiness" in his house (6). With that sanctuary defiled and Margaret's parents dead, the chaplain begins to fictionalize kinship but in a revealingly limited way. He tells his ward, "I will be your papa; and Laetitia [a servant] here, you know is very good to you, and will teach you how to make yourself fit for Heaven" (48). Even amidst family catastrophe, a servant cannot pass for a mother, and the chaplain, able to rely upon the hidden 15,000 pounds and an old friendship, soon places Margaret in another family, avoiding direct responsibility for her upbringing for fourteen years. That Margaret becomes a beautiful young woman and a Stuart loyalist owes more to her education than to her guardian; her reading is limited to "the high-wrought dignity of the old romance," and she avoids the "flimsy laxity of the modern novel" (63).

Even this perfect child sets basic epistemological and ontological challenges to the chaplain's "philosophy" once she returns to his presence. In a long discussion with him just prior to the supper party at which she will be poisoned, Margaret looks out upon a favorite part of her father's "grounds" and reveals to the chaplain that she is "well aware of the astonishing powers of imagination"; she knows "spirits" intervene in our lives (156). To the chaplain these views smack of "enthusiasm," and, thus, he tries to counter them, to redirect them. But Margaret dies before her reeducation can be attempted, and her "spirit," whose presence the chaplain has refused to recognize (195, 206, 208), finally triumphs over his obtuseness and Hacket's villainy. All the arguments the chaplain uses against Margaret's version of the "imagination" crumble when her spirit appears to him.

A critic schooled in the patriarchal etiologies that underlie the various "waves" of feminist criticism would (and should) point out that because of all this dying, the chaplain inherits Sir Gregory's property. Again, his is a position of privilege, but that privilege operates outside the "fragment"; we do not see the chaplain enjoying his property. Rather, at the fragment's end, he is left to explain to Sedley (who has been in London and then at his estate preparing for the wedding) what has happened. For the first time in the narrative, the chaplain is both resourceless and speechless as Sedley arrives at Sir Gregory's: "My heart beat with inexpressible sensations . . . when I beheld joy beaming in the countenance of Sir Charles Sedley, as he was looking out of the carriage window, expecting a welcome in the smile of Margaret" (234). No longer fortified by impercipience, the chaplain only can wonder how to treat Sedley's happy but misguided ignorance.

In the cataclysmic events of Margaret's final days, her natural father is absent, her figurative father impotent (except for the treasure he manages to hide). Margaret herself is both beautifully passive and definitively (albeit not defiantly) subversive. She comes into danger only because all of her siblings are dead, only because in her very being she prevents the "extinction" of the line. Her power is such that, even in her dying, she can command the chaplain to use her cash to rescue Sedley's properties (185). She is poisoned by a man, but by a man who represents "usurpation" (religious, political, and social) rather than patriarchy. Her life and her death cannot be accounted for only by an "etiology" of presence. Rather, like the female protagonists of Burney, Inchbald, and Lennox, she requires an etiology of absence if the conflation of power and peril in her life is to be understood.[30] As an example of Hale's "right of Representation" and of the impact of the demographic crisis, Margaret should be understood via both Henry James and Ian Watt, via both Northrop Frye and Michel Foucault. Her story, as unsophisticatedly as it is told, provides the template for the essays that follow. If those essays succeed, they will make reciprocally illuminative the structural and the social, the etiology of presence and the etiology of absence.

1

The "Quest for the Proper Name": *Don Quixote* and the Madness of "Fictive Kin"

When Tobias Smollett published his translation of *Don Quixote* in 1755, he joined a long if not always illustrious list of earlier English translators.[1] In the 150 years between the appearance of part 1 of the *Quixote* and Smollett's translation, Thomas Shelton, John Phillips (Milton's godson and an associate of Titus Oates), Peter Motteux, and John Ozell all translated at least parts of the *Quixote*. Shelton's translation of part 1 appeared in 1607, barely two years after the first Spanish edition. A translation of part 2, probably by Shelton, was published in 1620 and reprinted in 1652, 1675, 1725, and 1731. Phillips's translation, which the *Dictionary of National Biography* describes as "coarse and unfaithful," appeared in 1687 and, apparently, disappeared soon thereafter. The most popular eighteenth-century translation was Ozell's revision of Motteux's. Motteux's translation of part 1 first appeared in 1712; Ozell's revision of Motteux's part 1 and original translation of part 2 was first published in 1717. This translation, which reached its seventh edition in 1743, was the one Fielding read, the one Smollett hoped to supersede. James Mabbe's translation of Cervantes' *Exemplary Novels*, first published in 1640, was reissued in 1654, the same year as Edward Gayton's *Pleasant Notes Upon Don Quixote*. In 1694 both Thomas D'Urfey and John Crowne produced theatrical adaptations of material from the *Quixote*, as would Henry Fielding in 1734.

Against this background of translations and adaptations, we can sense how thoroughly "Englished" *Don Quixote* had become by the time of Fielding's adolescence in the 1720s. For writers like

Fielding, Smollett, Sterne, and Lennox, Don Quixote set a literary precedent as important as Aeneas or Telemachus. When they refer to him, they have a literary "Manner," a "Cervantick tone"[2] in mind. But Cervantes' relevance to English fiction goes beyond his "Manner." Don Quixote captured the imaginations of English readers and writers not only because he tilted at windmills but also because he revealed, in his naming, both the power and the danger of fictive versions of kinship. James A. Parr has pointed out that one of the great actions of the *Quixote* is the "quest for the proper name."[3] Cervantes will not say, definitively, whom Quixote is. He thus becomes an attractive, even inevitable, model for eighteenth-century British writers because he links questions of narrative provenance (Who tells the story?) with anxieties about status that were created by Charles I and Phillip II as they imposed religious uniformity upon a diverse society.

In *The Rise of the Novel*, Watt offers only five brief references to the *Quixote*, no doubt because as part of his definition of "formal realism," he asserts that the plots of novels are "non-traditional," that they neither derive from nor depend upon earlier works. McKeon, perhaps benefiting from Watt's example, devotes a chapter to *Don Quixote* but finally sees the book in terms of its "cultural layerings" or "cultural laminations" (McKeon, 277, 278, 292), in terms of its representing the social conflicts of golden age Spain. As McKeon claims that "the relationship between Don Quixote and Sancho Panza synoptically mediates the historical transition from feudalism to capitalism" (283), his argument is, as Duckworth notes, "somewhat reductive" (Duckworth, 65). The confidence with which McKeon talks about Quixote's social identity seems particularly misplaced when we note that none of us, McKeon included, knows Quixote's name. Seeking the knight's "proper name," we can see that *Don Quixote* is more than a representation of social change, even as it is more than an antiromance.

Parr, differing from Watt and McKeon, takes his lead from Gerard Genette[4] and outlines, even diagrams, the "very complex and sophisticated narrative strategies" (Parr, 6) Cervantes employs. He shows that the *Quixote* has both "diegetic" and "mimetic" (56) voices, that it is as much a book about how stories get told as it is a representation of life in *siglo de oro* Spain. Parr thus reveals how partial a reading of the *Quixote* McKeon's is. Parr, however, may frustrate readers who want to find more in the *Quixote* than narrative sleight-of-hand. Don Quixote's appeal is not only "intertextual" (5). In raising questions about its telling, the *Quixote* also raises questions about the power of fiction to alter, even to create, social status. These questions will loom particularly large for British writers from Defoe to Lennox. As we cannot figure out who narrates Don Quixote's story, so we also cannot figure out whom the story is about—that is, the subject's "proper name" and his patrimony and status. Cervantes' genius, in part, was to recognize that such uncertainties can be interesting and amusing rather than (as in classical and Renaissance drama) frightening and ruinous.

Parr works through the uncertain naming of Don Quixote in a passage that proclaims a basic but frequently overlooked truth and thus merits extended quotation:

> The archivist/collator vacillates regarding the last name. Other writers have given Quijada and Quesada, but it seems to him that Quejana is a more likely possibility. When the character assumes his knightly appellation, near the end of Chapter 1, the speaker inclines toward Quijada, since it most closely approximates Quixote; he apparently rejects Quesada, and makes no further mention of Quejana. When Pedro Alonso finds his befuddled neighbor hallucinating beside the road after the drubbing by the muleteer of the merchants of Toledo, he twice identifies him as Senor Quijana.
>
> The knight himself seems equally confused. In Chapter 49 of Part I, he claims to be a direct descendant of a Gutierre Quijada, but he subsequently reveals his niece's name to be Antonia Quijana and finally settles on Alonso Quijano for himself. We have to read more than a thousand pages to learn his first or Christian name, Alonso. The quest for the proper name of both persons and objects complements the quest for an authentic text, as well as the protagonist's own sense of mission. (93)

Parr links the uncertainty about Don Quixote's name with uncertainty about point of view, reminding us that the *Quixote* not only has "numerous narrative voices" (24) but that those voices continually subvert each other and thus subvert "narrative authority" overall (30). Even the chapter headings become problematic:

> It will obviously not do to say that the chapter headings derive from Cide Hamete's manuscript, since the Arab historian is referred to in third person in the heading of II, 28. . . . Likewise, the headings of the first nine chapters cannot be his. The ninth is the most problematical of all, since the first speaker has left his post and neither the second nor Cide Hamete has yet come on stage. Who wrote that ninth, phantom heading? (53)

A naive reader might answer Parr's last question much more readily than an academic critic trained in the various "narratologies" of Genette, Tsetvan Todorov, and Mikhail Bakhtin.[5] And the answer would be "Cervantes." For Cervantes writes the chapter headings as surely as he writes the story that they subdivide and summarize. Pursuing "diegesis," Parr becomes so involved in what E. M. Forster once referred to as "technical troubles" that he appears to forget that a story does get told. Not only that, the story gets told so well that Quixote becomes famous in his own time—his fame becoming one of the major motifs of Cervantes' second volume. Quixote's "quest for the proper name" anticipated the need of elite families in eighteenth-century England to invent fictive kin but also to lessen the status inconsistency inherent to such inventions. That Cervantes' narrative is, to use another phrase from Forster, "all to pieces logically"[6] only set a precedent for the illogicality of the "pious fictions" by which authors and families maintained the appearance of patrilinear succession.

If Parr narrows his focus to questions of narrative technique, McKeon narrows his to fit his social and epistemological categories. McKeon rightly emphasizes the ten-year interval between the two volumes of the *Quixote*, claiming that the interval reveals Cervantes moving "from naive empiricism to extreme skepticism, from romance ideology to conservative ideology" (McKeon, 292). For McKeon, "Don Quixote's terminal sanity requires that the essential aura of his own romance be obliterated, and in the final chapter he simply becomes Alonso Quijano once more" (485). Of course, having realized the mistake imbedded in the phrase "simply becomes Alonso Quijano once more," we can give social dimension to the only seemingly intertextual question of Don Quixote's lost name. By hiding Quixote's "true" name, Cervantes not only subverts and problematizes the various points of view within the novel, he also mimetically reenacts particular confusions about identity in sixteenth-century Spain—confusions that had special relevance to English life during the demographic crisis of 1650–1740.

Besides being divided into social classes, Spanish society also was divided into three religious groups: Jews, Christians, and Moors.[7] With the union of Aragon and Castile brought about by the marriage of King Ferdinand and Queen Isabella, the nation we know as Spain was born. Known as "los Reyes Catolicos," Ferdinand and Isabella not only dispatched Christopher Columbus to the New World in 1492, they also established religious uniformity; Jews and Moors were required to convert to Roman Catholicism or to suffer expulsion. Jewish converts came to be known as *conversos*, Moorish as *Moriscos*. After 1492, the distinction between "Old Christians," which Sancho Panza proudly claims to be,[8] and new Christians became crucial. Quixote, who describes himself as "a Catholic and faithful Christian" (130), never makes the claim his squire does. He also, while operating under a delusion, attacks a procession of priests (1:xix) and is "excommunicated for having laid violent hands on holy things" (130).

Throughout the reigns of Charles I and Phillip II, the *siglo de oro*, as Spain's colonies brought it wealth and power, the national administration became increasingly centralized. In 1543, Charles I promulgated a statute requiring purity of blood (*limpieza de sangre*) in both religious and public orders.[9] Only "Old Christians" could fill lucrative and powerful positions in the church or the civil service. As a result, a vast bureaucratic apparatus was set in place to investigate and to certify bloodlines. The "heteroglot" culture of sixteenth-century Spain was undergoing a foredoomed but nonetheless intense attempt at homogenization. If a "converso,"[10] Cervantes would have experienced firsthand both the importance and the provisionality of paternity in golden age Spain. Jews and Moors could become, indeed had to become, Christians; in that sense, social identity was fluid, unfixed. But Jews, unless they somehow passed rigorous scrutiny of their lineage, never could be "Old Christians," and Moors never could be more than *Moriscos*. In his "un-naming" of Don Quixote, Cervantes not only establishes narrative uncertainty (Who is speaking?) but social as well (Where are the records?). Eighteenth-century authors learned from Cervantes the uses—both diegetic and mimetic—of this "quest for the proper name." In the character of Don Quixote, Fielding, Smollett, Lennox, and Inchbald all could see both the beauty and the danger, the freedom and the folly, of fictionalizing kinship.

Is Don Quixote a hero or a fool?[11] The question has received (can receive) no final answer. But we can say that the question has arisen for generations of readers precisely because Quixote moves so readily between intervals of conventional and unconventional behavior; he is alternately mad and sane. What perhaps has not been sufficiently noted is that the society through which Quixote moves is almost equally unfixed—sometimes willing to share and to enjoy his delusions, sometimes ready to punish them. The question of Quixote's madness is a rich one, but one that typically has been approached intratextually. Critics assume that Don Quixote is the deranged version of Alonso Quijano and then chart the various ambiguities that his derangement creates. But once we realize that Quixote's "sane" identity is no more fixed than his mad identity, we can emphasize that his confusion is not his alone; it is shared, sometimes even embraced, by those around him. Rather than being seen in McKeon's terms as a "progressive" character whose "terminal sanity requires that the essential aura of his own romance name be obliterated" (McKeon, 286), Quixote may be seen to mediate between social conventions (much less rigid than McKeon would have them), social tradition (much less fixed in golden age Spain than many assume) and individual need. In this mediation between the public and the private, between a world of his own imagining and *the* world, Quixote engenders many of the protagonists of eighteenth-century British fiction—even though Alonso Quijano is unmarried, childless, and, in one provocative account, a virgin.[12]

When McKeon claims that the "terminal sanity" of Alonso Quijano requires the death of Don Quixote, he follows Michel Foucault[13] in assuming that changes in European society during the period 1600–1780 made madness and sanity antithetical, even inimical to each other rather than, as they once had been, mutually and equally human. To be sane, Quijano must destroy his old mad self. When we recognize that Quixote has no fixed self to get back to, we also can understand his madness in less Foucauldian, less Manichaean terms. Arthur Efron has argued almost the opposite case.[14] In his view, Quixote's problem is not the conflict between his delusion and the real; rather, his problem is that his world is "Dulcineated." Illusion and reality are confounded in advance of the illness that turns an unnamable Manchegan hidalgo into Don Quixote, and Quixote's actions bespeak only his participation in— not his initiation of—that confusion. Efron points us beyond the narrow dialectic that Foucault proposes and to which McKeon accedes.

While Foucault claims that in the Renaissance madness is "an undifferentiated experience" (Foucault, 28), Spanish society offers powerful evidence to the contrary. In his influential and widely translated *Examen de ingenios para las sciencias*,[15] Juan Huarte de San Juan, a sixteenth-century Spanish physician, applies with clinical precision humors psychology to human behavior (including madness). Huarte de San Juan assumes that "from the three qualities, hot, moist, and drie, proceed all the differences of men's wits" (51). He further assumes that these qualities have material causes and, thus, are subject to control, even manipulation: "The matter whereof man is compounded produceth a thing so alterable, and so subject to corruption, that at the instant when he beginneth to be shaped, he likewise beginneth to untwine and to alter" (322). As the last passage indicates, Huarte de San Juan's great interest is in what we today call eugenics. On the basis of his discussion of the origins of human personality, he offers various regimens by which prospective parents can control the character, even the sex, of their offspring. In his elaborate account, both diet and climate help to determine an infant's character.

Conception, however, does not end the relationship between physical circumstances and personality. Malcom K. Read puts the matter succinctly: "According to Huarte, the material world conditions the human body, and in turn somatic changes cause corresponding changes in the psyche."[16] Huarte understands madness to be caused by a preponderance of "heat" in the individual, a preponderance leading to excessive, if sometimes instructive, imaginativeness. While for Huarte all human beings are somewhat mad because all human "qualities" are, since the Fall, unbalanced, extreme cases are both diagnosable and treatable; they are not "undifferentiated."

As part of his study of personality, early in the *Examen* Huarte offers several accounts of madmen returned to their senses. These accounts reveal much about standard notions of insanity in the sixteenth century—notions very different from those Foucault assumes. They also suggest connections between Huarte and Cervantes[17] because they introduce characters similar to Don Quixote:

> A Page of one of the great ones of this realme, whilst he was mad delivered such rare conceits, resemblances, and answers, to such as asked him, and devised so excellent manners of governing a kingdom (of which he imagined himself to be soveraigne) that for great wonder people flocked to see him and heare him, and his very maister scarcely ever departed from his bed's head, praying God that he might never be cured. Which afterwards plainly appeared, for being recovered, his Physition (who had healed him) came to take leave of his lord, with a mind to receive some good reward . . . but he encountered this greeting: I promise you maister doctor, that I was never more aggreeved at any ill success, than to see this my page recovered, for it was not behoofful that he should change such wise folly, for an understanding

so simple as this, which in his health he enjoyed. Me-thinks that of one, who to fore was wise and well-advised, you have made him a fool again. (43)

The page is equally unhappy with the doctor's success, regretting that "to morrow I must begin againe to serve one, who whilst I was in my infirmitie, I would have disdained for my footman" (44).

While the performance of the page in his "folly" is admired, this should not lead us to overlook the status of madness throughout the case history. As the "maister" expresses regret over the page's cure, he does not argue that madness is or should be "undifferentiated." Rather, he expresses willingness to learn from the mad, to apply in "governing a kingdom" their "answers." The "maister" is at once both more and less tolerant of madness than Foucault's characterization of the Renaissance "experience" of madness would allow. Less tolerant in that he does label certain behaviors "mad" and thus permits their treatment and cure. More tolerant in that he feels neither social nor political pressure to repress "mad" behavior, even though the page's dreams of social glory—"there raigned no king on earth who was not my vassal" (43)—might lead him to do so.

Without attempting to resolve the difficult question of Huarte's influence upon Cervantes,[18] we can note that the case history of the page adumbrates major questions about the relationship between madness and civilization that are raised in Don Quixote. Foucault claims that "in . . . Cervantes, madness still occupies an extreme place in that it is beyond appeal. Nothing ever restores it either to truth or reason. It leads only to laceration and thence to death" (31). But particularly in part 2, characters and readers alike are asked to balance their judgment that Quixote is mad with their wonderment at the "rare conceits, resemblances, and answers" that he offers. Having read or heard about Quixote's adventures in part 1, characters in part 2 "flock to see him and heare him"; they have become part of a community with him, a community similar to that which gathers around the mad page. By overlooking this emphasis upon community, Foucault misreads the Quixote. He forces the Don's madness to be both more "undifferentiated" and more "lacerating" than it actually is. He does not recognize that Cervantes (and sixteenth-century physicians like Huarte) can treat madness (that is, differentiate it) but also learn from it (that is, tolerate it).

Foucault's distortion becomes manifest if we note that all readers find themselves in the position of Don Juan and Don Jeronimo,
the characters who introduce Quixote to Avellaneda's spurious
sequel. Having read the first part of his story, the two men question Quixote about his life since its conclusion:

> The amusement the two men derived from hearing Don Quixote
> recount the strange incidents of his history was exceedingly great; and
> if they were amazed by his absurdities, they were equally amazed by
> the elegant style in which he delivered them. On the one hand they
> regarded him as a sensible man, and on the other he seemed to them a
> madman, and they could not make up their minds where between
> wisdom and folly they ought to place him. (754)

Two points bear noting here. First, Don Quixote's madness is in
no sense "ultimate." Rather, it is proximate. Don Juan and Don
Jeronimo converse with Quixote, question him about Dulcinea,
judge him to be mad—but only after noting his "elegant style."
They are part of a community with the Don, sharing an inn with
him, an inn, significantly enough, that he does not mistake for a
castle. Second, because Quixote's madness is proximate rather
than ultimate, Don Juan and Don Jeronimo derive "amusement"
from it. While confused by Quixote, they are neither terrified nor
mystified by him. He occasions for them a judgment difficult to
render, but, in the very difficulty of the case, we can see how close
they are to him. The two gentlemen hardly can be said (as
Foucault's argument would require) to "subjugate" him.

In their response to Quixote, Don Juan and Don Jeronimo
repeat that of the priest at the opening of part 2. Having engaged
Quixote in a discussion of knight-errantry—a discussion that
reveals Quixote's madness to persist—the priest, rather than fighting to reverse the course of the conversation, "yield[s] to the
enjoyment of hearing such nonsense" (432); he asks a question
about earlier knights-errant and thus pushes Quixote toward his
third sally. Without going as far as Howard Mancing, who
impugns the motives of both the priest and the barber at the opening of part 2,[19] we can say that Quixote's madness, particularly in
part 2, is enjoyable for many who encounter him. Without accepting Efron's negative assessment of Quixote and his society, we can
profit from Efron's compelling insight that almost all the characters in the *Quixote* accede to the Don's madness (Efron, 12–31).
Quixote's world is, indeed, "Dulcineated" far beyond his ability
physically to coerce loyalty to his illusion.

As Quixote himself points out in a telling remark to the Duchess, that illusion can only survive with the complicity of those around him: "God knows whether there is any Dulcinea or not in the world, or whether she is imaginary or not imaginary. These are things the proof of which must not be pushed to extreme lengths" (Cervantes, 606–7). The ducal pair, spoiled and jaded by their wealth, continually "follow up their joke [upon Quixote]; for to them there was no reality that could afford them more amusement" (627). They briefly make Don Quixote's madness the center of their lives but only for their diversion and not for the good of Quixote or the other members of their court. In making Dulcinea's disenchantment depend upon Sancho's lashing himself (624), they attempt to drive a wedge between the knight and the squire, between the hidalgo and the *pechero*. Their villainy resides not in their playing a joke upon Quixote, but in their having "pushed it so far" (720). They, not Quixote, risk "social uselessness" (Foucault 1965, 58).

The ducal pair stands in sharp contrast to Don Antonio Moreno, who is "very fond of diverting himself" but only "in any fair and good-natured way." "Having Don Quixote in his house," Moreno, like the ducal pair, sets "about devising modes of making him exhibit his mad traits." Unlike the ducal pair, he pursues his diversion "in some harmless fashion; for jests that give pain are not jests, and no amusement is worth anything if it hurts another" (Cervantes, 768). Moreno's character comments negatively upon the characters of the ducal pair, but in both cases we find Quixote's "mad traits" in a house, not in an asylum. In both cases Quixote's madness delights and entertains rather than frightening and lacerating. Moreno establishes his moral superiority to the ducal pair not by submitting more completely to Quixote's illusion but by treating it with greater care.

It is left for Sanson Carrasco, in the guise of the Knight of the White Moon, to deal Don Quixote's fiction its death blow. But even after Quixote's defeat, the fiction retains power for the community, if not for Quixote himself:

"Oh Senor," said Don Antonio [to Carrasco], "may God forgive you the wrong you have done the whole world in trying to bring the most amusing of madmen in it back to his senses. Do you not see, Senor, that what is gained by restoring Don Quixote's sanity can never equal the enjoyment his delusions give. . . . And if it were not uncharitable, I would say may Don Quixote never be cured, for by his recovery we lose not only his amusing remarks but his squire Sancho Panza's too, any of which is enough to turn melancholy itself into merriment." (789)

Don Antonio balances the profit and loss of Quixote's "cure" in terms remarkably similar to those which the "maister" uses in Huarte's case history of the mad page. Having offered this forceful but temperate rebuke, Don Antonio then reports to the viceroy "what Carrasco told him, and the viceroy was not very well pleased to hear it, for with Don Quixote's retirement there was an end to the amusement of all who knew anything of his mad doings" (789).

Carrasco rides out of Barcelona (like the physician in Huarte's account) unrewarded and unpraised. He has pushed Quixote's illusion until it breaks. But the leaders of the community—the viceroy and Don Antonio Moreno—view Quixote's madness in less dualistic ways than do Carrasco or his postmodern descendants. For these golden age "maisters," madness brings "amusement" and "enjoyment." They see no need to incarcerate or to fear Quixote and are happy to have their reason revivified by his unreason. Carrasco reveals that he has learned the lesson Moreno would teach him when he eagerly, if belatedly, joins in Quixote's pastoral illusion near the story's end: "I'll be always making verses, pastoral or courtly or whatever may come into my head, to pass the time in those secluded regions where we shall be roaming" (824).

If Cervantes portrays Don Quixote's madness as more amusing than lacerating, so he also uses Quixote to raise questions of "status inconsistency" (McKeon, 171–75). As Huarte de San Juan describes the mad page, he anticipates the rich blend of attitudes toward social status in the *Quixote*. People "flock" to see the page, not because he rants and raves, but rather because he offers "so excellent manners of governing a kingdom." His "maister" prays that he not be cured because he finds so much political guidance in the page's "wise folly." When the page expresses regret for his cure, complaining that he now must "serve one, who whilst I was in my infirmitie, I would have disdained for my footman," he displaces both himself and his master in the social hierarchy. His imaginings bring into question the master-servant relationship and problematize golden age assumptions about where superiority and inferiority lie. But the page's final words also show that, even in his madness, hierarchy persists. In his delusion, he changes places with his master, but he still operates within social categories—"disdained for my footman."

In his madness, Don Quixote similarly subverts and reinstates social categories. Early in their adventures, Don Quixote and Sancho (1:xxi) discuss the rewards they may receive. Don Quixote turns to the model of chivalric romance, comparing himself to a knight who "conquers" and "triumphs" and then asks a king for his daughter's hand. At first the "king is unwilling," since he does not know who the knight is. But then, Quixote imagines, the knight "is proved to be the son of a valiant king of some kingdom, I know not what, for I fancy it is not likely to be on the map. The father dies, the princess inherits, and in two words the knight becomes king." His squire, much to Sancho's gratification, marries the "daughter of a very great duke" (148). In his fantasy, Quixote uses a "family romance"[20] to resolve incipient social conflict— conflict broached by the only seemingly "inconsistent" virtue of the knight (who is, after all, a prince).

As Quixote outlines his status, he alternately suggests that lineage is fixed and important, unfixed and unimportant. He also, as he adumbrates Freud, offers a complicated version of fictive kinship that will have important consequences for eighteenth-century fiction:

> It may be that the sage who shall write my history will so clear up my ancestry and pedigree that I may find myself fifth or sixth in descent from a king. For I would have you know, Sancho, that there are two kinds of lineage in the world. Some there are who trace and derive their descent from kings and princes, but time has reduced them little by little until they end in a point like a pyramid upside down. Others who spring from the common herd go on rising step by step until they come to be great lords. Thus the difference is that the former were what they no longer are, and the others are what they previously were not. Of these I may be one, so that after investigation my origin may prove great and famous, with which the king, my father-in-law to be, ought to be satisfied. Should he not be, the princess will so love me that even though she well knew me to be the son of a water carrier, she will take me for her lord and husband in spite of her father. (149)

Quixote, as always, fantasizes with remarkable force. But the vagueness of Cervantes' pronoun reference ("Of *these* I may be one") points to the larger social accommodations that Quixote's imaginings encourage. Just outside the fantasy is the possibility of Quixote's exercising brute force; given the power of "his arm,"

Quixote simply could "carry . . . off the princess." Or as Sancho observes, "Never ask as a favor what you can take by force." Within the fantasy, Quixote's most fervent wish is that his family records might be fictionalized, that a "sage" will rewrite his "history" such that he may claim descent from a king. All this despite Quixote's prefacing these remarks to Sancho by lamenting, "I do not know how it can be made out that I am of royal lineage, or even second cousin to an emperor" (149).

Quixote wants someone else to write/discover his "family romance," and this reveals his unwillingness to challenge social categories directly. While the syntax of his sentences—"the former were what they no longer are, and the others what they previously were not"—emphasizes the fluidity of social identity, the diction—"common herd," "great lords," "water carrier"— emphasizes the powerful hold of hierarchy. Unwilling to write and then sustain a version of fictive kinship, Quixote responds unpredictably to specific instances of status inconsistency. As he listens to the story of Basilio and Quiteria (2:xix), Quixote first claims that Basilio, who possesses many virtues, including "skill" with a sword, "deserves to marry, not merely the fair Quiteria, but Queen Guinivere herself" (527). But after Sancho approves of the marriage, Quixote takes the opposite tack, supporting the "right" of Quiteria's parents to marry her to the wealthier and better placed, if less talented, Camacho:

> If all those who love one another were to marry . . . it would deprive parents of their right to choose and to marry off their children to the proper person at the proper time. If it was left to daughters to choose husbands as they pleased, one would be for choosing her father's servant, and another, some one she has seen passing in the street and thinks gallant and dashing, though he may be a drunken bully. (527–28)

Quixote subsequently urges Basilio to "abandon the accomplishments he was skilled in, for though they brought him fame, they brought him no money. He should apply himself to the acquisition of wealth by legitimate industry" (544)—in other words, become more like Camacho, less like Don Quixote himself.

While Quixote responds erratically to status inconsistency, Dorotea, whose story unfolds in the second half of part 1, responds more purposefully. Probably the most remarkable figure in the *Quixote* apart from the Don and Sancho, Dorotea resolves (or at least manages) both Quixote's madness and the uncertainties about status that it suggests. Her story begins with an act of status inconsistency. Her parents are "vassals" to an Andalusian duke, "one of those who are called Grandees of Spain" (211). But her parents also are "so wealthy that if birth had conferred on them as much as fortune . . . I would have no reason to fear trouble like that in which I now find myself" (211–12). Indeed, Dorotea directly attributes "my ill fortune . . . to their lack of noble birth," revealing a fine sense of both the importance and the elusiveness of status:

> It is true that they are not so lowly that they have any reason to be ashamed of their condition. . . . [T]hey are peasants, plain homely people, without any taint of disreputable blood, and, as the saying is, old rusty Christians, but so rich that by their wealth and sumptuous way of life they are coming by degrees to be considered gentlefolk by birth, and even noble. (217)

Dorotea's strength is that she confronts so matter-of-factly the disparate social attitudes that lead Quixote to wish for a "family romance." Confident and clear about her parentage, Dorotea can benefit from social change ("coming by degrees"), even as she identifies herself as an "old . . . Christian" with untainted "blood."

This confidence does not spare her from temptation when the "younger son of the Duke," Don Fernando, is "smitten with a violent love" for her. While "it gave me a certain satisfaction to find myself so sought and prized by a gentleman of such distinction," Dorotea, urged by her parents, recognizes the "disparity between Don Fernando and myself" (213) and resists his advances. When Don Fernando invades Dorotea's rooms and embraces her, she initially offers powerful and eloquent resistance: "I am your vassal, but I am not your slave; your nobility neither has nor should have any right to dishonor my birth. Low-born peasant that I am, I have my self-respect as much as you, a lord and gentleman" (214). This resistance continues so long as Dorotea remembers the maxim, later (449) offered by Teresa Panza, "marriages . . . unequal never bring happiness." But it weakens with other, less categorical thoughts:

> I debated the matter briefly in my own mind. "I shall not be the first," I said to myself, "who has risen through marriage from a lowly to a lofty station, nor will Don Fernando be the first led by beauty or, as is more likely, a blind attachment, to marry below his rank. Conse-

quently, since I am introducing no new usage or practice, I may as
well avail myself of the honor that chance offers me." (215)

Dorotea gives in to Don Fernando not only because of "the charms
of his person and his high-bred grace" (216) but also because she
can see her action as not offending against tradition. The confusion that contributes to her seduction is much the same that
pushes Quixote to his family romance: social identity is simultaneously fixed and fluid.

Don Fernando breaks all his promises to Dorotea in order to
make a "brilliant match" with Luscinda. His plans are upset
because Luscinda has betrothed herself to Cardenio, "a gentleman
of distinction." Outraged, Fernando tries to stab Luscinda, fails,
and, as she flees, sets out after her. Cardenio, heartbroken by what
he takes to be the marriage of Luscinda to Fernando, also leaves
the scene. The four characters wander around la Mancha, meeting
unexpectedly at the inn of Maritornes, the inn most famous for
Don Quixote's night adventures—his battle with wineskins, his
subsequent fight with the landlord, and, proceeding through all
this, the story of ill-advised curiosity. In the midst of Quixote's
melees and one of Cervantes' more famous digressions, an important social accommodation occurs (290–91), one that sets a precedent for others.

As the four mixed-up lovers recognize each other, Dorotea has
her chance to sway Fernando:

> Consider, my lord, that the incomparable affection I bear you may
> compensate for the beauty and noble birth for which you would
> desert me. . . . [Y]ou were not unaware of my station in life, and well
> you know how I yielded wholly to your will. . . . [D]o not make the
> old age of my parents miserable. The loyal services they as faithful
> vassals have ever rendered your family do not merit such a return,
> and if you think it will debase your blood to mingle it with mine,
> reflect that there is little or no nobility in the world that has not trav-
> elled the same road, and that in illustrious lineages it is not the
> woman's blood that counts. Reflect, moreover, that true nobility con-
> sists of virtue, and if you are lacking in that, refusing me what in jus-
> tice you owe me, then even my claims to nobility are higher than
> yours. (289)

"Conquered" by this speech, Fernando releases Luscinda and
accepts "the injured Dorotea" as his wife. He receives universal
acclaim from the now rather large company that has gathered

around them, the priest reminding him "that beauty enjoys the privilege, provided virtue accompany it, of exalting itself to any rank, without any slur upon the man who places it upon an equality with himself" (291). (This helpful doctrine Richardson's Mr. B will repeat almost exactly.) Dorotea succeeds because she vindicates both egalitarian and elitist sympathies. She opens by suggesting ways she can "compensate" for her "birth," then suggests that "nobility" actually may be mutable, and concludes by proposing that "nobility consists of virtue," virtue as defined by "just" treatment of individuals rather than by class.

As Don Quixote's difficulties in defining his rank suggest, Dorotea's mediation between "peasant" and "grandee" is a special and rare achievement. Her social success finds an appropriate and important counterpart in her ability to manage Quixote. When the barber and the priest first tell her about "the strange nature of Don Quixote's madness" (221)—this just after she has recounted her brief liaison with Don Fernando—Dorotea promptly suggests that "she could play the distressed damsel . . . especially as she had with her a dress in which to do it to perfection. . . . She had read a great many books of chivalry and knew exactly the style in which afflicted damsels begged boons of knights-errant." Dorotea becomes the princess Micomicona, playing with "great ease of manner" the role of an "heiress in the direct male line . . . come to beg . . . [Quixote to] redress a wrong or injury that a wicked giant has done her" (222). The ruse, of course, allows her to lead Quixote home, but it also allows her to act the part she will assume as Fernando's wife. "Being quick witted" (227, 364), Dorotea finds in Quixote's madness a simulacrum for the social reality that she hopes to create. *Don Quixote* may be the antiromance that critics have claimed it to be,[21] but for the clever and graceful Dorotea, the romances are a means to enter Quixote's delusion and to profit from the invention of social status that the delusion allows.

Throughout the second day of adventures at the inn, Don Fernando, now reconciled to Dorotea, acts with great authority. When the innkeeper would disabuse Quixote of his delusion— "You were engaged with a couple of wineskins and not a giant"— Don Fernando tells him "to hold his tongue and not interrupt" (Cervantes, 295). Fernando's status now is in service to Quixote's illusion. He also protects Quixote after the latter attacks the officers of the Holy Brotherhood and brings total chaos to the inn (358). Only because they submit to "the rank of those with whom they had fought" (359) do the officers not arrest Quixote. Subsequently, they accept the priest's claim that Quixote is "a madman" (361) and thus not prosecutable. In the aftermath of Dorotea's triumphant handling of the two men, Don Fernando's status serves Quixote's madness.

The second day also brings to the inn Clara and Luis, two lovers of different social rank who reenact the bridging of social differences that Dorotea and Fernando barely, but now happily have achieved. Here again Fernando acts with confidence in his authority. Luis's "father is of such a lofty position and so wealthy" that Clara fears "he would think I was not fit to be even a servant of his son, much less wife" (343). Luis is traveling incognito in search of Clara, "in clothing . . . unbecoming his rank" (351). In a reunion scene, as he asks for Clara's hand and advises her father of "the wealth and noble birth of my parents," he also anticipates the freedom and power of young men in eighteenth-century Britain: "I am their sole heir." Clara's father, a "shrewd" judge, wants the marriage to be with the consent of Luis's parents because, while he can see how "advantageous" the match is, he also knows that Luis's father is "looking for a title for his son" (353). Don Fernando uses his prestige not only to give Luis "the welcome his breeding entitled him to" (359) but also to reconcile Clara's father to the match. With the Dorotea-Fernando precedent set, the Clara-Luis match is made more smoothly. Dorotea can confidently urge Clara to "trust in God" for "the happy ending that such an innocent beginning deserves" (343).

All the conflicts created at the inn by Quixote's delusions or by status inconsistency are resolved finally by "the great zeal and eloquence of the priest," who negotiates settlements, and by "the unexampled generosity of Don Fernando," who pays for all damages: "The inn no longer reminded one of the discord of Agramante's camp . . . but of the peace and tranquility of the days of Octavianus" (362). As part of this "golden" consensus, the "illustrious company . . . devised a plan that, without giving Dorotea and Don Fernando the trouble of going back with Don Quixote to his village under pretense of restoring Queen Micomicona, would allow the priest and the barber to carry him away with them" (365). The Micomicona illusion brings Don Quixote to submit gladly to being caged; it is an illusion that Dorotea (and now Fernando and the rest of the company) use with calculated detachment. Having achieved true social status, Dorotea steps out of the simulacrum of it. She stands as a woman of beauty, eloquence, and control, one who will not permit her story to be interrupted by the chaos around her, most notably by the emotional outbursts of Cardenio. Her beauty, wit, and will achieve a rare triumph over the dangers created by status inconsistency. The peasant and the grandee wed.

Such accommodations are not as easily made in the second part of the *Quixote*. The central figure here is the man in the green coat, Don Diego de Miranda. But he, in many ways the polar opposite of Quixote, suggests the unlikelihood of the mediation that Dorotea achieves—particularly for individuals who are not sensitive to (that is, both able to participate in but also to manage) Quixote's madness. Don Quixote is both decisive and effective during the interlude with Don Diego, in part because the mundane life of the latter gives focus and force to the madness of the former. Quixote triumphs over false knights (Carrasco) and real, if indolent, lions; he does not attack wineskins and then depend upon the "fair Dorotea" to clean up his mess. Strengthened by his antithesis, Don Diego, Quixote, for the first time in the narrative, speaks self-consciously about his madness: "No doubt, Senor Don Diego de Miranda . . . you look on me as a fool and a madman. It would be no wonder if you did, for my deeds bear witness to nothing else. But for all that, I would have you note that I am neither so mad nor so foolish as you might have thought" (517).

If Dorotea makes Quixote look confused, Don Diego makes him look heroic. Cervantes presents Don Diego as the representative of a sanctimonious suburban piety, a piety unable to manage or to profit from social change. His characterization of Don Diego carefully references social categories and, in its smallest details, points to the dead end at which the man in the green coat has arrived. Both Don Diego and Alonso Quijano (?) are avid hunters; both participate in this favorite pastime of the Spanish aristocracy (as scores of paintings in the Prado attest). But in Don Diego's case, while "my pursuits are hunting and fishing . . . I keep neither hawks nor greyhounds—nothing but a tame partridge or a bold ferret or two" (507). In other words, rather than hunting large game with dogs, or large birds with hawks, Don Diego hunts for rabbits in their burrows with ferrets. Defining his hunting by negation ("neither hawks nor greyhounds"), Don Diego offers "a decadent version"[22] of a noble pastime. Quixote suggests this when, as he prepares to beard the lion—the lion, it should be noted, is a gift to the king—he curtly dismisses Don Diego: "You go and mind your tame partridge and bold ferret. . . . This is my business" (513).

Brought into contrast with Quixote, Don Diego appears not as an upwardly mobile peasant (the role of Dorotea), nor as an upwardly mobile professional (the role of Clara's father), but rather as a hidalgo who pursues only a degraded version of the heroic past and has no future toward which to direct his small portion of energy. He is given to "leafing through" books and to defining his virtues negatively: "no taste for gossip" ; "no display of charitable works"; "I do not pry into my neighbors' lives, nor do I guess at others' motives." He values "entertainment being neat and well served" (507) and, thus, is troubled by his son's study of poetry because he cannot see that the king will "liberally reward" it (508). He rides a horse equipped "for field use," not for combat, and his spears are not "gilt but lacquered green" (505). When Sancho, impressed by Don Diego's material well-being, describes him as a "saint," Don Diego, ever negative, declines the appellation.

Don Diego complains of his son, Don Lorenzo, "not that he is a bad son, but he is not so good as I could wish" (508). He similarly observes of Quixote, "I have seen him act like the greatest madman in the world, and heard him make observations so sensible that they efface and cancel everything he does . . . though, to tell the truth, I am more inclined to regard him as mad than sane" (520). In both cases he reacts conventionally. He does not fear Quixote's madness; indeed, he invites Quixote to his home. But he also cannot be enlivened by it. While much changes for Dorotea, who enters Quixote's madness, nothing changes for Don Diego. While Don Quixote can hope a "sage" will rewrite his family history, the translator of the *Quixote* finally dismisses Don Diego as a candidate for literary rehabilitation:

> Here the author [Cide Hamete Benegeli] paints a detailed picture of Don Diego's mansion, displaying for us the whole contents of a rich gentleman farmer's house. But the translator of the history thought it best to pass over these and other details of the same sort in silence, as they were not in harmony with the main purpose of the story, the strong point of which is truth rather than dull digressions. (519)

Don Diego's life abounds in the domestic "details" through which eighteenth-century writers, in Watt's view, "individualize" their characters. For Cervantes, however, Don Diego is uninteresting because neither he nor his son (who apparently is more of a poseur than a poet) will enter Quixote's madness. Don Diego offers Don Quixote to his son as a problem to be solved: "Talk to him yourself and take the pulse of his intelligence. You are discerning so exercise your best judgment concerning his wisdom or folly" (520). But Don Lorenzo, like his father, cannot treat Quixote decisively and to some purpose: "All the doctors and clever scribes in the world . . . will not make sense of his madness, for it is an illegible scrawl. His is a madness streaked with lucid intervals" (522). As the odd but finally telling metaphor "illegible scrawl" indicates, neither father nor son is ready to "read" Quixote, neither is "quickwitted" enough to enter Quixote's romance as Dorotea does. As he departs, Quixote urges Don Lorenzo to "turn aside from the somewhat narrow path of poetry and take the still narrower one of knight-errantry." The latter, Quixote urges, "is wide enough, however, to make you an emperor in the twinkling of an eye." Both father and son see this as one more instance of Quixote's talking "sense at one moment and nonsense the next." Neither picks up on Quixote's suggestion that Don Lorenzo accompany him.

In describing Quixote's actions as an "illegible scrawl," the de Mirandas anticipate the failures in perception and sympathy of the ducal pair. But successful readers do appear—Dorotea in part 1 anticipating Don Antonio Moreno in part 2. However, the *Quixote* exerts a powerful influence upon eighteenth-century British fiction not because the misplaced knight-errant evokes different responses from different people. Rather, Cervantes showed later novelists that it was possible to link the social (the decline of the hidalgo) with the literary (the viability of the romance tradition at the intersection of the medieval and Renaissance periods). A witty and brave character like Dorotea can enter the madness and find in it a means to social elevation. Less forceful, less skillful characters can profess only amazement at the madness (Don Diego) or cruelly mistreat it (the ducal pair), in both cases only affirming, perhaps hastening, their social decline. (The ducal pair, we should remember, has fallen in debt to their steward, a debt their extravagant treatment of Quixote only increases.)

Cervantes binds together in *Don Quixote* the social and the literary confusions of golden age Spain. He bequeaths to the British novelists who follow him more than a few scenes (nighttime confusion at an inn becomes almost obligatory in eighteenth-century comic fiction) and characters (the types of the eccentric master and the commonsensical servant). He also provides a seminal example of "fictive kin" as a response both to literary and to social change. Foucault errs when he claims that Quixote's madness has to be suppressed, that Quixote's experience is both ultimate and lacerating. Quixote has the power to wander free, to build his own asylums because his madness is of great use. He reveals to a Spanish society undergoing the uncertainties of unification and to a British society undergoing the uncertainties of demographic crisis the efficacy of fictional versions of kinship, however mad, in mediating conflicts created by status inconsistency. If wanderers from Joseph Andrews and Tom Jones to Roderick Random and Humphry Clinker are Quixote's sons, women who fashion themselves, from Moll Flanders and Roxana to Pamela and Evelina, are Dorotea's daughters. Quixote's madness, like that of Huarte's page, was neither lonely nor, finally, anguished. He drew and then impressed a crowd.

2
Milton's Two Versions of the Patriarch: Mimetic and Anamnestic Plots

So spake the Patriarch of Mankind, but *Eve*
Persisted; yet submiss, though last repli'd.
With thy permission then, and thus forewarn'd
. . . I go . . .

—Paradise Lost, 9:376–80

John Shawcross has claimed that, for eighteenth-century British writers, "Milton does loom large as a given, a presence that does not have to be explained or detailed or justified."[1] In both the force of his claim and the erudition with which he backs it, Shawcross stands as a worthy successor to Raymond Dexter Havens, whose chapters on "The Attitude of the Eighteenth Century Towards Milton" rehearse in sometimes astonishing detail the wide sale of Milton's poems and his great effect upon the prosody, diction, and matter of poets from Pope to Thomson to Young.[2] How we will characterize Milton's "influence" upon later writers remains, of course, a crucial, even definitive, question: Harold Bloom centers his study of "misprision" upon the notion that Milton set a standard, at once enabling and baleful, for later poets;[3] Leopold Damrosch Jr., writing in the wake of George Lukács, argues that for novelists, Milton, insofar as he "psychologizes doctrine" and "individualizes myth," opens the way to the representation of "individual consciousness."[4]

Milton, beyond his effect upon their psychologies or their understanding of myth, bequeaths to eighteenth-century novelists two different versions of the relationship between fathers and sons. Insofar as these two narratives bespeak different attitudes toward the patriarch, they achieve political and social, as well as formal, significance. In charting these two plots, I assume, as Shawcross encourages us to do, that any study of eighteenth-century literature does well to begin with Milton. I also suggest that Milton is influential because, even more specifically than Cervantes, he raises questions about the nature and the bounds of patriarchal power. He thus anticipates fictional responses to the demographic crisis that began in the second half of his life. Paul Yoder has pointed out that Milton's influence upon Richardson, particularly in discussions of *Paradise Lost* as a source for *Clarissa*, has been a rich topic for criticism, a topic this chapter will address in its conclusion.[5] The differences between Milton's two versions of the patriarch, however, appear most clearly in a contrast between references to him by Fielding and Smollett.

In his version of what Ronald Paulson refers to as "the expulsion story,"[6] Fielding alludes specifically to Milton: "*The World*, as *Milton* phrases it, *lay all before him*; and [Tom] *Jones*, no more than *Adam*, had any man to whom he might resort for Comfort or Assistance."[7] Smollett, however, avoids "meaningful allusions to the Christian myth that lies behind Perry's [Peregrine Pickle's] exclusion" (Paulson, 68). Smollett will not point to his source, will not admit his allegiance because his fiction seeks to subvert the social and literary traditions in defense of which Fielding writes.[8] Smollett knows his Milton as well as Fielding does, but his is a different Milton.

As Smollett refutes David Hume's comments upon Milton in the latter's *History of Great Britain*, he reveals his "lifelong esteem for Milton"[9] and also makes a political statement:

> We think Mr. *Hume* is too severe on the character and abilities of *Milton*. He says "he prostituted his pen in factious disputes, and in justifying the most violent measures of his party."—We have a better opinion of Milton.—He was an enthusiast; but, surely no prostitute. Neither do we find his prose writings disagreeable; nor any of his poetical performances flat and insipid. We cannot think [as Hume claims] that near one third of his *Paradise Lost* is devoid of harmony, elegance, and vigor of imagination. (*The Critical Review*, December 1756, p. 388)

Smollett lives in literary history as a Tory, but his view of Milton's "prose writings" indicates that his Toryism is of the iconoclastic variety described by Donald J. Greene.[10] Smollett, like Samuel Johnson, espoused Toryism only to place himself apart from the mid-eighteenth-century Whig hegemony. Smollett's defense of Milton's political writing depends upon his distinguishing between a "prostitute" and an "enthusiast." While this distinction seems obvious enough, as Smollett willingly embraces "enthusiasm," he separates himself from the great Tories of the early eighteenth century—Swift and Pope—and from a centrist Whig of his own day—Fielding. Smollett only may appear to remind us that Milton, the great poet, also had a political career. But his description of Milton's prose (not "disagreeable") is in equal parts disingenuous and revolutionary. In mid-eighteenth-century England, Milton's views on divorce, censorship, and monarchical power all were far from mainstream, even though a grateful nation celebrated (and demanded almost yearly new editions of) his Christian epic.

When Smollett brings Milton's political writings into his defense of *Paradise Lost* or fails to mention Milton as one source for his "expulsion" story, he practices a distinctive type of remembering, a remembering very different from Fielding's more overt referencing of his sources. Smollett, celebrating the political Milton, the subversive Milton, remembers anamnestically rather than, as Fielding does, mimetically. While in classical rhetoric, anamnesis is synonymous with recollection or memory, with a calling to mind, the figure undergoes significant modification in its passage from Socrates to, more recently, Paul Feyerabend. In both the *Phaedo* and the *Meno*, Socrates uses the term in its noblest sense, arguing that in our memory resides the most powerful proof that we come from God, that we have souls. Recounting these dialogues, Plato discovers that learning and recollecting are one and the same. By the sixteenth century, anamnesis undergoes an important change in its connotation, if not in its meaning. Henry Peacham defines it as "a forme of speech by which the speaker calling to Remembrance matters past, doth make remembrance of them sometime matters of sorrow." For Peacham, anamnesis is recollection, but recollection of "what we have suffered." Peacham's emphasis upon sorrow intensifies in the eighteenth and nineteenth centuries, anamnesis becoming, in one definition, "the story which the patient tells of his illness." Outlining his "anarchistic theory of knowledge," Feyerabend, writing in 1975, uses anamnesis to designate a strategy of revolutionary scientists who hide the subversiveness of their findings by writing as if they remind us of what we already know. In the case of one of Feyerabend's favorite examples, Galileo, "the methods of reminiscence [anamnesis], to which he appeals . . . create the impression that nothing has changed and that we continue expressing our ideas in old and familiar ways."[11]

Trained as a physician and dubious about any claim that Plato might make to be "the great oracle of human reason,"[12] Smollett works between the versions of remembrance offered by Socrates, Peacham, medical texts, and Feyerabend. While all his longer prose fictions describe characters who are "on the road," their journeys are neither pilgrimages nor quests nor progresses. In his birth-mystery plots, as in his journey motifs, Smollett establishes but then confounds mimetic expectations about what characters can mean or can be. In his remembering, Smollett redacts one of Milton's plots. Particularly in *Paradise Lost*, Milton combines seemingly conventional reminiscence, the account of the Creation and the Fall in Genesis, with the undercutting of the very traditions to which he appeals. God's words find their way into Satan's mouth, hypocrisy (the false version of true virtue) is proclaimed to be impossible for even angels to discern (3:680–85), events that happen for God in an "eternal present" (3:170–80) happen for man and the fallen angels in a sequence of days and nights, a sequence that raises painful and, finally, impossible questions about "Fixed Fate, Free will, Foreknowledge absolute" (2:560–61). Indeed, the dual nature of Milton's plotting perhaps is best glossed by Boethius, who describes God foreseeing all in his "eternal present" while man acts freely in his "time": "The divine mind, looking down on all things, does not disturb the nature of things, which are present before it but are future with respect to time. . . . [T]he same future event is necessary with respect to God's knowledge of it, but free and undetermined if considered in its own nature."[13]

Milton's narrative reveals its dualism—as well as its importance for novelists with very different social motives—in its treatment of "Providence." Surely this must be an important word in an epic written to "assert Eternal Providence / And justify the ways of God to men" (1:25–26). Yet, while Milton does use the word in his opening and his final verse paragraphs, the word (and its variant "provident") is used only three more times in the poem, twice by Satan (1:162) and the fallen angels (2:559), and once by the fallen Adam (12:564). How can Milton "assert Eternal Providence" while using the word so sparingly? Without offering a final answer to this question, we can suggest that "Providence" does control one of Milton's plots, the plot of God the father whose son will "provide" for man's needs and eventually will "bruise" the head of Satan (12:223–24, 383–84, 430). However, in human time—that is, in Adam's story once he comes down from the mountain top with Michael—Providence is a latent, sometimes even seemingly absent force. In man's story, references to Providence function anamnestically, giving an appearance of conventionality to events that otherwise defy explanation. How, indeed, could God permit man to fall? Why do bad things happen to good people?

In his epic, Milton combines mimesis and anamnesis. He offers one narrative in which he does "justify" God's ways, another narrative in which those ways are difficult to see. He encourages his readers to achieve the great virtues—". . . add Faith / Add Virtue, Patience, Temperance, add Love, / By name to come call'd Charity, the soul / Of all the rest" (12:581–83)—even as he shows how easily those virtues are feigned, how difficult they are to name rightly, let alone realize in our lives. Fielding takes from Milton his mimetic plot, revealing the workings of Providence in what initially seem the multifarious events of his narrative. Smollett, an angrier, more marginalized writer than Fielding,[14] takes from Milton his anamnestic plot, using traditional devices of narrative (the birth mystery) and a traditional vocabulary ("Providence") but in ways that undercut their ability to account for events.

Of course, the distinction between mimetic and anamnestic plots is not absolute, nor do those plots occur in pure forms. For only one example, the events at the inn at Upton in *Tom Jones* reveal Fielding working in an anamnestic vein. Still, Milton's achievement in *Paradise Lost* does set important questions. Why do writers who come after him lack his scope? In particular, why do eighteenth-century novelists tend to divide his plots? Ian Watt has warned against "the terms 'genius' and 'accident,' the twin faces on the Janus of the dead ends of literary history" (9). While the case for Milton's "genius" is as strong as any, we can note that he reaches maturity before the demographic crisis through which Defoe, Fielding, and Smollett all live. Indeed, as the Stones have shown, life expectancy would not return to the level of Milton's young manhood until late in the eighteenth century (137). Also, as the poems "Ad Patrem" and "At A Solemn Music" reveal, Milton's father encouraged his literary career—supported him both emotionally and financially, supported him as perhaps only another artist (Milton Sr. being a noted amateur composer) could.

While Milton's relations with his wives and daughters are famous
for stories about their unhappinesses and difficulties, his relations
with his father avoided the anxiety that motivates the fictionalizing of kinship in eighteenth-century life and art.

"At A Solemn Music" opens with Milton noting that "Voice and
Verse" (l. 2) are sister arts and celebrating their "mixt Power" (l. 3)
in songs raised to God. Milton describes man's prelapsarian voice
as "undiscording" until "disproportion'd sin / Jarr'd against
nature's chime" and "Broke the fair music that all creatures made"
(ll. 18–19). Insofar as his art, "Verse," and his father's art, "Voice,"
join together, Milton sees the possibility to "renew that Song" (l.
25) lost with Adam's sin. "At A Solemn Music" links this "perfect
Diapason" (l. 22) to a right relationship with God. Milton associates working with his father with working towards God.

In "Ad Patrem," Milton celebrates the father with reference to
classical rather than to Christian history. The poem, addressed to
"venerandi . . . parentis," to "pater optime" (ll. 5–6), hints at the
difficulty Milton's father had in accepting his son's decision to be
a poet rather than an attorney. As Milton encourages his father not
to despise the poet's work—"Nec tu vatis opus divinum despice
carmen" (l. 17)—so he also suggests that the father's approval has
given him his language, even his voice: "Tu pater optime, sumtu /
Cum mihi Romuleae patuit facundia linguae" (ll. 77–78). To win
his father's approval, Milton recounts the heroic past of poetry. He
describes the poet's divine song preserving a spark of Promethean
fire and recalls bards singing at royal tables, "Carmina regales
epulas ornare solebant" (l. 41). As the father is a musician and,
thus, the heir of Arion, so the son has been born a poet, "me
genuisse poetam" (l. 61). Father and son pursue sister arts,
"Cognatas artes" (l. 63), and in their bond reunite Phoebus, that is,
they renew the classical God, who, in Milton's account, divided
himself up in order that father and son each might have a gift:
"Ipse volens Phoebus se depertire duobus, / Altera dona mihi,
dedit altera dona parenti, / Disiduumque Deum genitorque
puerque tenemus" (ll. 64–66). As the father-son partnership will
renew divine harmony in "At A Solemn Music," so in "Ad
Patrem" it will restore wholeness within the arts.

Throughout "Ad Patrem" Milton emphasizes that poetry is all
he has ("Quae mihi sunt nullae, nisi quas dedit aurea Clio" [l. 14]),
but that poetry partakes of the divine ("Sancta Promethae retinens
vestigia flammae" [l. 20]). Thus, his father's support of his work as
a poet is the greatest of gifts, one to be spoken of in the same

breath as Hyperion's giving his chariot to Phaeton. His father's support also contributes to, perhaps even originates, the great confidence with which the poem ends. Milton promises his father that, however obscure his present place, he eventually will win the laurel. While this confidence would be tested by political defeats, by discord in his own family, and by his blindness, Milton could take his relationship with his father as a model for man's relationship with "th' Almighty Father." In his mimetic plot, Jesus acts as a perfect son to God, a perfect father. Only in his anamnestic plot, does Adam, the later son of God, lose touch with the Father, falling into discord with both his maker and his wife.

Leopold Damrosch Jr. concludes that "For Milton the biblical story was the one true story of which all others were reflections. For Fielding it guaranteed a universal order which comic fiction could imitate, even if lived experience might not disclose it. Since Fielding's time it has proved impossible to recreate that order in fictive form, however much individuals might accept it as doctrine or ethical code" (302). Damrosch, however, perhaps oversimplifies Milton's attitude toward God's plot. Milton believed that the biblical story was, indeed, "the one true story," but in his life as a seventeenth-century controversialist—working for the commonwealth government, suffering opprobrium as "the divorcer"—he learned how difficult the "true story" was to identify in man's time. Damrosch rightly sees Fielding as the great comic heir of Milton's mimetic plot but fails to observe the anamnestic plot that Milton left to Smollett. In response to the demographic crisis that began in the second half of the seventeenth century, both Fielding and Smollett express considerable anxiety about fatherhood. In their fictions, fathers are either missing, impaired, or (the case of *Peregrine Pickle*) oddly displaced. In Fielding's fictions, insofar as "Providence" can be imitated, problems of succession can be overcome. Fictive kinship maintains familial, social, and literary order. In Smollett's fictions, "Providence" is used anamnestically. The word is either, as in *Paradise Lost*, conspicuously absent, or it is made synonymous with "Fortune." And succession remains problematic, even confusing, as familial, social, and literary order remain liable to rapid subversion.

Although the pairing initially seems implausible, Milton's two versions of the father appear clearly if we place *Paradise Lost* over against Robert Filmer's *Patriarcha*, a work written between 1635 and 1642 but not published until 1680.[15] Filmer's life and his politics were opposite to Milton's. Although both men were educated

at Cambridge, Filmer was the eldest son in a wealthy and large
family, or, as Peter Laslett puts it, "he was his own example of the
rights and duties of primogeniture" (2). He succeeded to his
father's estate in 1629 and wrote essays for limited publication to
share with his fellow members of the East Sutton gentry. While
Milton was a puritan revolutionary, Filmer was a royalist and
spent time in prison (1643–47) during the Civil War. While Milton
was a famous and energetic controversialist, Filmer "appears to
have maintained a deliberate attitude of non-intervention
throughout the whole struggle: all he did was to write a little and
to publish less" (5). The perfect Roundhead and the perfect Cavalier, Milton and Filmer might be expected to differ in all ways.
That their notions about patriarchy occasionally conjoin only
reveals how basic patrilineal succession was to the English elite
and how unprepared the English were for the demographic crisis
that began near the end of Filmer's life.

Filmer's version of patriarchy shares much with Milton's
description of the relationship between God and Christ; for all his
indisputable political and religious iconoclasm, Milton, in God's
plot, proceeds traditionally. Filmer differs from Milton in a small
but crucial way: he assumes that postlapsarian sovereigns exert
authority similar to that of prelapsarian God. In arguing against
"the Unnatural Liberty of the People," Filmer claims, "I see not . . .
how the children of Adam, or of any man else, can be free from
subjection to their parents." For him, "this subordination of
children is the fountain of all regal authority," because it sets the
model for the relationship between "Kings and their people" (57).

Filmer distances himself from Milton's anamnestic plot when,
after admitting that "Kings be not the natural parents of their
subjects," he attempts to justify royal sovereignty. As he anticipates the objection that the power of fathers over children does
not correlate with the sovereignty of kings over their subjects,
Filmer anticipates disputes about figurative language that are with
us even today:

> After a few descents, when the true fatherhood itself was extinct, and
> only the right of the Father descended to the true heir, then the title of
> Prince or King was more significant to express the power of him who
> succeeds only to the right of fatherhood which his ancestors did natu-
> rally enjoy. (61)

John Locke, in his *Two Treatises of Government*, has fun with and
reduces to absurdity Filmer's attempt to trace the sovereignty of

British kings back to the patriarchs of the Old Testament. And Filmer, insofar as he models all political power upon Adam's authority over his children, sets himself up for such an attack. But here we see the true basis for sovereignty as Filmer conceives of it. Even when the "true fatherhood itself . . . [is] extinct," Filmer contends that the words "Prince or King" signify "naturally" the "power" that the first father had. By the standards of postmodernism, Filmer practices the most naive of semiologies—but his naiveté will be shared by characters as diverse as Clarissa Harlowe and Smollett's Uncle Tom Bowling, by the narrator of *Tom Jones* and by Milton in the sections of *Paradise Lost* given over to God's story. Filmer believes that words and gestures can bespeak directly and truthfully a preexistent, if hidden, nature. As Locke attacks Filmer's version of political sovereignty in his *Two Treatises*, so he will attack Filmer's semiology in his *An Essay Concerning Human Understanding*.[16] Filmer assumes that political sovereignty is as natural and clear as the sovereignty a father exerts over a child: "If we compare the *natural* duties of a Father with those of a King, we find them all to be one, without any difference at all but in the latitude or extent of them" (Laslett, 63, my italics). His political confidence depends upon his faith that the words "Father" and "King" have natural and uniform signification.

As Milton's Christ offers perfect obedience to Milton's God, the events of *Paradise Lost* illustrate the "natural subjection" and the "natural power" to which Filmer repeatedly (72, 84, 113, 188, 194, and 210) refers—the "natural power" he finds vindicated in the writings of Aristotle as well as in the Old Testament: "That there is no monarchy but paternal" (229). Filmer takes this as his central and abiding truth, using it to dismiss republican notions of government by contract. "Even the power which God exerciseth over man," Filmer claims, "is by right of fatherhood" (233). This is the "power" that Milton portrays Christ as perfectly fulfilling, Adam and Eve as disrespecting. For Filmer, kings and princes represent "the supreme fatherly power," which can "regulate, limit, or assume the authority of inferior fathers." Only this "transcendent fatherly power" can grant children a dispensation "from obedience to subordinate [biological] parents" (269).

Filmer inherited his estate in 1629 and did most of his writing in the 1630s, before the demographic crisis that the Stones describe. This perhaps explains why he never asks the question that is basic to Adam's story in *Paradise Lost*, to Hale's *De Successionibus*, and to eighteenth-century novels: What happens if the father is distant, missing, impaired, or dead? For Filmer, any debate over sovereignty is easily and clearly resolved by the second commandment: "Whereas many confess that government only in the abstract is the ordinance of God, they are not able to prove any such ordinance in the scripture, but only in the fatherly power, and therefore we find the commandment that enjoins obedience to superiors given in the terms of honour thy father" (289). Novelists in eighteenth-century England will place characters outside this patriarchal model by giving them fathers who are, in a variety of ways, as far removed as Milton's God. The second commandment does not apply as clearly to foundlings and orphan heiresses as it does to first sons like Filmer. Near the end of the century, Elizabeth Inchbald and Frances Burney achieve popular and critical success with novels about young heiresses who cannot find in their guardians adequate surrogates for their absent fathers. For Inchbald's Miss Milner and Burney's Cecelia Beverley, Hale, not Filmer, defines their legal and social status: their gender is more important than their sex.

Because Filmer reads the second commandment as the "natural" basis for all sovereignty, he can accept with equanimity the accidents and usurpations that constitute so much of political history:

> The obedience which all subjects yield to Kings, is but the paying of that duty which is due to the supreme fatherhood: many times by the act either of a usurper himself, or of those that set him up, the true heir of a crown is dispossessed, God using the ministry of the wickedest men for the removing and setting up of Kings: in such cases *the subject's obedience to the fatherly power must go along and wait upon God's providence* who only hath the right to give and take away kingdoms, and thereby to adopt subjects into the obedience of another fatherly power. (289)

From Filmer's "The Anarchy of a Limited and Mixed Government" written in 1648, this passage comes early enough to spare Filmer, who died in 1653, from arguing for obedience to Oliver Cromwell and the Commonwealth. However, the passage contains within it a rationalization, even a vindication, for the indignities and losses that Filmer suffered at the hands of Cromwell's army. Having had his estate ransacked and having spent time in prison (5–7), Filmer did not support actively or publicly the cause of Charles I. Rather he kept the faith, the faith that the second commandment does hold the true basis of sovereignty and that God's power finally will bring all right. He will "wait upon God's providence" rather than fight, because he believes that he can identify and understand the workings of Providence. Eighteenth-century fiction offers many an example of "the true heir . . . dispossessed" by "a usurper." But the appeal to "providence" is not one that all novelists will make. As God's order is hard for the fallen Adam to see, so anamnestic writers like Smollett and Henry Mackenzie will confuse or fragment their action such that references to Providence ring weak and empty. Only characters who have not lived Roderick Random's life will happily attribute his final good "Fortune" to "Providence." Only the sentimental Harley will attribute the old soldier Edwards's reunion with his grandchildren to "Providence" without wondering where God was when Edwards lost his farm and the rest of his family. Filmer "waits upon" Providence because he wishes to avoid "a variety of interpretations and disputations" (293) in matters of law and sovereignty; he wants succession to occur within Noye's "etc." Neither Milton nor eighteenth-century novelists will share his faith in a single, "natural" understanding of man's governments and laws.

As Adam and Eve debate in *Paradise Lost* book 9 whether Eve will work alone in the Garden, they reveal the narrowness of Filmer's account of sovereignty. For Filmer, Adam and Eve are the great source of both paternal and monarchical power: "Neither Eve nor her children could either limit Adam's powers, or join others with him in the government; and what was given unto Adam, was given in his person to posterity" (283). Milton argues that even in prelapsarian Eden, submission is difficult to understand and to enact. When Eve proposes that she and Adam "divide our labors" (9:214), Adam pleas that she not leave his "faithful side" (9:265), lest she fall prey to "danger or dishonor" (9:267). Eve reads Adam's response as betokening "Thy . . . fear that my firm Faith and Love / Can by his [Satan's] fraud be shak'n or seduc't" (9:286–87). In a magnificent redaction of Milton's famous defense of a free press in *Areopagitica*—"I cannot praise a fugitive and cloistered virtue, unexercised and unbreathed, that never sallies out and sees her adversary" (728)—Eve asks Adam, "And what is Faith, Love, Virtue unassay'd / Alone, without exterior help sustain'd?" (9:335–36). This argument leads Adam to give up his: "Go; for thy stay not free, absents thee more" (9:372).

In his dialogue with Eve, Adam may be "the Patriarch of Mankind," and Eve may be described as "yet submiss." However, Eve has "Persisted" in defining and defending her wish, and she has led the patriarch to change his mind. While Filmer might read Eve's fall as foreordained in her refusal to submit to Adam's power, Milton sets the scene such that Eve takes her leave from Adam, saying, "With thy permission, then . . . I go" (9:378–82). Of course, we still could argue that Eve fails to understand the difference between fallen and unfallen worlds. The lines from *Areopagitica* that ring with so much force even today have no place in Eden. However, this does scant justice to the chronology (how can Eve know of the fallen world?) and to the splendid inclusiveness of Milton's poem. In God's plot, Filmer's version of sovereignty is perfectly realized. God is a flawless father, and Jesus a son who immediately understands and promptly does what his father wants. In man's story, however, and even before the Fall, Adam is God's other son, his second son, and like so many second sons in seventeenth- and eighteenth-century England, he lives without full access to his father's estate, his father's power. Eve loves Adam, but, as she questions his motives and, finally, takes her hand from his and goes her own way, she shows that she does not see him as God's natural representative. If God truly were in this man, then Raphael would not need to educate him.

Eve ventures out to her Fall paraphrasing Milton, but this does not reveal Milton to be qualifying or correcting his life's work. Rather, it reveals Milton, in his anamnestic plot, showing us how difficult it is to identify, let alone "wait upon God's providence." In man's story, the word occurs only three times and in debased usages because God's hand is hard to see in events. In God's plot, the word is unnecessary because Christ participates fully in God's wisdom and power. Milton uses the word in opening and in closing the poem that he spent his lifetime preparing to write. However, this is only his boldest claim to prophetic power, to special sight. He, indeed, can see the Providence that others cannot. He, in the greatest poem in English, integrates the pagan and the Christian, the Greek, the Latin, and the Hebraic. He also integrates the mimetic and the anamnestic: the son who perfectly represents and bravely fulfills his father's will, and the son who, unable to embody the father's sovereignty, goes against his "better Knowledge" and fails to obey the Father's commands.

Peter Laslett has written of Filmer's work:

Half a century went by between the time of the formulation of his position and the time of its entrance into the tradition of political thinking. Yet when *Patriarcha* appeared in 1680 its thesis had a cogency which it might have lacked in any other year in English history. Charles II, his Court and ministers and the whole body of opinion which favoured the continuance of the Restoration stood in desperate need of an argument which would vindicate legitimacy. (33)

Filmer's brief and posthumous fame ended "when the rightful heir went into exile, and the cult he [Filmer] upheld retired into the country houses of the Tory squires and into the studies of the non-juring parsons" (34). Filmer's day in the sun would not last long,[17] largely because his notion of patriarchal power was irrelevant to a society that, in 1688, invented a new version of monarchy, a society whose elite families, from 1650 onward, would rely upon fictive versions of kinship to maintain themselves. In Eve's prelapsarian investigation of Adam's power, in her winning his "permission" to be tested on her own, Milton expresses the "individualism" that Ian Watt places at the heart of the novel and that Filmer's political theory denied. In sending Eve to a test that she will fail speaking his words, Milton indicates his fundamental likeness with her, his belief that the second commandment cannot solve (as it does for Filmer) all questions about sovereignty.

In sending Eve away with his "permission," Adam participates in her Fall in advance of his sharing with her forbidden fruit. While in Filmer's version, Eve is absolutely subordinate to Adam ("Neither Eve nor her children . . . could limit Adam's power"), in Milton's version, Eve, with Adam's permission, takes a risk. While Sandra Gilbert claims in a famous and influential essay that Milton "cuts woman off from the spaciousness of possibility,"[18] we might say that Milton gives Eve some of his most famous words and leaves her, having failed a great and difficult test, with the "World . . . all before" (12:646) her. In book 9, Eve, rather than being victimized by "a barrage of angry words,"[19] wins an argument and converts Adam to her view. Filmer might well deserve Virginia Woolf's image of a "bogey," but Milton's case is more complicated.

Milton's sympathy with Eve anticipates Richardson's with Clarissa Harlowe. Because of the connections between Milton's Satan and Richardson's Robert Lovelace,[20] many critics have proposed that Richardson drew upon *Paradise Lost* when writing *Clarissa.* Yoder astutely observes, however, that "this reference to

Milton's epic suggests a story in which the central character suffers a moral defeat by surrendering to temptation, a suggestion that accommodates neither Clarissa's resistance to Lovelace nor the moral victory that Richardson saw in Clarissa's 'triumphant death.'" (Yoder, 87). Yoder suggests that *Clarissa* depends more upon *Paradise Regained* than *Paradise Lost* and proposes that Richardson, by making his figure of perfect virtue a woman, attempts to redeem Eve in a way that Milton's male-centered epics could not. In this suggestion, Yoder overlooks the anamnestic dimension of *Paradise Lost*; he also overlooks the work of Milton's that is most similar to *Clarissa—Comus*. Richardson uses *Paradise Lost* mimetically in his characterization of Lovelace's perfectly satanic villainy, but he uses *Comus* and *Paradise Lost* anamnestically to present Clarissa as a character who, like Milton's Eve, remains virtuous despite her violation of the second commandment.

The comparison between Lovelace and Comus can be briefly summarized, even as the comparison between Lovelace and Satan is directly stated. Both Lovelace and Comus (and Satan as well) are masters of disguise. Both Lovelace and Comus use a "potion" to commit their most heinous crimes. Both Lovelace and Comus will transform themselves as well as others, Comus using magical dust to make himself into a "harmless Villager" (l. 166) when he hears the lady's song. Both Comus and Lovelace manipulate the appearance of their victims' surroundings. Upon discerning the approach of a virgin, Comus transforms his dreary wood into an enticing garden: "Thus I hurl / My dazzling Spells into the spongy air, / Of power to cheat the eye with blear illusion" (ll. 153–55). In order to control completely Clarissa's environment, Lovelace lodges her in a brothel, where he can be certain the women will act as he commands and thus make the house appear reputable. After she sees through Lovelace's designs, Clarissa echoes *Comus*: "Ever since I knew you . . . I have been in a wilderness of doubt and error" (Richardson, 777). Finally, both Comus and Lovelace try to justify their behavior by appealing to the code of the rake, in particular arguing that sexual pleasure is part of the nature God has given to man. "Beauty," Comus tells the Lady "is nature's coin, [and] must not be hoarded," lest "Th'all-giver would be unthank't . . . / Not half his riches known" (ll. 724, 739). Lovelace advocates polygamy and annually renewable marriages.

The Lady and Clarissa are paragons of virtue and chastity, but the equation between them is not as precise as that between

Lovelace and Milton's villains. Both women face their trials alone and, though penetrated by evil, remain unsullied. Using his magic, Comus immobilizes the Lady and fills her ears with impure arguments. The Lady asserts, however, that although Comus can pollute her body, he cannot touch her mind. In a remarkable and powerful anticipation of Clarissa's various dismissals of Lovelace after he rapes her, the Lady tells Comus: "Fool, do not boast, / Thou canst not touch the freedom of my mind / With all thy charms, although this corporeal rind? Thou hast immanacl'd" (ll. 663–65). Her soul inaccessible to Comus, the Lady comes back "To triumph in victorious dance / O'er sensual Folly and Intemperance" (ll. 975–76). Lovelace boasts to Belford that Clarissa's "silken wings are . . . so entangled in my enormous web that she cannot move hand or foot" (Richardson, 887), but Clarissa, "armed with conscious worthiness and superiority" (534), vehemently asserts her moral superiority—"My soul is above thee man" (646)—and finally, at least in Lovelace's account, defeats him: "Whose triumph now!" he rhetorically asks Belford after the rape, "HERS, or MINE?" (901).

The cases of the Lady and Clarissa diverge, however, in the circumstances of their testing. Both women happen into perilous circumstances through the fault of their brothers. The Lady is left alone and unprotected in Comus's Wood, but only because her brothers have gone to seek nourishment for her. Although her brothers make a mistake, they persist in their concern for her and urge Sabrina to rescue her. The brothers play an important part in rescuing the Lady from Comus's grasp and in returning her to the welcoming arms of her family. James Harlowe Jr. purposefully separates Clarissa from her family in order to pursue his "interest." Because of the effects of demographic crisis within his family, James stands to inherit the estates of his uncles, his godmother, and his father. Uniting these inheritances, he hopes to ascend to the peerage. But when Clarissa's grandfather, the patriarch of the Harlowe family, dies, he leaves the dutiful Clarissa part of his property and thus she becomes a potential threat to James Jr.'s plan. As I will argue in greater detail in chapter 6, the impairment of patriarchal power brings Clarissa to her test.

While both women triumph over their deceivers, Comus ends happily, Clarissa tragically. This is largely because the Lady is not, as Clarissa must become, an independent character. With the exception of her brothers' mistake, she is supported by her family throughout, family support that garners her crucial supernatural support as well. The Lady's dependence, then, facilitates the masque's ending happily, with the restoration of social order. Because of her brother's "instigations," Clarissa is alone; abandoned by her dysfunctional biological family, she ends her life building a "house" of her own. She is, as Ian Watt points out, "without allies, and this is fitting since she is the heroic representation of all that is free and positive in the new individualism" (Watt, 222). Indeed, Clarissa is so individualized that she becomes "the sole judge of insults offered to my person" (Richardson, 826), "the *only woman in the world*," according to Lovelace, "who would have made such a rout" (1032). She becomes so individualized that the significance of her story cannot be defined, as Lovelace's can, by reference to an earlier story.

In its characters and its plot, *Clarissa* bears a remarkable resemblance to *Comus*. However, Milton's influence does not operate as directly or as definitively as critics seeking mimesis will expect. In *Clarissa*, Richardson reexamines Milton's faith that true virtue is inviolable, placing virtue outside allegory and inside everyday eighteenth-century family life. Rather than type Clarissa, Richardson anamnestically redacts Milton's story by placing his heroine amidst a crisis in patrilinear succession that changes the roles of men and women, of brothers and sisters, in families. Lovelace is Richardson's fine imitation of Milton's Satan, a character briefly empowered by his "glozing Tongue." But Clarissa, whether compared to Comus's Lady or to Eve, departs from the literary precedents that she suggests.

This departure, however, does not challenge Milton so much as it recapitulates his achievement. In Milton's mimetic narrative, in God's story, authority is, indeed, patriarchal and cold. As thousands of students have complained, it is hard to like this God who sees all but will not save Eve, this God who leaves Eve "free to fall," this God who will not "cut [Eve] off from . . . possibility," however unhappy. But in his anamnestic narrative, Milton reveals life to be difficult precisely because "Providence" finds its way into the mouths of fallen angels. God's design, difficult to see, is almost impossible to "wait upon"—unless one is gifted with special prophetic powers. In this anamnestic narrative, man's only course is that recommended in *Areopagitica* and first expressed by Eve: woman only can realize her virtue by testing it, by winning it through painful labor. Milton's poem thus opens out onto the eighteenth-century novel by establishing both mimesis and anamnesis as legitimate literary representations of man's relationship with the Supreme Father. In the years after 1650, as England's demographic crisis intensifies, fictional patriarchs will descend directly from Adam and only indirectly from God. Patriarchs in the fictions that we call novels will be absent or impotent, dead or impaired. And in the wake of the patriarch's decline—a decline registered most intensely by his failure to produce heirs—novelists will move between mimetic and anamnestic plots, struggling towards (but rarely achieving) the great harmony that Milton, who was blessed with both a wonderful father and a revolutionary spirit, achieves.

3

Dorotea's Daughters: *Moll Flanders,* *Roxana,* and the Perils of Fictive Kinship

At first glance, the novels of Defoe may not appear relevant to the themes of this book: the crisis in patrilinear succession and the turn to fictive versions of kinship as a response to it. With the exception of his *A Journal of the Plague Year,* Defoe's fictions unfold untouched by demographic crisis; his heroines are notably, even famously, fecund. Moreover, while his heroines are notorious for their pursuit of money and, in the case of Roxana, a title, they tend to seek cash rather than land. Indeed, for all their upward mobility, Defoe's heroines are, by and large, familyless, and, thus, do not participate directly in the fictionalizing of kinship described by the Stones or in the "right of Representation" described by Hale. Inchbald's *A Simple Story,* Lennox's *The Female Quixote,* and Burney's *Cecelia* all provide much more direct treatment of the problems (and opportunities) presented to female protagonists by failures in patrilinear succession. While we can say that the stories of Miss Milner and Lady Mathilda, of Arabella, and of Cecelia Beverley all are precipitated by their being "the only survivor of the . . . family,"[1] Defoe's heroines have difficulty figuring out to what family they belong. The remarkable opening statement of *Roxana* understatedly reveals the extent of her alienation: "I was born, *as my Friends told me,* at the City of Poictiers."[2] An orphan, even as she claims a family, Roxana learns the details of her birth from her "*Friends,*" not from her parents.

It is precisely because of their uncertain backgrounds—what Ian Watt would call their "non-traditional" status—that Defoe's women can be so mobile, both physically and socially. While Watt emphasizes Defoe's lack of a classical education, we can note here that Defoe did know the *Quixote*[3] and that Cervantes' Dorotea charts, although much more happily, the difficult path that Defoe's heroines follow. The characters whom we know as Moll Flanders and Roxana both, in their pursuit of status, bring into question the social categories by which they would identify (and thus know) themselves; Cervantes spares Dorotea from struggling with the paradox of her using the vocabulary of status to describe her ascension, but Defoe is not so kind to his heroines. In the early parts of their stories, they profit (materially if not spiritually) from dysfunction in the families of others. Their freedom to advance their interests, however, eventually brings them to the brink of ruin, ruin that Moll escapes but that Roxana cannot. In the transition from Moll to Roxana, then, Defoe reveals his own doubts about fictive versions of kinship as a response to status inconsistency.

The options available to Moll and Roxana, were they to be "good" girls, are notably unappealing. Young Moll is told that she must "go to Service," while Roxana, her husband having bankrupted and deserted her, faces starvation. As young Moll resists the future that her status dictates for her, she sets the theme of status inconsistency, even as she offers an English version of Dorotea's aspiration: "Why what, says she [Moll's guardian], is the girl mad? what would you be a Gentlewoman? Yes *says* I, and cry'd heartily, till I roar'd out again."[4] Moll's "roar," however revealing of her discontent, does not change her situation. She avoids "that terrible Bug-bear *going to Service*" (12) only because her nurse, while waiting on the town's mayor, talks about her: "At last my Story came up, and my good Nurse told Mr. *Mayor* the whole Tale: He was so pleas'd with it, that he would call his Lady, and his two Daughters to hear it, and it made Mirth enough among them, you may be sure" (11). Here Moll, only for the first time in her life, is rescued by the power of narrative ("Story," "Tale"). Moll later understands that one reason her story is so appealing is because her nurse, the mayor, and his family "meant one Sort of thing, by the Word Gentlewoman . . . [while] I meant quite another" (11). Moll's version of gentlewomanliness is a childish invention. But insofar as it brings her to the attention of the mayor and, eventually, into his household, it frees her from the servitude that she otherwise inevitably faces.

Defoe understands that characters who invent identities for themselves (typically by fictionalizing kinship relations) confer

great power upon themselves; their wishes, even their most childish wishes, may come true. But with that power may come a
potentially tragic uncertainty about identity. If gentlewomanliness
can be achieved through storytelling, then how substantial or
enduring are family ties that confer status? Roxana's case is essentially the same as Moll's in that, once she fictionalizes kinship, she
no longer can say who she is. She achieves great wealth by accepting the names and the titles that a series of wealthy men offer her.
But she cannot recognize her daughter, lest she admit how insub-
stantial is her hard-won status. Moll's two voyages to Virginia
give her a way out of the dilemmas created by her upward mobility, but Roxana, with her daughter in needful and close pursuit of
her, cannot escape so easily or happily the consequences of her
fictionalizing.

When Moll discovers that her husband is her brother, her
horror perhaps is genuine (although it also seems that she eagerly
grasps an indisputable reason to separate from him and return to
England), but this incident of incest only culminates a series of
close calls to which Moll's fictionalizing brings her. We should
recall that she explicitly describes her first marriage as incestuous;
in love with an older brother while married to a younger, she says
of herself: "I never was in Bed with my Husband, but I wish'd my
self in the Arms of his Brother. . . . In short, I committed Adultery
and Incest with him every Day in my Desires, which without
doubt, was as effectively criminal in the Nature of Guilt, as if I had
actually done it" (47). The eagerness with which Moll accuses
herself here, the rapidity ("In short") with which she summarizes
the situation—these should not cause us to overlook, as she herself
seems to, that her situation in the mayor's home has been equivocal, then illicit, throughout. Once inside that household, she
subverts the very social category, "gentlewoman," by which she
hopes to identify herself:

> I had . . . all the Advantages of Education that I could have had, if I
> had been as much a Gentlewoman as they were with whom I liv'd,
> and in some things, I had the Advantage of my Ladies, tho' they were
> my Superiors; but they were all Gifts of Nature, and which all their
> Fortunes could not furnish. First, I was apparently Handsomer than
> any of them. Secondly, I was better shap'd, and Thirdly, I sung better
> . . . in . . . the Opinion of all that knew the Family. (16)

Simultaneously describing her natural "Advantages" and deferring to the mayor's daughters as her "Superiors," Moll only seems

to achieve a fine irony. Actually, her tone here involves no protest and little complaint. Instead, in accepting the conventional "Opinion," Moll reveals (unwittingly, I believe) the equivocations that reside within fictive versions of kinship, which inevitably "denature" the claims of family and blood that they seek to preserve. Indeed, as becomes apparent in the novels of Inchbald and Lennox, families lacking a male heir will rewrite the incest taboo in order to maintain the appearance of patrilinear succession.

References to incest persistently accompany Moll's fictionalizing of kinship relations, even after her return from Virginia. Moll goes to Bath, "a place of Gallantry" where men "find a Mistress sometime, but very rarely look for a Wife" rather than to Redriff, where "some honest Sea Captain or other might have talk'd with me upon the honourable terms of Matrimony" (84). Freed from the burdens of being "honest," Moll immediately fictionalizes her circumstances, particularly her financial situation, and comes to the attention of a "Gentleman" whose wife is "distemper'd in her Head" (86). Moll and her landlady work to stimulate the gentleman's interest in Moll, the landlady even "makes a Story of her own inventing" about Moll's losing money due her from the "Virginia ships" (87). Moll is unhappy with this fiction, but only because it seems too forward. It does, however, prompt the gentleman to come to Moll's aid. They begin a Platonic relationship in which the gentleman provides Moll with money, and Moll, during an illness of his, nurses him "as much and as carefully as if I had been his Wife; indeed If I had been his Wife I could not have done more" (89). For an extended period, this gentleman will lay with Moll but not copulate with her, "altho' all the familiarities between Man and Wife were common to us, yet he never once offered to go any farther, and he valued himself much upon it" (91).

The motives for the gentleman's seemingly odd behavior appear as Moll recounts a common event in illicit relationships, the renting of a room:

> The Master of the House going up with us to show his Rooms, and coming into . . . [a] Room, said very frankly to him, Sir, *It is none of my business to enquire whether the Lady be your Spouse or no*, but if not, *you may lie as honestly in these two Beds as if you were in two Chambers*, and with that he pulls a great Curtain which he drew quite across the Room and effectively divided the Beds; well *says my Friend*, very read-

ily, these Beds will do, and as for the rest, we are too near a kin to lye together, tho' we may Lodge near one another; and this put an honest Face on the thing too. (90)

With his opening disclaimer, the landlord makes the gentleman's reference to incest both gratuitous and crucial. The gentleman apparently "values himself much upon" his control over his fictionalizing. He has a *real* wife and a fictive wife; the distinction between them is guaranteed by his otherwise unlikely decision to not copulate with the latter. So he invents incest as a check upon any confusion that might be created by his illicit/fictional relationship with Moll.

As Moll embraces her gentleman's lie, "and this put an honest Face on the thing too," she acts consistently with her earlier references to incest—her harsh self-accusation during her marriage to Robin; her atypical horror at the discovery of her husband/brother in Virginia. For Moll, incest makes things "honest"; it consistently remains the one check upon Moll's "casuistry,"[5] upon her ability to justify any behavior, however illicit. Her references to incest, particularly in situations in which it is not a possibility, bespeak her complicated and powerful wish both to fictionalize kinship relations and to maintain the status that kinship designates. When Moll and the gentleman, on a night in which they both are "a little more in Wine . . . than usual," do make love, Moll describes the event as owing to her wickedness, and recalls it "*with shame and horror of* Soul" (91). The act ruins the "value" both set upon their platonic relationship—"This harden'd us both" (92)—because it proves incest to be an empty threat. Moll tells us, "I wanted nothing but to be a Wife, which however could not be in this Case" (93). Her verb is revealing, for she is, in all ways now, the gentleman's wife, but she still "wants" the word to designate a substantial and fixed condition, a fixity that her own behavior subverts. Not even the invention of incest, in Moll's case, can save her from denaturing precisely those categories by which she hopes to live.

For all its references to spiritual "hardness" and to "horror of Soul," *Moll Flanders* remains a comedy because Moll's impulse to fictionalize is unflagging, and her fictions assure her material well-being. In her second trip to Virginia, Moll deceives (once more) her Lancashire husband about her finances and about her brother/husband (256). She repeatedly refers to her son by her brother as her "only Child." Having met her son and discovered that her mother has left her an estate, she begins "secretly now to wish that I had not brought my *Lancashire* Husband from *England* at all" but then, recalling her "love" (262) for the indolent Jemmy, she invents stories that allow her to have him and her newfound wealth. She reports "to my Husband all the particulars" of her good fortune, "except that I called my Son my Cousin" (264). She also invents a story for the son whom she loves so dearly, telling him, upon news of her brother/husband's death, "that I believed I should marry a Gentleman who had a Plantation near mine." When her son visits the putative newlyweds, he "happen'd to be there when my Cargo from *England* came in, which I let him believe belong'd all to my Husband's Estate, not to me" (267). She gives her son a watch, hoping that he will "now and then kiss it for my sake," but undercuts her sentiment by adding, "I *did not indeed tell him* that I had stole it from a Gentlewoman's side" (264). Upon her return to her Lancashire husband, she claims, "I had lost my Watch" (265).

In her final paragraph, Moll does tell Jemmy about her husband/brother, but this openness comes only after she has used her money to guarantee his ease. He is more than willing to justify her behavior, describing the episode as "a Mistake impossible to be prevented" (268). The half-truths, lies, and deceptions practiced upon her "only Child" go uncorrected. As Moll makes clear in her story's opening sentence, we never will know her "True Name." This is the price of her "story"—that she "dare [not] own who I have been, as well as who I am" (7). Roxana comes to a tragic end because her fictions finally cannot ameliorate the conflicts between the self she has constructed and the desire of her daughter and namesake to discover "who I am." Although the revelation comes late in the story and only when she is under considerable duress, Roxana, unlike Moll, does tell us her name: "*Susan*, (for she [her daughter] was my own Name)" (247–48). Given its tragic consequences, Roxana might well wish to treat this information as parenthetical, even superfluous. However, it is crucial.

Moll Flanders has good reason to hide her name. As the title page indicates, she has been "Twelve Year a *Thief*, Eight Year a Transported *Felon*"; shame, even prosecution for crimes, might follow from her openly identifying herself. The title page of the book we call *Roxana* redacts the "Vast Variety of Fortunes" found in Moll's story, but at a different social level: "The Fortunate Mistress or, a History . . . of *Mademoiselle de Beleau*, Afterwards Call'd The Countess *de Wintelsheim* . . . known by the Name of the

Lady Roxana" (33). With the possible exception of her machinations with the English jeweler's effects, none of Roxana's activities have been illegal. But should she reveal her name, she would jeopardize the versions of kinship—most notably with the five (or six) children she deserted but then returned to through Amy— that she has constructed. Even more threatening, should Roxana/ Susan reveal her name, she will prove her "natural" bond with Susan and, in effect, testify to the social distance she has traveled.

We come to the heart of Roxana's tragedy if we ask why Susan, in asking Roxana to "own" her, threatens her. Roxana describes only one direct encounter with Susan, on board a ship on which the Dutch merchant (now her husband) has booked passage for them to the continent. Susan, a friend of the captain's wife, happens to be on board when Roxana comes to inspect her cabin. Roxana feels "a secret Horror" at this meeting and musters her "full Presence of Mind" to avoid any discovery of her "Surprize" (323). But she, like Moll, also describes herself responding with powerful emotion to her child. When Moll first catches a glimpse of her son after her return to Virginia, she, like Roxana, dares not "take any notice of him," but she only barely "restrain[s] . . . yearnings of Soul I had in me to embrace him and weep over him . . . I thought my Entrails turn'd within me, that my very Bowels mov'd." Eventually, she kisses "the Ground that he had set his Foot on" (252). Despite her fears, Roxana responds similarly to Susan:

> When I came close . . . to salute her . . . it was a secret inconceivable Pleasure to me when I kiss'd her, to know that I kiss'd my own Child; my own Flesh and Blood, born of my Body . . . and much ado I had, not to abandon myself to an Excess of Passion at the first Sight of her, much more when my Lips touch'd her Face; I thought I must have taken her in my Arms, and kiss'd her again a thousand times, whether I wou'd or no. (323)

What threat can Susan pose to Roxana that it overmasters desire so powerfully expressed? Important to recall here is the memorandum from Amy to Roxana (274–76) in which Amy, doing detective work on the continent, reports to her mistress upon the men in her life—from the Dutch merchant to her first husband— indicating that neither her husband (who is dead) nor the Jew (who has fled) can threaten her anymore. The Dutch merchant has suffered financial losses, but these only make him more amenable to Roxana's will. She can (and will) tell him anything. Susan herself wants nothing from Roxana other than recognition; she makes no financial claims, no threat of public revelation. Again, the question arises: why can't Roxana kiss her daughter as many times as she wants?

Moll's transportation to America is fortunate because Virginia offers a fresh scene for her fictions as well as providing her with a son who is "a handsome comely young Gentleman in flourishing Circumstances" (252). Moll sails away not only from the scene of her crimes but also from her confusion about what it means to be a "Gentlewoman." Susan interrupts Roxana's departure and threatens Roxana's very being because Roxana immediately recognizes her as "my old Cook-Maid in the *Pallmall,* and as . . . neither more nor less than my own Daughter" (322). While it might be odd, it certainly is not criminal to employ one's child as a servant, and scandal hardly seems to threaten Roxana, particularly since she has taken care of and placed her other children. Susan threatens Roxana, however, because her "downward" mobility reveals how far Roxana has traveled in her "upward," even as Susan's case brings into doubt the power of family ties: what good did her mother's beauty and wealth do her, even in her mother's house?

The threat Susan poses to Roxana, then, is not legal, familial, or social; rather, it is personal, even, in the vocabulary of our time, psychological. As she thrills to the kiss of her child, "my own Flesh and Blood," Roxana verges upon a recognition of how artificial, how fictional her hard-won status is. In her pursuit of a filial bond with her mother, Susan raises a question about status that Roxana's fictions have barely avoided: how substantial is a title if it can be bought? Once she hears from Amy, mistakenly it turns out, that the French prince still is interested in her (276), "the Notion of being *a Princess*" begins "to make strange Work" with Roxana, finally leading her to become "as truly craz'd and distracted . . . as most of the People in *Bedlam*" (287). Possessing enough wealth "to live like a Princess," Roxana realizes she is "not a Princess." In this case, her financial acumen, her focus upon the "bottom line," gives way to the irresistible attraction that "the Name of *Princess*" (279) has for her. Susan haunts her, however thrilling it is to kiss her, by suggesting that the title is empty.

Defoe arranges events such that the threat of Susan arises simultaneously with the Dutch merchant's preparations to buy Roxana a title: "He had a Nephew, the Son of his Elder Brother, who had the Title of Count . . . and . . . he had frequently offered

to make it over to him for ... not a great-deal of Money" (285).
The merchant's account, at once prosaic and equivocal, of how he
will get the title smooths over contradictions that Susan will
render tragic:

> He told me that Money purchas'd Titles of Honour ... tho' Money
> cou'd not give Principles of Honour, they must come by Birth and
> Blood; that however, Titles sometimes assist to elevate the Soul, and to
> infuse generous Principles into the Mind, and especially, where there
> was a good Foundation laid in the Persons; that he hop'd we should
> neither of us misbehave, if we came to it; and that as we knew how to
> wear a Title without undue Elevations, so it might sit as well upon us,
> as on another. (285)

Before cataloging all of the Dutch merchant's equivocations, we
should note that he tells Roxana exactly what she wants to hear.
She recounts his words (makes them her own, in effect) with no
qualification, and she is ready immediately to act upon his offer:
"I was not a little tickl'd with the Satisfaction of being a *Countess*,
tho' I could not be a *Princess*." She then, after a talk with Amy,
decides to buy titles both in England and in Holland, for, as Amy
jokingly suggests, "then you will be really *a Princess*; for sure to be
a Lady in *English*, and a Countess in *Dutch*, may make a Princess
in *High*-Dutch" (286). Roxana takes the joke seriously and the
morning after the Dutch merchant presents her with "Patent for
Baronet" and some valuable jewels, she marries him, declaring
"Thus I put an End to all the intrieguing [*sic*] Part of my Life"
(287).

Roxana wants her achievement of a "title," a "Surname," to end
her story. She compares herself to a colonizer of the Indies,
returned to England after great danger and struggle, who has "the
Pleasure of saying, he shall never venture upon the Seas anymore" (288). Only in his adroit fudging of natural and fictive
versions of kinship does the Dutch merchant, after "eleven Years"
(288), finally discover what Roxana/Susan wants. She wants full
freedom to become whomever she wants to be, but she also wants
to name herself definitively and permanently through social categories. In equal parts, Roxana believes that only "Birth and Blood"
can confer "Honour" and that "Honour" is hers to buy. She
prefers the title "Countess" because it is "in the Family," but she
also wants the English title, the title that is only bought. The
merchant hopes vaguely that the "Title" may "elevate the Soul,"

even as he undercuts the virtue of a "Title" by lamely concluding that "it might sit as well upon us, as on another."

Susan's sister sees Roxana in disguise—"dress'd-up in a *Quaker's* habit" (378)—and this daughter profits materially by participating in what the reader knows to be a fiction. Susan's need is too great for such an accommodation, and she frightens Roxana, Amy, and even the virtuous Quaker precisely because her motives are, by their standards, unfathomable. Indeed, Susan's psychology seems outside Defoe's ken as well. She moves through the book's final pages, relentless and implacable, battling through all the disadvantages that Roxana's various fictions and her now-considerable wealth present. Her lament, "She is my Mother! and will not own me" (352) is finely ambiguous. It obviously points to Roxana's refusal to recognize Susan, despite her desire to "kiss . . . her . . . a thousand times." But perhaps less obviously, the lament reveals why Susan is such a difficult and intransigent character. Unlike her brother and sister, she will not let Roxana, through Amy's ministrations, reinvent the kinship relationship. Roxana places her son by the jeweler with an Indies merchant and, against his wishes, buys him a wife. Roxana wants no direct contact with him ("I did not let him know me" [309]), but, allowed to define her obligations in her own terms, she treats this son with paternal, if not maternal, kindness. Susan, who will not be "owned," wants "her Mother," her mother as she was prior to the failure of the father with which *Roxana* opens.

Susan's lament leads inevitably to tragedy because it confines both social and personal crisis within such a small and intimate space ("own"). While elite families throughout England were fictionalizing kinship relations to assure that the ownership of great estates and houses stayed within families, Susan and Susan/Roxana reveal how oxymoronic, even equivocal is fictive kinship. Given the power of Susan's need to know her mother,[6] Roxana cannot escape from England (and save her gift for fiction) as Moll does. Like Susan, Robinson Crusoe, Moll Flanders, and Roxana are orphans with parents. While Susan is the grandchild of an émigré, Crusoe is the child of one; Roxana was born in France, and Moll was raised by gypsies. In each case the protagonist stands outside any fixed or clear relationship to English customs. As outsiders, Defoe's characters have great and unprecedented freedom to fashion themselves. As Crusoe's father goes from Kreutznaer to Crusoe, Crusoe journeys from being a slave to being a king. As Roxana's father moves from prosperity in France to even greater prosperity in England, she journeys from near starvation to a title, a title roughly as legitimate as Crusoe's. Moll's mother directly anticipates Moll's rise from transported felon to gentlelady. How this mobility "shipwrecks" social and familial institutions has been cogently described by Ian Watt (92).

What perhaps has not been sufficiently noted is the price the characters pay for their "success." Crusoe, the earliest and happiest version of the character, returns to England to take "my two nephews . . . into my care. The eldest having something of his own, I bred up as a gentleman, and gave him a settlement of some addition to his estate, after my decease; the other I put out to a captain of a ship."[7] He anticipates Moll's desire to be "a Gentlewoman," Roxana's desire to buy status. He also anticipates Susan's desire to reestablish the family ties that were sundered by his mobility. Crusoe makes a point of describing what he does for his brother's sons but says nothing about his own children or about his wife—whom he marries "not either to my disadvantage or dissatisfaction" (298).

Defoe blesses Crusoe with a happy impercipience to the implications of his story. Crusoe early on (36–37) mentions Jonah and the prodigal son as scriptural precedents for his setting out from his father's house, but he never worries about the failure of his story (at least in terms of financial profit) to conform to Christ's parable. He purchases two sorts of identity, gentlemanly and entrepreneurial, without troubling over the conflicts between them. In the New World, Crusoe finds status beyond Roxana's wishing, but only his isolation protects him from the latent dangers of his fictions. Like Roxana, he fancies himself "the prince and lord of the whole island; I had the lives of all my subjects at my absolute command; I could hang, draw, give liberty, and take it away, and no rebels among all my subjects" (157). That Crusoe's "subjects" are animals reveals both the extent of his fictionalizing and the safety from its consequences that his isolation provides. Trying to rule human subjects, Crusoe does not fare so well, even though he invents elaborate codes for them. Unlike Roxana, he can sail away when the kingdom he has invented shows signs of failure. He leaves his title, "Governour," and his "castle" very readily because England beckons. Roxana's problem cannot be solved by a return to England. Indeed, she needs to leave it because Susan haunts her there.

Susan threatens Roxana/Susan so powerfully because she embodies Roxana's desire (however much obscured by her wealth and her "rise") to identify herself as a mother and a wife, as Susan. For all the eagerness with which Roxana embraces and profits from fictive versions of kinship, her narrative repeatedly indicates her doubts about such inventions. Prior to her first liaison, the jeweler and Amy both offer Roxana ample opportunity to pretend she is the jeweler's wife.[8] Roxana responds to Amy:

> Don't talk any more of your Cant, of its being Lawful that I ought to marry again, and that he ought to Marry again . . . 'tis all Nonsence . . . there's nothing in it, let me hear no more of that; for if I yield, 'tis in vain to mince the Matter, I am a Whore . . . neither better nor worse, I assure you. (74)

Roxana's resounding insistence that, all appearances to the contrary, she is a "Whore" bespeaks her need to keep the designation "Wife" substantial, even pure. In one of the most famous and provocative episodes in her narrative, Roxana forces Amy to sleep with the jeweler, claiming "Had I look'd upon myself as a Wife, you cannot suppose I would have been willing to let my husband lie with my Maid, much less before my Face" (81). Amy's "ruin," insofar as it confirms Roxana's view of herself ("I thought myself a Whore") protects the title "Wife."

In her liaison with the French prince, Roxana has even more difficulty maintaining social categories. As part of his blandishments, the prince tells Roxana that he wants "to lay aside my Character; let us talk together with the Freedom of Equals; my Quality sets me at a Distance from you, and makes you ceremonious; your Beauty exalts you to more than an Equality" (98). What is "Character" that it can be laid "aside"? The prince here renders problematic the relationship between social status, "Quality," and personal merit, "Beauty." Roxana describes the "Temptation" offered by the prince as of a different and more dangerous order than the temptation offered by the jeweler; the latter tempts her "Poverty," but the former tempts her "Vanity" (100).

Vanity here is more than pride of person. The prince tells Roxana that she is the most beautiful woman in France, and while Roxana is glad to hear this, it merely confirms what she long has known. However, the prince becomes a particularly seductive and dangerous figure (he places Roxana within a series of paradoxes from which she never will escape) by suggesting that her beauty can translate into status. In his phrasing, "Beauty" becomes the syntactic equal of "Quality," and as he argues that her beauty "exalts" Roxana, he offers her wealth and power. But finally the translation of beauty into quality cannot take place; even in the prince's speech, he only can "lay aside my Character," not confer character upon her. She is offered "more than an Equality" but, significantly, no fixed rank. In his last words to her before she confers "the Last Favour" upon him, the prince reminds Roxana that "Princes . . . if repuls'd . . . made no second Attacks; and indeed, it was but reasonable; for it was below their Rank, to be long battering a Woman's Constancy" (100, 101). The seduction that opened with the prince laying aside his "Character" ends with him reminding Roxana of his "rank." Once exalted to "more than an Equality," she finally must sleep with him—graciously and flatteringly coerced, but coerced nonetheless. "You may be beautiful, but you only get one chance," or so I would translate the prince.

Roxana submits to this coercion, she reminds us, not because she is poor ("I was mistress of ten Thousand Pounds") or because her head is turned by the words she has heard. She submits to the coercion because he *is* a prince, because she is excited "to be treated as a Woman fit for the Bed of a Prince" (100). The prince's character finally and definitively does matter. Having bedded a prince and, eventually, a king, Roxana spends the rest of her life trying to become a princess: "I that was so willing once to be Mistress to a KING, was now ten thousand times more fond of being Wife to a Prince" (283). This desire flourishes apart from material motives; as Roxana herself notes, "[With] the Wealth I was Mistress of . . . I was able to live like a Princess, tho' not a Princess." What Roxana needs is "the Name of *Princess*" (279); what Roxana wants is that "Character" the prince lays aside. For Roxana to end comically, Roxana/Susan would need to sustain her fictive title of "Princess" but under much more difficult circumstances than Moll sustains her title of "Gentlewoman": she must sustain her fiction in England, a place where she can be known; she must act at the very top of European society, where questions of status may be hotly contested. Roxana's tragedy is not that she has been a whore; rather, it is that she has passed so easily for a princess.

Her children placed, Roxana might also pretend to be a virtuous Quaker: "I talk'd like a *Quaker* too, as readily and naturally as if I had been born among them; and . . . I pass'd for a *Quaker* among all people that did not know me" (256). Roxana's problem, then, is not, as some accounts would have it, that she "is torn between the virtuous poverty of a respectable Dutch merchant and the sinful prosperity of London's West End." She easily moves in both worlds. Nor does her "emotional tug-of-war" occur because she "is fatally tempted by aristocratic wealth and flattery but yearns for middle-class respectability."[9] She can redact convincingly both behaviors. Rather, Roxana is torn between fictive versions of kinship (which offer wealth, excitement, and, in the case of the prince, good sex) and her powerful, if less obvious desire to define kinship relations in other than fictive terms and to feel "secret inconceivable pleasure" when kissing "my own Child; my own Flesh and Blood, born of my Body." As the attempts by both the prince and the Dutch merchant reveal, the two versions of kinship can be reconciled only through equivocation and doublespeak: rank establishes "Character," but "Character" can be set aside; money can purchase titles of honor, but principles of honor reside apart, although the mere title can "elevate" the Soul such that the "Principles" then can enter the "Mind." Rank matters, then does not matter, then matters very much. Fiction confers power, but the gift is, as Roxana's response to Susan reveals, as liable to be a curse as a blessing.

Defoe's contribution to eighteenth-century fiction has been variously described: Ian Watt places him as the precursor of "formal realism"; critics from J. Paul Hunter and George A. Starr to Leopold Damrosch Jr. describe him as a mediator between Puritan devotional literature and the novel;[10] Virginia Woolf praises his work as an adumbration of modern psychological realism.[11] I would add that Defoe places fictive kinship (the opportunities and problems it creates) at the very center of his work. He does not resolve the questions about "Quality" created by the problematic lower-class virtue of Moll and Roxana; rather, he bequeaths the theme of status inconsistency to the men and women who followed him. In the very unresolvability of Roxana's life history, the eighteenth-century novel finds both its central action and its great theme. Defoe's life, although energetic, varied, and, thus, difficult to summarize, particularly suited him to set the agenda for the eighteenth-century novel. He clearly was a man driven by his desire for status—status as traditionally defined in the society into which he was born. His drive led him to frequent financial catastrophes and to his frenetic, even desperate reliance upon the resources of fiction, all other resources failing him.

In the less than nine years between his marriage in 1684 and his first bankruptcy in 1692, Defoe converted his wife's dowry of

3,700 pounds into debts equal to 17,000 pounds.[12] Paula R. Backscheider shows that "the most traumatic, influential experience in Defoe's life was not the pillory but his bankruptcy" (535). Yet, as Backscheider also points out, the bankruptcy, however traumatic, did not change Defoe. In 1724, as an active if ailing sixty-three year old, Defoe repeats the financial mistakes he made thirty-five years earlier. Having through his work as a psephologist and a writer achieved a happy rural retirement at Stoke Newington, he once again ruins himself by giving his money and time to "Projects and Designs" that he lacked the managerial patience (as well as the capital) to make profitable. Why couldn't Defoe be happy with 3,700 pounds? Why, with several bankruptcies behind him, couldn't he enjoy the "prosperous, serene life of the prominent citizens of Stoke Newington" (465)? Why is it, my students always ask, that Roxana, her financial problems solved by the jeweler, couldn't retrieve her children immediately?

Defoe, like Roxana, is betrayed continually by his desire to convert wealth into status, to find, amidst fictive versions of kinship, an "ancient" title to bequeath to his family. Defoe risked his wife's magnificent dowry to pursue status. That dowry lost many times over, he wrote millions of words (351, 504) not only to survive but to continue his quest for "Quality." For Defoe, as for Roxana, the correlation between fictive kinship and ancient title never became sufficiently exact; incongruities abounded. For example, in 1703, the year he stood in pillory, Defoe published an edition of his selected works bearing an engraving of himself:

> Below the picture was a coat-of-arms, now a sign of hard-won and fading prosperity. In order to qualify Defoe had needed to prove to the College of Arms that he had either "lands and possessions of free tenure to the yearly value of 10 l." or "moveable goods" worth 300 l. (128)

But what did a coat of arms signify if it could be bought, particularly in a society in which women like Mary Raby, purportedly one of the models for Moll Flanders, could be twice "burnt in the hand for acting quality in disguise" (482)? Characters who become criminals as they illicitly assume a place among the "Quality" perhaps engage Defoe so powerfully because they act out his own deep need. Defoe was made fun of for his rich dress, his "affected display" of a pinky ring, his ample wig—all bespeaking, to his critics anyway, his would-be lordliness. Defoe, apparently, chose to suffer derision rather than to cede his dream of status.

As a spy for Robert Harley and as a writer of prose satire, Defoe practiced the art of disguise. He boastfully writes to Harley that he has won credibility in Scotland by having "Caused it to be spread that I am fled hither for Debt and Can not Return."[13] Inventing a fiction to hide his identity as a government agent, he finds use for the event that wounded him most. "His power to penetrate diverse groups," Backscheider claims, "ranks him among the greatest spies of all time" (232). Much the same can be said of Defoe the novelist. His fictions endure in large part because of his chameleonlike ability to fit into any group. His social aspirations are displaced but not sublimated in his remarkable female protagonists.

Backscheider cites a passage from Defoe's *Tour of Great Britain* in which he describes London merchants buying country estates and looks forward to "another age" in which these families "will equal the families of the ancient gentry." She comments:

> Here is Defoe's dream. His family would come to "equal" the ancient families and take its place among the settled prosperous leaders of the country. His descendants would even have a base from which to be elected to parliament. (469)

But the "equality" that Defoe sought finally was impossible to achieve, for the "ancient gentry" were special precisely because their titles had not been bought; their titles, whatever fictionalizing was necessary to maintain them, were valued for the "Birth and Blood" to which they purportedly bore testimony. Defoe's sad and remarkable fate was to repeatedly bankrupt himself in his attempts to buy a "Title." In a lifetime of great achievements and stunning failures, he apparently never recognized that, once it could be bought, the title might lose its value.

After 1724 Defoe would write no more books in the *Crusoe*, *Moll Flanders*, *Roxana* vein, even though he remained astonishingly prolific. Earlier critics account variously for this change.[14] I suggest that, in *Roxana*, Defoe discovered the limits of fiction in modifying status. Those limits were not set by the weakness of fiction but rather defined by its strength. That Defoe, like Roxana, could "be" anybody finally threatens who he is. Having discovered through Crusoe et. al. his ability to generate satisfying and seemingly endless simulacra of "natural" kinship relations, Defoe, through Roxana, discovers the threat that fiction poses to the very notion of "Blood." As David Blewett has shown, Defoe's pamphlet

The Great Law of Subordination Consider'd (1724) reveals his fears about the diminishing power of masters and "the increasing equality and extravagance of servants"—all this in a work contemporary with *Roxana*. Defoe concludes that when "Order is inverted, Subordination ceases, and the World seems to stand with the Bottom upward."[15]

As Defoe worries about the disorder created by maids and mistresses sharing clothes, he seems to bear eloquent testimony against his own heroines: Moll, who "roars" out against going into service; Roxana, who brings her maid to her lover's bed. Defoe himself profited greatly by pretending to be or by creating characters who pretend to be someone else. But Moll's incest and Roxana's parricide reveal Defoe's sure sense of the dangers that await those who fictionalize kinship—a sense as powerful in his novels as in his pamphlets. The values he expresses explicitly in *The Great Law of Subordination* are implicit in his fiction—as early as the lecture by Crusoe's father upon the virtues of "the middle station" (28). As Crusoe achieves great wealth and buys his nephew status, he seems to discredit his father's teachings. He comes home very differently than the prodigal son does in Christ's parable. But Crusoe insists upon reading the events of his life as part of a spiritual autobiography[16] (rather than, for example, as part of a rags to riches fairy tale), and this bespeaks his powerful sense of the justness of his father's example.

Backscheider takes as her epigram Defoe's claim in his *Elegy on the Author of the True Born Englishman*: "The God that gave me Brains will give me Bread." In her interpretation of Defoe, Backscheider sees him responding to the recurrent setbacks in his life by working harder as a writer, using the combined power of millions of words to win his bread. Backscheider no doubt is correct to take the frenetic pace of Defoe's writing as a persistent response to his several ruins. But the problem of "Bread," however pressing, usually is solved quickly by Defoe and by his characters. While Crusoe is an exception who can be shown to prove the rule, the great female characters achieve their full significance, their compelling equivocality, *after* they win prosperity. The excitement with which they achieve wealth soon gives way to their difficult, finally tragic need to transmute wealth into status. Moll and Roxana both follow Dorotea, using their beauty and wit to elevate themselves. Unlike Dorotea, they internalize the status inconsistency their success creates. They hope to fix their identities by using the very terms ("Gentlewoman," "Princess") that their beauty and talent have caused others to "lay aside." The God who gave Defoe his brains did, indeed, give him an almost unfailing source of income. But neither God nor his bread could satisfy Defoe's yearning for a title—for land, a coat-of-arms, a family seat. Moll and Roxana become compelling characters after they achieve great wealth precisely because they show that lots of bread, for example 3,700 pounds, guarantees neither happiness nor (even more important) a sure sense of who one is.

Writers after Defoe use a variety of literary devices (the birth mystery and the redefinition of incest among them) as they try to avoid a confrontation with Susan, the tragic lost child whose mother cannot "own" her lest mother and daughter destroy the fiction by which the mother would know herself. Roxana thrills to Susan's kiss, but obeisance to nature would have left her to starve, would have left Moll to serve. Roxana's fictions are more exciting, more liberating than her blood ties. But her fictions cannot offer (though she tries to make them) the certainty and the stability that blood provides. That Defoe will not let Roxana escape England and refashion herself abroad reveals his sense that her dilemma is his and his nation's. Having reached a point at which his fiction no longer can mute the problems that inhere to lower-class virtue, Defoe stops writing "novels." It is left for later writers, Fielding in particular, to return to the comic mode the confusions (and the freedoms) offered by Defoe's fictionalizing of kinship.

4

Night Moves: Henry Fielding and the Birth-Mystery Plot Under Stress

My body is my winning lottery ticket.

—Deion Sanders, circa 1988

Your sister, my Lady Desmond, is now suing for divorce of your brother, accused of that I have heard few Filding's guiltie of, insufficiencie to please a reasonable woman.

—G. Filding to Lord Feilding, 12 April 1635

From their time to ours, the roles of Defoe and Fielding in the origins of the novel have been clear. Defoe, a champion of religious dissent and an often-failed businessman, discovers the new literary territory of religious and economic individualism. He peoples that territory with characters both memorable and isolated, characters who *are* memorable precisely because they go against conventions of church and family. Fielding, trained in the classics at Eton, friend of Pitt and Lyttelton, cousin of the earls of Denbigh, takes the "new Species of Writing" from Defoe and Richardson and gives it a classical patrimony. Describing "not Men but Manners; not an Individual but a Species" (*Joseph Andrews*, 189), Fielding blunts the subversive thrust of the new men Defoe and Richardson by giving his characters broader historical and literary reference. All this is true enough, but it is important to remember that Fielding's background was only tenuously aristocratic, that, to put the matter perhaps too simply, the dowry of 3,700 pounds that Mary Tuffley brought to Defoe in 1684 is more money than Fielding ever had in his life.

If Defoe had ready cash, however, his only status was that which he bought. Fielding, improvident and chronically in debt, in his very being stood close to the status that Defoe's characters so eagerly (and in Roxana's case tragically) seek. Fielding's grandfather was the younger brother of the 3d Earl of Denbigh, and I believe that one reason for Fielding's notorious improvidence was his sense that his body might be his winning lottery ticket. At this late date, we only can guess what plans the Feilding/Denbighs made to assure patrimonial succession. The family tree suggests that Fielding stood within two or three deaths of being very close to the title and its estates, a long shot by today's standards but not so wild a dream in the demographic crisis of 1650–1740.

In Fielding's three great novels, estates wait for heirs. Sir Thomas Booby's rapidly announced death in *Joseph Andrews* provides a fine synechdoche for the quick changes that high mortality rates brought to eighteenth-century England. Allworthy, who "had three children, all of whom died in their infancy" (35), and Western are without male issue. Amelia's father is long dead, his estate, again because he leaves no male heir, subject to the machinations of a selfish child and an unscrupulous attorney. The happy endings in Fielding's novels may bespeak his deep wish that the accidents of mortality might bring him to a great estate. William, the 5th Earl of Denbigh, the earl during Fielding's adult life, had only one son; William's brother Charles had only one son as well. Not until a later generation would the earldom pass to a "second son," but the possibility existed earlier.[1]

Fielding's greatest achievement, the book we know as *Tom Jones*, was titled *The History of a Foundling*. Criticized in Fielding's day for its "lowness,"[2] the title points to the narrative technique Fielding favors as he attempts to manage status inconsistency. As Northrop Frye points out, Fielding takes the "birth-mystery plot"—a plot that goes back as far as the plays of Plautus and the story of Moses—as his "constructive principle of storytelling" (51). When the character we know as Tom Jones discovers his parentage, he solves not only a personal and a literary problem but a social problem as well. The concluding paragraphs of *Tom Jones* are easy to overlook because they are so formulaic: the hero gets the girl and the property too. Upon Tom's marriage to Sophia, Squire Western "hath resigned his Family Seat, and the greater Part of his Estate to his Son-in-Law . . . *Allworthy* was likewise greatly liberal to *Jones*." The continuity of the two estates assured in Jones's being and in Sophia's "already" bearing "him two fine Children, a Boy and a Girl" (981), the novel ends by bringing Tom, Sophia, and the world they sustain into one focus: "There is not a Neighbour, a Tenant, or a Servant, who doth not most gratefully bless the Day when Mr. *Jones* was married to his *Sophia*" (982). That all this goodwill and preservation of property is owing to the discovery that Jones is Bridget Allworthy's illegitimate son bears eloquent witness to the lengths to which families would go to sustain the fiction of kinship. On one hand, any male will do; on the other, that male must have, through his mother, some connection, however indirect, to the family. Tom rescues the squirearchy, but he is the creation of Bridget's sexuality and her willingness to go outside social proprieties to gratify it. Tom's potency descends to him from his mother, not from his uncle.

The birth mystery in *Tom Jones* is shaped by a complicated, sometimes divided social agenda. *The History of a Foundling*, like Defoe's stories, reveals how arbitrary social categories can be, how little, sometimes, the patriarch is able (Allworthy) or willing (Western) to see. Fielding spells his surname "ie," the Denbighs spell it "ei"; in many ways, *Tom Jones* suggests, status may depend on little more than the order of vowels.[3] Jones, the illegitimate child, is handsomer and more virtuous than the legitimate Blifil Jr. How important, then, can legitimacy be? Why should "a Neighbour, a Tenant, or a Servant" celebrate Jones's rescuing of a patriarchal system that privileges the foolish Western and the virtuous but sometimes impercipient Allworthy? The very fineness of the distinction Fielding/Feilding, insofar as it brings the author close to the earldom, makes the title important for him. Although a foundling, Tom always sees himself (and is seen by others) as a gentleman. His illegitimacy aside, Jones can make a more substantial claim to the estates than any "Neighbour . . . Tenant, or . . . Servant." The birth mystery in *Tom Jones* serves a comic purpose because it allows Fielding to bring together the attitudes that tragically divide Roxana. Fielding both subverts and vindicates the claims of patriarchal order, enacting, through Jones, his own dream of status.

Fielding's social agenda manifests itself differently in the birth mysteries of *Joseph Andrews*, *Tom Jones*, and *Amelia*. The former uses the plot to handle problems of status inconsistency with clarity and force; the latter shows the power of the plot (and the power of the patriarch) to be waning. Along with his working out of his birth mysteries in these novels, Fielding also offers three

Cervantick night-scenes. From Parson Adams's "Night Adventures" at Booby Hall, to the confusion during Tom Jones's overnight stay at Upton, to Amelia's "visit" to a masquerade, these scenes become more insidious. Personal virtue increasingly is threatened by the confusion of social categories.

Joseph Andrews offers Fielding's most confident redaction of the birth mystery. The small piece of gold that Joseph carries with him (64–65) and that, once mentioned, disappears, the strawberry birthmark (225) that Wilson describes upon his lost son—these are clear signs to any reader versed in the romance tradition that Joseph eventually will assume the higher rank that his nature deserves. And while Fielding labels his squire a "Booby," the effects of demographic crisis are limited in *Joseph Andrews*; the recently deceased Sir Thomas has a nephew ready to take his place. That the new Squire Booby is married to Pamela Andrews—to Richardson's Pamela—typifies the freedom that demographic crisis brought to young heirs. Fielding uses the birth mystery to sort out the confusions created in *Pamela* by Mr. B's freedom from parental constraint. Parson Adams, perhaps Fielding's single most famous character, is both a potent and a benevolent patriarch—an Abraham and an Adam rolled into one man. But his tattered clothes and chronic financial need reveal his version of patriarchy to be one whose day is rapidly passing.

Richardson's Pamela resurfaces in the conclusion of Fielding's novel so that he can redirect Richardson's attempt to deal with the revolutionary implications of her progress.[4] Richardson would ameliorate status inconsistency by changing Pamela's "Creator" and her rank; Fielding accomplishes the same end but does so by restoring Joseph and Fanny to their biological parents and thus to their rightful places. Although he seems to attack it through much of his story, Fielding finally implies that social hierarchy, by and large, has value.[5] Richardson's egalitarianism is not so easily suspended. Until her elevation, Pamela's character and rank never bear any relation to each other, and she remains, even after her marriage, a social anomaly. With almost painful regularity, onlookers marvel at the accomplishments of a girl of such humble origin. Beau Didapper to the contrary (and he is rendered comically impotent), once Fielding straightens out his characters' identities, their ranks and natures roughly correspond. Joseph's fair skin and good looks do, indeed, belong to a gentleman. He discovers his parents and eventually lives next door to them rather than cutting himself off from them. Joseph does profit from

Pamela's rise, but even here Fielding blunts the revolutionary thrust of his story. The "Fortune" that Mr. Booby gives to Fanny, and that Joseph lays out in "a little Estate," is owing to "unprecedented Generosity" (343–44). Joseph and Fanny come to their rightful place through the good auspices of a great aristocrat; they do not stage a long, protracted rebellion prior to their reward. Fielding offers a resolution through restoration, Richardson a resolution through transmutation.

In permitting important contradictions to reside latent in his characterization of Adams, Fielding not only attempts to improve upon Richardson, he also reveals how special, even miraculous, is Adams's version of patriarchy. Adams, who once attacked "the Luxury and Splendour" (82) of the clergy, accepts from Booby a profitable living and hires a curate. Can Fielding's figure of moral rectitude be guilty of pluralism? While Adams is famous for his sermons on submission—a fact of which his long-suffering wife reminds him—he refuses to follow Lady Booby's orders concerning Joseph and Fanny (306). Most tellingly, Adams himself splits his personality, declaring that "Mr. *Adams* at Church with his Surplice on, and Mr. *Adams* without that ornament, in any other place, were two very different Persons" (342). One Adams challenges and rebukes the elite; the other is their servant, sometimes their victim. One Adams stands (in clerical garb so tattered it barely identifies him) as a Christian of simple virtue, following Benjamin Hoadly in the belief that Anglican ritual must be demystified (83);[6] the other insists that Joseph and Fanny marry in accord with church law (340).

Adams shares in, even as he rises above, the spiritual egalitarianism and social elitism that rive *Pamela*. Like Joseph, Adams (outside the pulpit) is a gentleman in disguise. His clothes, his eating and drinking habits, his spontaneous benevolence—all hide his rank. They open him to contact with all social types and place him in situations in which he suffers from injustice and hypocrisy within the social order. But Adams, however unwittingly, relies on the definitions of place and privilege that his character seems to overturn. Facing unjust imprisonment, he is rescued by the discovery not of his virtues but of his rank (149). Unable to pay the bill he ran up because of the lying gentleman's promises, he is pardoned by an innkeeper who honors "the Clergy too much to deny trusting one of them for such a Trifle" (177). While he finds no charity in his fellow clergyman Trulliber, he praises the good that Lady Booby has done in the parish. His sense of her religious failings in no way blinds him to her social virtues (101). Adams's wholeness depends upon the particular orientation of his Christianity toward understanding the parish as an extended family that the parson educates and guides. Underlying both his challenges to his superiors and his submission to the status quo is his unflagging conviction that, as a clergyman, he is "a Servant of the Highest" (342), a role that combines both humility and deference to rank ("Servant of") with an egalitarian assertion of quality ("the Highest").

In no other scene is Adams's patriarchal power more tested than in the "Night-Adventures" at Booby Hall. Discovering that Adams has spent the night in the bed of the woman he loves, Joseph will feel "Rage." Adams himself will believe that the "Devil" has been at work in all the confusion (335). But Fielding, as Mark Spilka observes, uses the scene to "put a kind of comic blessing upon the novel."[7] Fielding's debt to the night scene at the inn of Maritornes is clear here, a debt he acknowledges on his title page when he proclaims his "history" to be "Written in Imitation of the Manner of Cervantes" (1). Parson Adams, in his "Night-Adventures," like Quixote, engages in physical combat in the dark and misidentifies his opponents. Placed between the revelations that Joseph and Fanny are brother and sister and that they are *not*, the "Night-Adventures" risk but then purge the story of illicit sexuality. Adams's virtue is both untainted and unchallenged by the confusion that is, in part, of his own making: "I know not whether," he tells an astonished and then enraged Joseph, "she is a Man or a Woman" (334). Only Joseph's "great Opinion of *Adams*" (335)—that is, only Joseph's respect for the head of the parish—gives him enough pause that he discovers an explanation for the events and saves the scene from violence.

As the events at the inn of Maritornes result in a reconciliation between Dorotea and Fernando and leave the grandee's son in a position of great power, so Fielding's "Night-Adventures" are part of the rehabilitation of the social elite that occurs throughout the second half of *Joseph Andrews*. The "Adventures" begin with Beau Didapper, who still hopes to bed Fanny and sneaks into what he takes to be her bedroom, imitating Joseph's voice. However, he is in Mrs. Slipslop's quarters. Didapper almost immediately "perceive[s] his Mistake" (331), but Slipslop wants to use him to prove her chastity and screams "Rape," even as she will not let Didapper escape. Adams enters the scene to rescue virtue in distress, but mistakes Didapper's "soft" skin for a woman's and

Slipslop's "rough Beard" (332) for a man's. He thus exchanges blows with Slipslop as Didapper manages a naked escape. One need not have read Mikhail Bakhtin's work on the carnivalesque[8] to see that conventions of gender and of class are turned upside down in these events.

"Lady *Booby*, who was as wakeful as any of her Guests," no doubt because she has Joseph under her roof, acts with a "bold Spirit" and brings "Light" into Slipslop's room. As Adams and Slipslop unsuccessfully attempt to explain the event, Lady Booby "casting her Eyes on the Ground, observed something sparkle with great Lustre, which, when she had taken it up, appeared to be a very fine pair of Diamond Buttons for the Sleeves. A little farther she saw lie the Sleeve itself of a Shirt with lace Ruffles." Lady Booby alertly solves what remains a mystery to Adams, and she is blessed with "Laughter" (333). Earlier a figure of weakness, Lady Booby here is a figure of "Spirit" and perceptiveness. The "Night-Adventures," for all their subversion of categories of gender and class, reestablish her authority. The "Adventures" also vindicate the perfect if rough virtue of Adams. In the darkness, he almost kills Slipslop (332) and almost comes to know Fanny in a very intimate way. But his innocence and his power emerge unscathed from these close calls.

As the birth mystery in *Tom Jones* is not as neat as that in *Joseph Andrews*, so the night at Upton, while finally vindicating the narrator's control of events and English common law, does so only after confusion and terror even more intense than Fielding visits upon Adams et. al. The "Adventures" at Booby Hall involve the naked Adams, and so the adventures at Upton begin with the naked Mrs. Waters. As decorums of dress are suspended, so are distinctions based on class. Tom and Partridge fight together, Sophia and Mrs. Honour travel together. The servants, as they speak for their betters, play crucial roles in Tom and Sophia's communication (or lack thereof). Indeed, the confusions about class lead to breaches of decorum. The landlady at the inn dislikes Mrs. Honour's putting on upper-class airs and criticizes her in "foul Language . . . it scoured out of her Mouth as Filth does from a Mud-Cart, when the Board which confines it is removed" (542). Mrs. Honour, reporting Tom's infidelity to Sophia, "discharge[s] . . . a Torrent of Abuse" (543) upon him.

With hierarchy and etiquette displaced, confusion and violence follow. Tom's visit to the inn begins with a fight that involves him, Partridge, the landlady, the landlord, and their maid—a fight caused by the landlady's unwillingness to serve or to lodge a naked woman. In short succession, a coachman and a sergeant fight in the kitchen, and Jones and Mr. Fitzpatrick fight when the latter mistakenly interrupts Jones and Mrs. Waters. On the morning after all the fisticuffs, Fielding offers "a Scene of universal Confusion" (551) with Squire Western, Mr. Fitzpatrick, and Jones meeting in the kitchen and abusing each other as they seek their loved ones.

When Mr. Fitzpatrick takes Squire Western to the bed of the woman whom he supposes is Sophia, the confusion reaches its greatest, most frightening intensity: "The poor Lady [who actually is Mrs. Waters, who actually is Jenny Jones] started from her Sleep with as much Amazement as Terror, and beheld at her Bed-side a Figure which might very well be supposed to have escaped out of Bedlam. Such Wildness and Confusion were in the Looks of Mr. Western" (552). Western's "Wildness" and Mrs. Waters's naked-ness would be frightening—would break Fielding's comic "envelope"—were it not for the care with which Fielding frames the events at Upton. For one example, the landlady beats Jones with her broom only because she wants to maintain her inn's reputation as a place frequented "by Gentry of the best Quality" (580); she fears that the naked Mrs. Waters will besmirch its good name. The fight ends when a coach and four arrives at the inn and requires the combatants' services. "Quality" is served in all this battling, not subverted. The interlude at Upton ends with English common law, not carnival chaos, in force. Jones goes on trial for stealing Sophia's muff. At first the case is confused, but the rules of evidence are applied, the truth gets told, and Jones (for one of the few times in the book to this point) is vindicated.

More significant than the suggestions of order within the scene of confusion is the scene's placement within the narrative as a whole. Fielding brackets the events at Upton with the stories of the Man of the Hill and Mrs. Fitzpatrick. These stories, as Frederick W. Hilles and Martin C. Battestin have argued,[9] show us potentially negative courses for Tom and Sophia. Fielding, coming out of the tradition of Augustan satire, offers a series of negative alternatives to imply a positive mean. Indeed, in his influential essay, "Fielding's Definition of Wisdom: Some Functions of Ambiguity and Emblem in *Tom Jones*," Battestin shows that the scene atop Mazard Hill, which opens the adventures at Upton, is staged by Fielding to emblematize both a definition of prudence and Tom's failure to achieve that virtue. That deficiency, as it leads to his infidelity with Mrs. Waters, stands as the source of much of the confusion at the inn.

Partridge repeatedly identifies Jones as Allworthy's nephew and mistakenly relies upon Jones's status to protect him. But, of course, Jones *is* Allworthy's nephew. Partridge's mistake, like the confusion to which it contributes, is superficial rather than substantial. All the confusion at Upton is contained within a birth mystery of both traditional and elaborate contrivance. That plot is conservative—the good-natured and handsome foundling turns out to be a gentleman after all. Besides the birth-mystery plot, Fielding's narrator also plays a crucial and conservative role. For all the fame of the scene at Upton, one of its most basic features long has gone unnoted: the narrative of the events runs from book 9 to book 10. This allows the narrator to speak to us midway through the scene in chapter 1 of volume 10. Amidst all the confusion, he reminds us that the history has a "design," that the "Whole is connected" (521).

The night moves in *Tom Jones* stand between the reassuring safety of Parson Adams's "Night-Adventures" and the insidious masquerade in *Amelia,* a work that makes confusion about "Quality" its great theme, even as it makes deception so universal that its heroine cannot innocently or safely engage in such. The character most like Joseph Andrews in *Amelia* is Sergeant Atkinson, but Atkinson, while finally rewarded for his virtue, is almost fatally wounded by the conflicts to which those virtues lead. He needs a birth-mystery plot to place him but never finds one. Fielding's uncertain treatment of Atkinson reflects his growing doubt about the health of the British body politic, his fears of corruption in the political and social constitution he long had celebrated.[10] In *Joseph Andrews* and, to a lesser degree, *Tom Jones,* Fielding uses the birth mystery to protect himself from systematic criticism of British life. Of course, as long as the identities of Joseph and Tom are unknown, their physical comeliness and generosity of spirit do comment negatively upon the physical stuntedness and mean spiritedness of their social betters—the Boobies and Didappers, the Bellastons and Fellamars. But once Fielding reveals the identities of Joseph and Tom, the seeming disparity between their noble natures and humble places disappears, and Fielding invites us to see the Boobies et. al. as individual aberrations, not as symbols of a corrupt order.

Eschewing a birth mystery, Fielding proceeds more equivocally in his treatment of class distinctions.[11] At first glance, *Amelia* appears to attack vigorously conventional notions of quality. Usually this attack is twofold, with characters first asserting the value of sentiment and then the equalizing force of sentiment— that is, the ability of any person at any rank to enjoy it. Miss Matthews speaks for all the characters in *Amelia* when she cries, "A Cottage . . . A Cottage with the Man one loves is a Palace" (86). Amelia cannot proclaim too often her willingness to share any condition with Booth, and he responds in kind, at one point describing himself waiting to meet her with "such a Delight, that I would not have exchanged my poor Lodgings for the finest Palace in the Universe" (81). Mrs. Bennett (later Mrs. Atkinson) and Dr. Harrison give a religious rather than a sentimental justification for it, but their egalitarianism is equally forthright. She declares, "Religion . . . professes to know no Difference of Degree; but ranks all Mankind on the Footing of Brethren. Of all kinds of Pride, there is none so unchristian as that of Station" (305). Harrison criticizes "the Custom of the World; which instead of being formed on the Precepts of our Religion to consider each other as Brethren, teaches us to regard those who are a Degree below us, either in Rank or Fortune, as a Species of Beings of an inferior Order in the Creation" (377).

No one will be surprised to learn that Miss Matthews's claim is empty. Rank is crucial to her throughout the story, most notably in her complaints about attending the theater with her landlady's daughter: "A Girl indeed of good Sense, and many good Qualities: but how much beneath me was it to be the Companion of a Creature so low!" (57). Fielding's problem with status inconsistency looms large when we realize that, in this instance anyway, the other characters are little better than Booth's seductress. One again, a "Night-Adventure," in this case Mrs. Atkinson's attending a masquerade pretending to be Amelia in disguise, initiates conflict.[12] During the masquerade, Mrs. Atkinson speaks to a corrupt peer who would seduce Amelia and gets him to promise a commission for the sergeant. Upon hearing this, Amelia protests, "You may have blown up my Reputation by your Behaviour," while Mrs. Atkinson accuses her of "Prudery" (445). As Booth and Atkinson enter, and the argument intensifies, the point at issue changes. Booth, "in a violent Rage," charges Mrs. Atkinson with "Insolence" and "Presumption," and she cries out to her husband, "Do you tamely see me insulted in such a manner, now that you are a Gentleman and upon a Footing with him?" Booth rejoins, hinting at the (im)possibility of a duel, "It is lucky for us all, perhaps . . . that he is not my equal," and then Mrs. Atkinson gets the last word: "You lie, Sirrah . . . he is every way your Equal; he is as good a Gentleman as yourself, and as much an Officer" (447). When her husband, who throughout the scene wants only "to procure Peace" (446), fails to back her, Mrs. Atkinson leaves the room, angry that he has permitted her to be "insulted" (448).

Terry Castle describes this scene as only a "minor disturbance," perhaps overlooking that it gives lie to all the egalitarian claims made in *Amelia*. For here rank matters greatly. Confusion and anger have followed from Mrs. Atkinson's posing as her better (but so also has opportunity); and Atkinson, no matter what his military title, never will be Booth's social equal. The narrator discredits Mrs. Atkinson's cause, telling us that she has taken "a Sip too much that Evening" and describing her anger as "a Rage little short of Madness" (447). She is punished by a serious illness that immediately befalls her husband. Upset by the quarrel, he drinks "a whole Bottle of Brandy" and develops a fever that leads his wife to fear for his life. Having found him "in a raving delirious Fit," Mrs. Atkinson comes abjectly to ask for Amelia's help, noting, as part of the request, that she has been to see the peer: "I have . . . set all to Rights—Your reputation is now in no Danger" (480). Atkinson's illness allows the two families to reconcile without mentioning again the incident that led to it.

But the sickbed meeting between Amelia and her foster brother raises once more the problem of rank. Atkinson, who "wish'd to kill himself" after the quarrel and "is sure he will die" (480), wants to return a miniature of Amelia that he stole when he was eighteen. When he then begs to kiss her hand, his devotion overwhelms Amelia. The narrator describes tears running "plentifully from her Eyes with Compassion for the poor Wretch" (482) and then offers this explanation:

> To say the Truth, without an Injury to her Chastity, that Heart which had stood firm as a Rock to all the Attacks of Title and Equipage, of Finery and Flattery, and which all the Treasures of the Universe could not have purchased, was yet a little softened by the plain, honest, modest, involuntary, delicate, heroic Passion of this poor and humble Swain; for whom, in spite of herself, she felt a momentary Tenderness and Complaisance, at which *Booth*, if he had known it, would perhaps have been displeased. (482–83)

Amelia's confusion here offers a synechdoche for Fielding's. On one hand stand equalizing sentiment and the virtuous Atkinson, on the other the elitism of "Title and Equipage." Atkinson is worthier than the evil peer who would seduce Amelia, and she feels "Tenderness" for him. Yet this feeling must be "in spite of herself," must be, as the narrator describes it, improper. Of course, one reason for its impropriety is that Amelia is a married woman. But Atkinson, at death's door, hardly seems a threat to her fidelity,[13] and I think Fielding's adjectives define the tension under which Amelia labors. "Plain," "modest," "poor," and "humble," Atkinson is a swain, a child of a rural cottager. Even though the same woman nursed him and Amelia, he cannot get too close to the heroine, lest all distinctions vanish. Having narrowed the distance between Amelia and Atkinson, Fielding struggles, sometimes awkwardly, to reestablish it; in one instance Amelia, preposterously enough, will not "recollect her Foster-Brother, till he was introduced to her by *Booth*" (182).

Like his namesake Joseph Andrews and like Tom Jones, Atkinson combines humble social origin with "heroic passion" and virtue.[14] From his first appearance as "a Boy of very good natural Parts" (87) to subsequent descriptions of him as "one of the handsomest young Fellows in *England*" (107) and "notwithstanding the Meanness of his Birth . . . a noble Fellow" (182), Atkinson's virtue is incommensurate with his place. Most readers probably would agree with his wife that he *is* "as good a Gentleman" as Booth, probably better: while equally courageous and generous, he avoids Booth's weaknesses. But Mrs. Atkinson is nearly "mad" to make such a suggestion, and the sergeant-now-captain proves his virtue by not rising to her defense. Instead, he moves silently through the story; a troubling anomaly, he advances, in his career and in his social life, by awkward half steps.[15] The marriage to Mrs. Bennett elevates him, and she, with Amelia's encouragement, rejects considerations of rank to make it. Amelia here is at her most egalitarian, claiming, "I should not be ashamed of being the Wife of an honest Man in any Station.—Nor, if I had been much higher than I was, should I have thought myself degraded, by calling our honest Sergeant my Husband" (305). Yet, her own "Tenderness" for Atkinson will fill her with confusion and guilt, and her diction—"station," higher," "degraded"—shows how thoroughly she has absorbed the norms that she seems to challenge.

The marriage itself, while all see it as an advancement, is not a reward for virtue as complete as those of the other Joseph and Tom Jones. Coupled to an intermittently shrewish wife, Atkinson, when we last see him, "upon the whole hath . . . a very happy Life" but not the "ten Years" of perfect bliss that Booth receives. Perhaps Atkinson's most awkward half step comes in this same final account of him, when the narrator notes, "He is lately advanced to the Rank of Captain" (532). With Booth out of the military and safe in rural retirement, Atkinson's military rank no longer can cause trouble. Fielding apparently is so relieved by this that he promotes Atkinson to the rank that the corrupt peer once had bestowed upon him. Not only do the Booths and the Atkinsons forget their quarrel and its cause; so too, apparently, does Fielding. The good sergeant rises, then, but neither as smoothly nor as grandly as do Andrews and Jones. Because Atkinson's lineage never changes, his progress has limits.

In Atkinson's case, Fielding has a fine opportunity for a birth-mystery plot—the nurse's background is obscure, as are the reasons Amelia became her foster child. A revelation that Atkinson really is the gentleman he appears to be would surprise us no more, I think, than the revelations about Joseph and Tom. But the birth mystery, particularly as Fielding earlier used it, endorses a society based on rank by proposing that the father's mark is upon the son. The virtuous ultimately do turn out to be the great; the social system, once the lines of patrilinear succession are uncovered, works. This affirmation is one that Fielding will not allow himself in *Amelia*, not just because his years at Bow Street had broken his spirit, or because Mandeville had captured his mind, or even, as I once proposed, because his political faith in Henry Pelham caused him to view the British "Constitution" more pessimistically.[16] Rather, Fielding in *Amelia* no longer can sustain patriarchal power. Harrison is one of his finest characters, a man of intelligence and virtue. All goes relatively well when he is on stage; all falls apart when he is off. Unlike Abraham Adams, who always is in the center of the action, Harrison frequently is absent. He is the prototype for the patriarch in novels by women in the century's second half—powerful perhaps, but frequently away on business. Childless himself, Harrison's force is within himself rather than, as is Adams's, fungible. In the absence of the patriarch, the birth mystery no longer can work, no matter the "Fildingesque" procreative successes of Booth and Atkinson, to the former of whose children Harrison "will leave his whole Fortune" (532). Martin C. Battestin argues that Booth's conversion, his progress to a happy ending, depends upon his mastering his passionate nature by reading the sermons of Isaac Barrow, one of

Adams's favorite divines.[17] While Barrow is always present for Adams, Booth's encounter with him is owing to "Fortune" (532), and while we and Fielding take joy in his good luck, we can sense the distance between his faith and that of the patriarch of Booby Hall.

Fielding drops the birth mystery in *Amelia* because he senses the diminution of patriarchal power, the distance between Billy Booth's Barrow and Abraham Adams's. As an odd corollary to his dropping the birth mystery, he also, in a famous and revealing gaucherie, damages his heroine's nose.[18] Amelia must have "her lovely Nose . . . beat all to pieces" in order that she and Booth can discover their love for one another. Booth never thinks of approaching Amelia while she is surrounded by suitors of "the highest Rank," and she does not discover him until her shattered nose causes those suitors to flee. At his first vision of Amelia, Booth feels that she is "absolutely out of my Reach" (66). The injured nose places her within it.

Just as a birth mystery involving Atkinson would have spared Amelia's feelings, so one elevating and enriching Booth might have spared her nose. Incapable of offering the vindication of patriarchal power (and social hierarchy) that such a plot would require, yet equally incapable of attacking uninhibitedly the traditions that might metamorphose him into an earl, Fielding finds himself in an unsatisfying and difficult position.[19] He either bites his tongue, cataloguing examples of vice but accepting vicious behavior,[20] or he equivocates, turning to narrative contrivances to ameliorate the conflict he suggests. He marries Amelia and Booth and challenges notions of rank,[21] but first he damages Amelia. His attacks on the peerage are qualified (after all, he might hope to become one of them), even as his faith in the correlation between virtue and rank wavers (this novel's Joseph is not to be placed as easily as his first Joseph). Amelia's shattered nose finally is a phenomenon of the same order as Fielding's dropping the birth mystery. Both are results of the disjunction between his satiric sense of the flaws in the British "Constitution" and his hesitation to destroy that "Machine."

In *Amelia* Fielding's egalitarian and elitist sympathies do not find the comprehensive mediation that they do in *Joseph Andrews*. In recognizing the happy blending of literary and social conservatism in *Joseph Andrews*, however, we also should recognize that it depends on a faith inexplicable, rare, and strong. Adams's rising above a seemingly classic split personality is a miracle. When his wife points to the disparity between his sermons and his deeds (306–7), he makes no response. The division cannot be debated or investigated, only observed. We may wonder how Adams can be one person in church and another out; he does not. We may note the potential hypocrisy of his accepting a living from Booby; he does not. When these seeming moral dilemmas arise, his faith blesses Adams with a happy impercipience, an impercipience made credible by its less beneficial counterparts: Adams's naiveté in his dealings with villainous, deceitful men and his inability to recognize the strength and virtue of arguments that his opponents use.[22] A latter-day version of the Old Testament patriarchs, Adams can neither ask nor accept questions about his power (even when offered by his wife) lest it, under analysis, disappear.

Pamela Andrews, at least in her notions about chastity, is memorably different from Defoe's heroines. Pamela, however, like Defoe's Moll and Roxana, reveals the revolutionary potential of lower-class beauty and virtue. In response to the "new" writing of Richardson and Defoe, Fielding in 1742 affirms social, religious, and literary traditions (witness the classicism of his preface to *Joseph Andrews*), but the conflicts latent in Adams's double personality and in the "natural Gentility" of Joseph and Fanny could not be put off forever. Political revolution and literary Gothicism await only the weakening, the attenuation of the patriarchal power (already tattered and impoverished) that Adams embodies. Richardson, although less accomplished than Fielding, was more successful. His abrupt shift from egalitarianism to elitism (and the large scope he gives to democratic themes) better fit the political and literary worlds to which demographic crisis was giving rise. Fielding's righting of Richardson's resolution actually set him apart from great historical and literary trends. Having centered his story upon a patriarch and his plot upon a birth mystery, he stands, in his own age, somewhat like Parson Adams—marvelous but outdated, possessed of latent conflicts whose importance later writers (including himself in *Amelia*) will limn.

5

Roderick Random's "Agreeable Lassitude" and Smollett's Anamnestic Fiction

Much of the history of eighteenth-century English fiction could be written according to distinctions among journey motifs. . . . [W]e may roughly classify the strands readily available to Fielding in mid-century in three versions: a PILGRIMAGE emphasizes arrival and the necessity of steady application or fortitude in overcoming obstacles, and its meanings are essentially internal and religious; a QUEST emphasizes attainment of an object and the relation of search to desert, and its meanings are cultural; a PROGRESS describes growth and accumulation of judgment and skill, and its meanings are individual, but often with contextual reference to the individual's social setting.

—J. Paul Hunter, *Occasional Form:*
Henry Fielding and the Chains of Circumstance

While not the staple of literary criticism that the Fielding-Richardson comparison has been, the Fielding-Smollett comparison has had a long and instructive life. In most cases, the comparison has been made at Smollett's expense. Tuvia Bloch's 1967 essay, "Smollett's Quest for Form," nicely summarizes this tendency; Smollett seeks but only occasionally achieves the "form" that Fielding has.[1] John Richetti, rather than apologizing for Smollett's various interpolations, digressions, and infelicities, takes the violence that Smollett does to traditional notions of literary form as interesting in its own right. Claiming that Smollett's work "has its own narrative virtue," Richetti connects Smollett's narrative structure (or lack thereof) with social motives. In Richetti's view, Smollett uses "comic violence and satiric distortion" to express his "disaffection from the conservative ideology that governs Field-ing's narrative practice."[2]

More recently, Aileen Douglas has linked Smollett's narrative practice to his "uneasy" representation of the "body."[3] She places Smollett between Foucauldian "conceptual complexities of human physicality"—the notion that even our bodies are socially "constructed"—and an angry, even feral sense that "physical experience" is "absolute and irreducible" (xx). In a fine summary, she claims:

> The materialism of Smollett's characters is neither simple nor totaliz-ing. In his work he accompanies the shock of physical contact, the immediacy of physical experience, with an awareness that the body becomes an object of knowledge through the discourses of law, medicine, and philosophy. (xxii)

So Smollett sees the human impulse to narrate as both natural and socially determined. He will use Frye's "constructive principles of storytelling" even as he establishes his distance from them. Douglas describes Smollett reminding us, "If you prick a socially constructed body, it still bleeds" (xxii). Similarly, Smollett's stories proceed with a fierce impulsiveness—flying chamber pots, flying brains, near lethal hits from behind—that only seem to place them outside the conventions available to him.

Following the leads of Richetti and Douglas, I want to offer a basic difference between Fielding and Smollett, a difference both formal and social. Fielding's art of fiction, as critics like Frederick W. Hilles, Robert Alter, and Martin C. Battestin among many others have shown, is mimetic.[4] Fielding as author imitates the providential design of God's creation. Jerry C. Beasley helpfully summarizes this view of Fielding: "The conspicuously orches-trated intricacies of his works . . . furnish ample evidence of his conviction that the artist's responsibility to moral purpose and his responsibility to form were indistinguishable, that the homiletic and the aesthetic functions of the novel ought to *mirror* one another as *reflections* of the author's ordered *vision of life*" (my italics).[5] Hunter points out that even when Fielding complicates mimesis by offering "more than one version of journey" (Hunter 1975, 148)—the case of *Tom Jones*—the journey still is toward an earthly reward that adumbrates a heavenly.

Smollett's fiction, rather than being mimetic, is anamnestic. Adapting Milton's story of Adam, he works between the versions of remembrance offered by Socrates, Henry Peacham, and Paul Feyerabend. While all his longer prose fictions describe characters who are "on the road," their journeys are neither pilgrimages nor quests nor progresses. In his birth-mystery plots, as in his journey motifs, Smollett will not fit the mimetic categories that are relevant to Fielding, even when those "motifs" are described as comprehensively as Hunter does. What Richetti sees as Smollett's "defiant lack of structure"[6] actually is structure, but structure that is anamnestic and thus of a different sort than that which literary critics are accustomed to describe. An "uneasier" writer than Fielding, Smollett, in concluding his birth mysteries, will not rescue patrilinear succession.[7]

The conclusion of *Roderick Random* [8] provides a fine example of Smollett's referencing the body such that he can present his subversions as commonplaces. Roderick, having dropped off a cargo of slaves that he has carried from "the coast of Guinea" to South America, begins to "breath with pleasure the pure air of Paraguay" (410) and to dream of a reunion with his beloved Narcissa. He meets an English gentleman for whom he immediately feels "a profound veneration" (411) and "surprising attraction" (412). Roderick, eager to learn the "particulars" of the gentleman's life, is revealed through an accidental reference by his uncle, Tom Bowling, to be the gentleman's son. The *anagnorisis* accomplished, Roderick's father and uncle celebrate the reunion, offering praises to the "Mysterious Providence," the "infinite goodness" (413) that rules their lives. Writing within the tradition of Frye's "birth mystery," Smollett seems to move his story briskly towards its comic resolution: Roderick and his now wealthy father return to Scotland to reassume their birthright; Roderick overcomes financial and familial barriers and marries Narcissa. Before all that happens, however, the usually indomitable Roderick suffers a revealing setback:

On this great, sudden, and unexpected occasion . . . I fell sick, fevered, and in less than three hours, became quite delirious; so that . . . the joy of the family converted into grief and despair.—Physicians were instantly called, I was plentifully blooded in the foot, my lower extremities were bathed in a decoction of salutiferous herbs; in ten hours after I was taken ill, I enjoyed a critical sweat, and the next day felt no remains of the distemper, but an *agreeable lassitude*, which did not hinder me from getting up. (414, my italics)

Roderick's illness departs sharply from the birth mystery as Fielding employs it. Fielding, as he restores characters to their rightful social places, makes the discovery of paternity the means to health, individual and communal. Once Joseph's strawberry birthmark reveals him to be Wilson's son, the story proceeds rapidly to its happy ending. We discover that Joseph has been a gentleman all along albeit a gentleman in disguise. As he learns of his birth, Tom Jones also learns that he is illegitimate, but this discovery still does place him, does win him Sophia (the mimetic representation of wisdom), and does allow him to become the center of a viable and prosperous community.

Moreover, Fielding sets up his birth mysteries such that readers, if sufficiently watchful and sufficiently grounded in earlier versions of the plot, can solve them quite early in the narrative. Joseph Andrews's "whiteness . . . of skin" and talismanic piece of gold are early signs that he is a birth-mystery protagonist. Betty the chambermaid's somewhat lascivious nature hardly disqualifies her judgment that Joseph has the physical attributes of a gentleman. Fielding not only gives Tom Jones the obvious signs of being well-born—fair skin and good looks, he also repeatedly has him cross paths with lawyer Dowling, the man who knows and inadvertently reveals Bridget's secret.[9] Fielding's birth mystery, however complicated, is always there to be solved: if only Joseph were not asleep during Wilson's story; if only Tom "took" Dowling "at his word." In Roderick's story there is not as much a mystery to solve as an accident waiting to happen.

Whatever the sources of his "epical resentment,"[10] Smollett will not join Fielding in acts of social accommodation. Many critics, Lewis M. Knapp and Ronald Paulson perhaps most notable among them,[11] have pointed out that Smollett's intentions and his methods remain those of a satirist, at least until *Humphry Clinker*. This satiric bent would hardly distinguish him from Fielding, himself an author capable of moments of "savage indignation." But insofar as Smollett's anger leads him to pursue anamnesis rather than mimesis, it also leads him to modify significantly the birth-mystery resolution. Roderick's sudden illness suggests that he cannot join in his father's easy proclamation of a happy ending. Even his father notes that, whatever the good fortune that has restored Roderick to him, his wife, his beloved Charlotte, is dead—a victim of Roderick's grandfather and his refusal to accept a marriage between people of different social classes (even though of the same family). Lacking a detached, semiomniscient, self-conscious, first-person narrator like Fielding's to bring order to them,[12] the events of Roderick's life are, indeed, random, and the discovery of his father, following hard upon his miraculous rescue by his uncle, presents itself as a good break after a series of bad ones. The appeal to Providence is weakened by Roderick's "agreeable lassitude," and any reader of *Bleak House* can see danger in his concluding "certainty" that he will recover Narcissa's estate.

Roderick's illness and subsequent "lassitude" are not the only signs that his birth mystery serves anamnestic rather than mimetic ends. Fielding's heroes—Joseph, Tom, even Billy Booth—are last seen as the benevolent proprietors of happy rural seats. Jerry Beasley, who offers an astute and comprehensive reading of Fielding's conclusions, tries to see the same pattern in Smollett: "It is something like this journey to Eden, rendered in the form of a comic novel, that Roderick completes at the end of his story when he travels to Scotland and settles tranquilly into his now happy ancestral estate together with his father and his bride."[13] While Roderick and his father are granted a triumphal homecoming, Roderick's description of the event casts doubt upon the patriarchal order that his father revives: "As there is no part of the world, in which the peasants are more attached to their Lords than in Scotland, we were almost *devoured* by their affection in getting out of the coach." In the welcoming crush, people "crowded together so closely to see us, that several were in danger of *being squeezed to death*" (434, my italics).

Rather than "tranquillity," Roderick emphasizes danger, even death, and in the novel's final sentence, only Narcissa's pregnancy prevents him from rushing off to London to litigate with her brother. Smollett, in a famous and telling metaphor, uses a bouncing tennis ball to figure the life of Roderick Random (1). We may sense, at the story's end, that a ball placed under such pressure— the crowd of peasants serving as an anamnestic symbol for the expectations and requirements of patriarchal order—either will bounce again or explode. Roderick, rather than "questing" for status (for social "form"), actually is uneasy, even unhappy with it. For Roderick, the money in Scotland is very good; he is wealthy beyond his wildest dreams, but his compulsion to lay claim to Narcissa's estate may reveal that only the money holds him to his fraternal homestead.

Besides the important differences of his conclusion from Fielding's, Smollett also treats subversively two of Fielding's great themes: status inconsistency and providential order. Throughout his career, Smollett not only attacks Fielding's "conservative ideology," as Richetti has described, but he also refuses to frame social questions as Fielding does. In Fielding's novels, the problem of class (How can servants and foundlings be so talented and so virtuous?) is contained in a dialectic between lower-class virtue and upper-class vice—a dialectic that the birth-mystery plot, along with other devices, finally completes.[14] While Fielding will satirize roasting squires, booby peers, and uneducated justices of the peace, he also renders what we call upward mobility unproblematic because it is unnecessary.[15] Virtuous lower-class characters really are upper-class characters.

Smollett's differences with Fielding appear most clearly in the *Critical Review* paragraph on Admiral Charles Knowles that landed Smollett in jail. Most earlier critics, if they bother to cite this passage, see in it a direct and courageous attack upon Knowles for what Smollett believed to be his incompetence. I suggest that the attack got Smollett in trouble not only because he libels Knowles but also because he discredits both sides of the social mediation that writers like Fielding mimetically achieved:

> We have heard of a man [Knowles] who, *without birth, interest, or fortune, has raised himself from the lowest paths of life to an eminent rank* in the service; and if all his friends were put to the strappado, they could not define the quality or qualities to which he owed his elevation. Nay, it would be found upon enquiry, that he neither has, or ever had any friend at all; (for we make a wide distinction between a patron and a friend); and yet for a series of years, he has been enabled to sacrifice the blood, the treasure and the honor of his country, to his own ridiculous projects. Ask his character of those who know him [and] they will not scruple to say . . . that *in every station of life he has played the tyrant with his inferiors, the incendiary among his equals,* and commanded a sq-----n occasionally for twenty years, without having even established his reputation in the article of personal courage. (my italics)[16]

The magnificent vituperation of this attack, which I have abridged, should not blind us to its mercurial subversion of Fielding's social categories. Knowles has friends; he has no friends. He is the very type of upward mobility; he is the very type of incompetent elitism. As he is placed in this paragraph, Knowles has no good options. When he operates within the military hierarchy, he is a "tyrant." When he pushes to raise his status among his equals, he is an "incendiary." Smollett places virtue outside Knowles's seemingly admirable raising of himself "without birth, interest or fortune . . . from the lowest paths of life," nor is it to be found in his seemingly admirable and loyal ("twenty years") service to an established institution. A discovery that Knowles is well-born could not solve the problem of status inconsistency here because Smollett pillories not just Knowles but the options—upwardly mobile lower-class virtue and flexible but strong social elitism—that mainstream writers like Fielding were attempting to reconcile. Virtue resides only in a "personal courage" that exists outside of social categories.

   Roderick Random provides a broad fictional version of the rapid shifts in the Knowles paragraph. Roderick, a victim of his grandfather's elitism, relies continually upon Strap's deference to him as a gentleman: "To be sure, Mr. Random, you are born a gentleman, and have a great deal of learning. . . . On the other hand, I am a poor but honest cobbler's son" (95). While Strap finally receives a "reward" for his deference—marriage to the former prostitute Miss Williams and "five hundred pounds to stock a farm" (435)—through most of the novel he must watch uncomplainingly as Roderick squanders his money. If Strap's deference seems foolish, "new men," as seen in a character like Mr. Cringer, M. P., also are denigrated. Cringer mistreats Roderick, who asks his help in securing a position as a surgeon's mate, even though "this very individual Mr. Cringer had many a time rode before my grandfather's cloak-bag in quality of a footman" (74). Cringer, who represents vile social climbing—Roderick, in his last reference to him, describes him as "this upstart, proud, mean member" (74)—is countered by Captain Weazel, who bodies forth empty elitism. Unwilling to share a wagon with servants and with Scotsmen, threatening always to get his sword but cowering before a highwayman, Weazel finally is seen as "a little thin creature, about the age of forty, with a long, withered visage, very much resembling that of a baboon" (50).

   Weazel also reveals the thoroughness of Smollett's remembering. In chapter 11 of *Roderick Random*, a typical night scene in the manner of Cervantes, Strap briefly and accidentally winds up in the bed of Weazel's wife. The next morning Weazel threatens Strap with a "drawn sword," swearing "he must either fight him, or he would instantly put him to death" (53–54). Roderick notes that "the more submission that appeared in Strap, the more implacable seemed the resentment of Weazel" (54). "Seemed" carries weight here because Weazel's threats are empty and cowardly. That Strap's "submission" is misdirected becomes apparent as Roderick intervenes and suggests different means of combat. Because "it could not be supposed that a poor barber lad would engage a man of the sword at his own weapon" (54), boxing, cudgeling, fighting "at sharps" (with knives)—all are proposed and all rejected by Weazel. Weazel finally declines to enter into any combat with Strap because "it was beneath any gentleman of his character to fight like a porter, or even to put himself on a footing, in any respect, with such a fellow" (54). Weazel is portrayed as Knowles was, using his status to hide his cowardice.

When Roderick subsequently uses a meat spit to duel with Weazel and to defeat him, the implication of this contretemps might seem clear. The virtuous character of relatively little social status defeats the supercilious would-be aristocrat. The spit might be read as a Fieldingesque "emblem" for the social synthesis that Smollett achieves, but the episode ends, not with Roderick triumphant but with Strap "on his knees," once more asking "pardon for the mistake he had committed" (55). Weazel is both discredited and triumphant. He soon disappears from the story, but the subversion of his claims to status continues, finding its culmination in an episode involving Roderick himself.

After participating in the Battle of Cartagena, Roderick is "dropped" back in England (having won a fight with Crampley but then been knocked unconscious from behind) with nothing but the shirt on his back. Everyone, including a clergyman, refuses to care for him, until he is taken in by Mrs. Sagely, "who was suspected of witchcraft" (240). At this juncture, and for motives he never announces, Roderick takes an alias, "John Brown," and also meets a woman "whose name for the present shall be Narcissa" (218–19). Perhaps one reason for all this coyness about identity is that Roderick, to support himself, must become a servant in Mrs. Sagely's household; she "bid the maid to order a new suit of livery for me and instruct me in the articles of my duty" (218). Assuming that Smollett practices mimesis, we might suggest that Roderick must change his name in order to distinguish his servant self from his "real" self. But Roderick himself brings the utility of both his old identity and his new into question: "How often did I curse the servile station, that placed me so infinitely beneath the regard of this idol of my adoration [Narcissa]! and how often did I bless my fate, that enabled me daily to enjoy the sight of so much perfection!" (219). In the midst of his dilemma vis-à-vis Narcissa, Roderick "unwittingly" conquers the affections of "the cook-wench and dairy maid" and thus wins the enmity of the "coachman and gardener, who paid their devoirs to my admirers . . . and [were] alarmed at my success." When the coachman challenges Random/Brown to a boxing match, the novel reaches an anamnestic high point, with Roderick spurning the invitation in almost the exact words that Weazel used to spurn Strap's: "I would not descend so far beneath the dignity of a gentleman, as to fight like a porter." Roderick's response is validated by Smollett to the extent that it brings about good results: the coachman is frightened off, the servants begin to call Roderick "Gentleman John," and Narcissa and Mrs. Sagely express their approval by occasionally honoring him with that sobriquet (227).

If Smollett's goal were to restore a virtuous young Scot to his rightful place, this episode would seem out of place, sloppy—choose whatever pejorative term critics have applied to Smollett's "form." Just as we later may wonder how our hero can engage so easily in the slave trade, so here we may wonder how he can act like a "Weazel." Since Smollett, as the Knowles paragraph indicates, explodes Fielding's dialectic of virtuous servants and salvageable booby squires, the echo of Weazel has a perfect, if anamnestic, appropriateness. The servants at Mrs. Sagely's are not particularly virtuous, and Brown is not a gentleman. That Roderick *is* a gentleman only adds fine irony to Smollett's subversion of social categories. The pretend gentleman is actually a real gentleman who, in the past, has fought against the gentlemanly pretensions of Weazel who, finally, has those pretensions vindicated by Strap's submission. Weazel's claims to status are no more empty (and no more substantial) than are Roderick's claims to be a virtuous and upwardly mobile servant.

Most confusing about the Weazel-Random/Brown connection for critics operating from mimetic assumptions is that it deprives the appearance-reality distinction of importance. That John Brown is not what he appears to be matters not here, just as, albeit to a lesser degree, the revelation of Weazel's cowardice has no impact upon his social standing. Fielding, from the beginning of his career in his poem *The Masquerade*, writes to distinguish between truth and sham, to arrive at convincing representations of crucial (for him) moral terms: charity and chastity in *Joseph Andrews;* prudence in *Tom Jones;* fidelity in *Amelia*.[17] Smollett, instead, suggests that virtue resides outside the language available to him.

While he frequently discovers sham, he neither prevents his characters from, nor punishes them for, participating in it.

Fortune, in Fielding's religious theme, has a role analogous to sham in his social; fortune is the mask, the disguise that prevents Tom Jones from seeing right. Thus, the plot of *Tom Jones* turns upon Jones's recognition in prison that his seemingly horrible fate is not accidental but instead is owing to his failings: "But why do I blame Fortune? I am myself the Cause of all my Misery. All the dreadful Mischiefs that have befallen me are the Consequences only of my Folly and Vice" (916). This admission made, Jones can lay claim to "prudence" and win "Sophia" (wisdom).[18] Smollett favors the words "fortune" and "Providence," but he has his hero repeatedly use them synonymously, thus subverting the distinction which Fielding hopes to reinforce. In Roderick's description of the early stages of the Battle of Cartagena (the events during which Knowles's incompetence, in Smollett's view, cost the British their slight chance for victory), Smollett makes a typical transmutation:

> Providence stood our friend upon this occasion, and put it into the hearts of the Spaniards to abandon the fort. . . . And while our soldiers took possession of the enemy's ramparts, without resistance, *the same good luck* attended a body of sailors, who made themselves masters of fort St. Joseph. (185, my italics)

In a later description of the conduct of the English at the Battle of Dettingen, Random will claim that "Providence or Destiny acted miracles on their behalf" (248) although incompetent leaders again waste the opportunity. Moreover, as Roderick judges his own life at the time of Dettingen, he distances himself from notions of providential order: "I resolved all the crimes I had been guilty of, and found them so few and venial that *I could not comprehend the justice of Providence* which after having exposed me to so much wretchedness and danger, left me prey to famine and lost in a foreign country" (270–71, my italics).

Besides this tendency to declare Providence the "same" as luck, Smollett also subverts the fortune-Providence distinction by making fortune an indifferent rather than an evil force. Throughout *Roderick Random*, gaming is a recurring activity, and cheating (sham) is, for Roderick, an inevitable part of gaming. During his first journey to London, Roderick watches a clergyman strip two farmers of "all their cash in a very short time"; when one of the countrymen suggests that the clergyman may cheat, Roderick, rather than expressing anger or surprise, merely notes: "I did not wonder at all to find a cheat in canonicals, this being an animal frequent in my own country" (39). Later, as part of his courtship of the wealthy Melinda, Roderick plays cards with her and "with great cheerfulness [but to Strap's horror] suffered myself to be cheated" of eighteen guineas (282–83). Significantly enough, Roderick also wins at the gaming tables. Indeed, the 150 guineas he wins in chapter 52 allow him to travel to Bath, where he has a crucial meeting with Narcissa.

Such luck cannot last, and when Roderick, after Narcissa's brother takes her away, tries to win a fortune at the gaming tables, he loses all. Tellingly, he blames "providence" for his losses, credits "fortune" for his brief success:

> Melancholy and despondence took possession of my soul; and repining at the providence which by acting the stepmother towards me, kept me from the fruition of my wishes [Narcissa], I determined . . . to risk all I had at the gaming table. . . .
>
> Actuated by this fatal resolution, I engaged in play, and after some turns of fortune, found myself . . . worth a thousand pounds; but it was not my intention to stop there . . . I continued my career, until I was reduced to five guineas, which I would have hazarded also, had I not been ashamed to fall from a bet of two hundred pounds to such a petty sum. (368–69)

Roderick's "shame," the only control on his gaming besides lack of ready money, is not providential but social. He feels no guilt for his losses, only embarrassment. "Providence" here is not an enabling and beautiful larger order but a blocking force. When Roderick reports his disaster to Banter, the latter has the last word on the episode: "Fortune would probably be one day weary of persecuting me" (371).

At this point in the story, Roderick's course may seem similar to that of Tom Jones. His arrest for debt immediately follows the gambling episode, and the scene of the novel shifts to prison, then to his rescue by his uncle, then to his meeting with his father. However, Roderick never comes to the recognition that Jones makes in his prison cell. Rather, Roderick will persist to the story's end in his commingling of fortune and Providence. When he becomes ill almost immediately upon his father's thanking "Mysterious Providence" and asking him to pray (413–14), Roderick sets a pattern. Almost without exception, it is others who speak of "Providence," not Roderick. He, rather than praising Providence, will continue to report the vicissitudes of fortune—vicissitudes he is protected from only by his father's wealth. The wind that blows him back to England becomes an anamnestic figure for fortune as it affects Roderick. While the wind now brings him "joy," Roderick, as he describes it, emphasizes its indifference. When it "shifts" and forces Bowling to anchor at Spithead, it brings "mortification" to thirty of the crew who "were immediately pressed on board a man of war" (420).

During his reunion with Narcissa, Roderick notes that "fortune hath at length recompensed me for all my sufferings," leaving to her the task of establishing the providential dimension of his story: "[She] congratulated herself and me upon my good fortune, and observed that this great and unexpected stroke of fate seemed to have been brought about by the immediate direction of providence" (425). While in the penultimate chapter Roderick will refer to Narcissa as "this inestimable gift of providence" (429), in the final chapter he will repeat his claim that "Fortune seems determined to make ample amends for her former cruelty." In effect, he reads the events of his life in Banter's terms, not in those of the mature Tom Jones. When he ends his story by claiming, "I shall certainly recover my wife's Fortune," and then describing that fortune as the "crown [of] my felicity" (435), he reveals how far he is from providential notions. Smollett has not unwittingly and ineffectively confused fortune and Providence. Rather, he has subverted the distinction upon which Fielding grounds his hero's salvation, even as he employs diction and plotting that sound familiar, diction and plotting with which readers in both the eighteenth and the twentieth centuries are comfortable.

In Smollett's final novel, *Humphry Clinker*, the anamnesis is kinder and gentler perhaps—Smollett wrote the novel sure that his life was nearing its end. The occasionally milder tone makes the subversiveness of the novel less noticeable and, thus, all the more powerful. The modification of the birth mystery is even more telling than in *Roderick Random*, and the power of the plot to vindicate patriarchal power is correspondingly diminished. Clinker, at his first appearance, has the telltale fair skin of the birth-mystery protagonist, but we see it only because his tattered clothes cause him inadvertently to "moon" the Bramble entourage. As our first sight of his bare skin suggests, Clinker never will become a gentleman. Indeed, at the story's end, although Clinker has found his father and gotten married, he still does not fit any social category. Bramble wonders what occupation he can find for his son and refers to him almost as if he were an animal, "stout and lusty . . . very docile" (329). Smollett also subverts the conservative impact of the birth mystery by having its resolution change not only the son's identity but the father's as well. We discover that Bramble, the novel's staunch social conservative, is a social climber. Matthew Bramble, we learn, along with Clinker, really is Matthew Loyd; the name change was made in order that Bramble could inherit an estate. His status only marginally less equivocal than Clinker's, Bramble does "progress" toward health, both physical and psychic, but the sense of Humphry's journey is unclear, even at his story's end.

As *Roderick Random* does, so *Humphry Clinker* treats anamnestically the great themes of status inconsistency and providential order. Initially, Bramble's social commentary seems unequivocal. All that is wrong in England—at least in Bath and London—is owing to the pernicious effects of leveling:

> The general tide of luxury . . . hath overspread the nation, and swept away all, even the very dregs of the people. Every upstart of fortune, harnessed in the trappings of the mode, presents himself at Bath . . . as in the very focus of observation . . . usurers, brokers, and jobbers of every kind; men of low birth and no breeding, have found themselves suddenly translated into a state of affluence, unknown to former ages; and no wonder that their brains should be intoxicated with pride, vanity, and presumption. (36)

Bramble, who finds many activities "despicable," reserves the category of most despicable for any "man of birth, education, and fortune, [who will] put himself on a level with the dregs of the people, mingle with low mechanics" (102). Even before the revelation that Bramble is Loyd, Smollett carefully subverts his elitism. In the encounter with Lord Oxmington, for one example, Bramble responds angrily to the superior airs of the peer, who invites him to dinner but then controls how much he eats and drinks. Bramble sends a challenge to Oxmington, who responds in the vein of Weazel and Random: "What! a commoner to send a challenge to a peer of the realm!—Privilege! privilege!—Here's . . . a challenge from the Welshman that dined at my table—An impudent fellow!—My wine is not yet out of his head"(283). When Bramble finally wins an apology from Oxmington, his triumph, while perhaps gratifying to him, undercuts his prior assertions concerning the importance of rank. Significantly enough, the Oxmington episode is reported in a wry letter written by Jery Melford; Bramble will not, perhaps cannot, report upon this instance of status inconsistency.

Similarly, the conflicts created by Clinker's Methodism—conflicts social as well as religious—never are resolved. Bramble orders Clinker to stop preaching, and Clinker does. But when Clinker claims that "the new light of God's grace [may] shine upon the poor and the ignorant in their humility, as well as upon the wealthy, and the philosopher in all his pride of human learning," Bramble overcomes him only by narrow-mindedly asserting his financial privilege. Offended that his sister has been listening to his servant sermonize, Bramble ends the brief debate by claiming, "I will have no light in my family but what pays the king's taxes" (138). Offended by "the presumption of his lacquey" (137), Bramble can require his servant to "submit" (139), but he cannot require him to change his beliefs. Humphry can "recall" those parts of Christianity that Bramble countenances but must leave unspoken their subversive import, particularly their elevation of "the poor and the ignorant." Clinker does not break his emotional ties to Whitfield, who, of course, is a persistent target of Fielding's in both *Joseph Andrews* and *Tom Jones*, in the latter suffering the ultimate defamation of becoming part of Blifil's final scheme. For all the happy good will at the end of the story, the feeling lingers that Humphry won his argument with Bramble. Tabby, as Bramble himself notes, attends "Wesley's meeting in Newcastle" (207) and another in Glasgow (238). Jery lists "the methodist doctrines of the new birth, the new light, the efficacy of grace, the insufficiency of works, and the operations of the spirit" (225), showing familiarity with them but not contempt.

The extent of Smollett's variation of Fielding becomes powerfully clear when we note from whom we hear claims that "Providence" is at work in the concluding events of the story: the romantic Lydia (330, 334) and the foolish and weak Baynard (340). Bramble and Clinker cannot use the word because their understandings of it differ so radically. Bramble's is the Providence of divine order mimetically realized within social order; Clinker's is the Providence of mysterious and amazing grace realized outside of any social, theological, or philosophical conventions. Proceeding anamnestically, Smollett names the "expedition" after a character who writes none of the letters that constitute it; he titles his book after a character who knows the truth but cannot speak it.

Even the oldest of literary devices—the birth mystery—here cannot rescue either social or religious order, cannot give Clinker a place. We last hear of him as a confusing anomaly, "Mr. Clinker Loyd" (345), who has discovered his father but cannot take his father's name. His father is ready to offer him "indulgence" but cannot find him work.

I earlier criticized Jerry Beasley's reading of the conclusion of *Roderick Random*, but he first observed an important truth about Roderick's return to England after the Battle of Cartagena and the fight with Crampley: "Interestingly enough it is at this moment, when he is reduced to nakedness, that Mrs. Sagely comes to his relief, he meets Narcissa, and the real course leading to his final happiness is actually begun—*at almost the exact midpoint of the novel* (my italics).[19] The detail noted by Beasley is interesting not as part of a move toward a Fieldingesque "final happiness." We have seen that such is not the case in *Roderick Random*. But while Smollett will not offer a mimetic rendering of the journey motif (what virtue or faith can we claim that Roderick's experiences bring him?), he still places events with great calculation. When Tom Jones stands with the Man of the Hill atop Mazard Hill, he is both midway through his journey and placed such that "the emblematic projection of Fielding's theme," the definition of "prudence" is there for him to see, if only he will.[20] Midway through his story, Roderick not only meets Narcissa but also becomes John Brown; the confusions about status and identity at Mrs. Sagely's set Smollett's anamnestic agenda as surely as the view atop Mazard Hill (or lack thereof in Jones's case) sets Fielding's mimetic.

Roderick Random and *Humphry Clinker* have received more attention from critics, in the eighteenth century as well as the twentieth, than any of the other works in Smollett's large and diverse canon. Anamnesis, however, is not unique to them. Indeed, one of the finest examples of this tendency comes in Smollett's lesser known *The Life and Adventures of Sir Launcelot Greaves* (1762), an attempt to adapt *Don Quixote* to eighteenth-century England. Fielding uses his night scene "in Imitation of the *Manner* of Cervantes" (Fielding 1967, 2) to confer a "comic blessing" upon *Joseph Andrews*. Smollett reads Cervantes as carefully as Fielding does, perhaps, his translation of the *Quixote* suggests, even more carefully. But as his Milton is different from Fielding's, so is his Quixote. Thus, while Greaves is an eighteenth-century imitator of Quixote, he is an imitator who almost immediately proclaims his distance from the original. Greaves is Quixote without delusion:

> I am neither an affected imitator of Don Quixote, nor, as I trust in
> heaven, visited by the spirit of lunacy so admirably displayed in the
> fictitious character exhibited by the inimitable Cervantes. I have not
> yet encountered a windmill for a giant; nor mistaken this public house
> for a magnificent castle . . . I see and distinguish objects as they are
> discerned and described by other men. (50)

Greaves shares with his model only an old set of armor and a commitment to do battle against the "foes of virtue."

As Smollett here bends the literary precedent that Cervantes establishes, so he spurns acts of social accommodation. Estates will be inherited in this novel (one of them passing through the beautiful heroine Aurelia Darnel), but Smollett jokes vulgarly about the "entail" in his opening chapter (42–45) and suggests throughout that the "law" operates at the mercy of caprice and whim. Anamnesis continues in the story's "Chapter the Last" with the revelation that a young tavern maid, "Dorothy Cowslip, is in fact Dorothy Greaves, daughter of Jonathan Greaves." This discovery has no effect upon the outcome of Sir Launcelot's story; the birth mystery loses the central role that it plays in Fielding, here involving only minor characters. The misnaming is attributed to the death of Greaves's uncle "before he [Launcelot] came of age" and to some mislaid "memorandums" (253). Greaves welcomes Dolly to his family, but all this happens only after his marriage to Aurelia and their reclamation of their estates.

This final chapter describes Greaves celebrating the "birth of a son, destined to be the heir and representative of two worthy families." It also describes him bidding good-bye to an unscrupulous Hobbesian political writer named Ferret, who has played a small but important role in the story's resolution,[21] but whose "misanthropy" will not allow him to share in the "easy circumstances," the "happiness" that Greaves's marriage has brought to the countryside: "He could not bear to see his fellow creatures happy around him; and signified his disgust to Sir Launcelot, declaring his intention of returning to the metropolis, where he knew there would always be food sufficient for the ravenous appetite of his spleen" (254).

In Smollett's anamnestic version of the "happy ending," Ferret's malevolence is irremediable, unconquerable by Greaves's goodness. Even as Smollett's ending "looks like" a Fielding ending, Smollett empties the birth mystery of its power to fix status. *Sir Launcelot Greaves*, one of his lesser novels, reveals his persistent urge to explode Fielding's artful elevation of the virtuous poor. Only Greaves's potency—only his producing a son—assures that his and Aurelia's estates will not become prey to the villainous schemes, to the bad laws that have threatened them. Should demographic crisis recur, the ravenous Ferret abides, ready to seek his malevolent advantage. If the last chapters of *Joseph Andrews* and *Tom Jones* offer comic versions of the reward that all virtuous men and women will receive from God, Smollett suggests instead that the happiness of Greaves and Aurelia, however richly deserved, neither is a product nor a reflection of a larger order. Rather, like Roderick Random's homecoming, Greaves's happiness arrives only because good fortune has followed bad, only because the "ball" for once has bounced right.

Aileen Douglas contrasts *Sir Launcelot Greaves* to Smollett's *Ferdinand Count Fathom*, arguing that *Greaves* is "insistently public and communal," that Sir Launcelot reestablishes the power and the preeminence of the aristocratic body that Fathom, spectral and private, brings into question (116). She perhaps overlooks the thinness of the thread upon which the "happy ending" for Launcelot and Aurelia hangs. In *Greaves*, as in the "major" novels, Smollett's anamnesis is as deft as Fielding's mimesis. He takes in with a sharp and baleful glance the opportunities for venality, cruelty, and deception in the inheritance of estates—opportunities created by failures of patrilinear succession. Fielding crafts his novels as secular imitations of God's Providence. Smollett takes the Palladian superstructure that Frederick Hilles attributes to Fielding—the birth mystery, the "journey motif," the Cervantick paradigm—and sets a Weazel, then a Ferret loose to burrow underneath it.[22] He weakens the foundation of the noble house by anamnestically suggesting that what some see as "Providence" may be nothing more than "Fortune," that the discovery of paternity may not right the random injustices to which property and succession are liable in eighteenth-century England.

6

Clarissa's Pregnancy
and the Fate of Patriarchal Power

> As to the question required of me to answer, and which is allowed to
> be too shocking either for a mother to put to a daughter, or a sister to
> a sister; and which, however, *you* say I must answer—Oh sir!—and
> must I answer?—This then be my answer: "A little time, a much less
> time than is imagined, will afford a more satisfactory answer to my
> whole family, and even to my brother and sister, than I can give in
> words."
>
> —Samuel Richardson, *Clarissa or The History of a Young Lady*[1]

Thus Clarissa Harlowe responds, in a letter to her uncle Anthony,
to this question put to her by her uncle John: "Your mother can't
ask, and your sister knows not in modesty how to ask; and so I
must ask you, if you have any reason to think yourself with child
by this villain? You must answer this, and answer it truly, before
anything can be resolved upon for you" (1192). Clarissa responds
two months to the day (June 13 to August 13) after her rape by
Robert Lovelace—that is, if we can conclude that Lovelace did,
indeed, rape Clarissa. In a 1977 essay, Judith Wilt proposed that
Lovelace is impotent and that any sexual abuse Clarissa suffers is
at the hands of Mrs. Sinclair and the "women below." Terry Castle
concedes to Wilt "that nothing *in* the text definitively refutes" her
interpretation but concludes, "I read Clarissa with the belief that a
heterosexual rape does take place, with Lovelace as the rapist, yet
I am also aware that, technically speaking, this is as much a
construction as is Wilt's."[2]

As Castle locates an "ultimate unverifiabilty" in the case of
Clarissa's rape, I find a similar "indeterminacy" in the case of

Clarissa's pregnancy. Clarissa's response to her uncle is frustrat-ingly evasive. She writes less than a month before her death on September 7. The twenty-five-day interval truly is "a little time," "much less time" than her family and friends imagine is left to her. But how does Clarissa answer her uncle's question by dying, particularly since she demands in her will that "my body . . . not on any account . . . be opened" and that it "be put into my coffin as soon as possible"? What will "time" tell us about Clarissa's condition when she allows only her family a "last . . . look" at her and demands that "I may not unnecessarily be exposed to the view of anybody" (1413)? While we occasionally read newspaper stories about women who go to hospitals fearing an ulcer or appendicitis only to give birth to a child, in most cases pregnancy is relatively easy to detect or suspect two or three months after conception. But Clarissa will not offer a simple "yes" or "no."

I want to consider the implications of "yes," not because of any conclusive evidence in the text but because a pregnant Clarissa raises basic questions about male potency and patrilinear succes-sion. While Clarissa can shape her end such that she, ever a paragon of virtue, avoids the sin of self-destruction, a pregnant Clarissa, at least by the standards of eighteenth-century Anglican-ism, verges on the crime of abortion.[3] If we ask why Richardson, however covertly, risks this association, we can appreciate the opportunities that his hints at pregnancy create. As Lovelace and the Harlowes respond to the possibility, they chart the decline of patriarchs, particularly of Lord M. and James Harlowe Sr. In describing these weak men, Richardson writes with remarkable prescience, adumbrating commentary upon "patriarchy" by writ-ers as influential as Susan M. Gilbert, Sandra Gubar, Terry Castle, and Nancy Armstrong.[4]

Castle's widely cited reading of Clarissa as overborn by "patriarchal power" in her "fight" with Lovelace[5] is challenged by Clarissa's "pregnancy"—at least insofar as the pregnancy empha-sizes what Armstrong refers to as a "historical condition": in this case, male impotence in the period 1650–1740. And insofar as his response to Clarissa's pregnancy reveals Lovelace to be not the agent of patriarchy but rather a Derridian angel who would mock it, the pregnancy again works against Castle's thesis. But Claris-sa's response to her victimization by Lovelace is to rebuild her "father's house," to seek solace in the "perfectly paternal." And this response perhaps reveals Richardson to understand, well in advance of Jacques Lacan's *école freudienne*, that men and women

both are marked by patriarchy apart from the historical condition
of specific patriarchs. In her silence about her condition, Clarissa
simultaneously tempts us to and warns us against the conflation
of "patriarchal power" with individual men, the conflation of, in
Lacan's vocabulary, the phallus and the penis.[6]

By thinking about Clarissa's "pregnancy," we can reconfigure a
major difficulty with which *Clarissa* confronts its interpreters: that
is, the tendency of the novel, in its prolixity, to undercut the major
antitheses by which it seemingly asks readers to understand it.
Terry Eagleton partially defines this tendency when he notes,

> The paradox of *Clarissa* is that Clarissa's writing is "masculine"
> whereas Lovelace's is "feminine". It has been claimed that men and
> women under patriarchy relate differently to the act of writing. Men,
> more deeply marked by the "transcendental signifier" of the phallus,
> will tend to view signs as stable and whole, ideal entities external to
> the body; women will tend to live a more inward, bodily relationship
> to script. Whatever the dangers of such stereotyping notions, nothing
> could be more appropriate to *Clarissa*. Clarissa herself exerts the fullest
> possible control over her meanings. . . . Lovelace's writing is mercu-
> rial, diffuse, exuberant. Clarissa's letters are signs of a unified self. . . .
> Behind them stands a transcendental subject. . . . Lovelace, by contrast,
> lives on the interior of his prose, generating a provisional identity
> from the folds of his text, luxuriating in multiple modes of being.[7]

Eagleton here proceeds with somewhat dizzying but instructive
doubleness: *Clarissa* renders paradoxical the dichotomy between
"male" and "female" writing, but that dichotomy remains "appropriate" to the opposition between Clarissa and Lovelace. If we
only turn upside down the male/female categories (which Eagleton derives from Luce Irigaray and Michele Montrelay), *Clarissa*
makes sense. Eagleton assumes that Clarissa and Lovelace, the
Harlowes, Belford, and Anna Howe—all are "men and women
under patriarchy" (my italics). For Irigaray and Eagleton, the
patriarch is ever and always a strong force for repression. But
Richardson understands and represents patriarchy in ways that
Irigaray cannot see. Confusions about "writing," "class," and
"gender" in Clarissa ultimately derive from the impairment rather
than the exercise of patriarchal authority, an impairment that
families in England had struggled with at least from the mid-
seventeenth century onward. From the failings of fallible and
weak patriarchs Richardson builds his story.

Clarissa and Lovelace live through and are affected by the

"demographic slump" that the Stones have described. As the inheritances that await James Harlowe Jr. and Robert Lovelace reveal, the demographic crisis of 1650–1740 did complicate "the descent of property and seats from generation to generation" (Stones, 101). Lord M., who would be a "father" (*Clarissa*, 664) to Lovelace but is not, can exert no influence upon his nephew's choice of a bride and is reduced to merely hoping that Lovelace will marry. James Harlowe Jr., while his father and uncles are alive, controls them (at least in Clarissa's account) and will make a marriage where he sees the family's advantage to lie. Failures "in the male line" privilege Lovelace and James Jr. because they force families—Lovelace's aunts Betty and Sarah, Lord M. himself, and James Jr.'s godmother—to develop "strategies of indirect inheritance . . . to save the principle of family continuity" (Stones, 104).

In the course of *Clarissa*, Lord M. writes one letter to Belford, two to Lovelace, and initials a letter of apology/explanation sent by the ladies Sadleir and Lawrance to Anna Howe—apology for the arrest of Clarissa. M. also participates in the "trial" of Lovelace (1029–30) and in the confrontation between Lovelace and Colonel Morden (1280–87), although, in both cases, Lovelace recounts and controls the events. In his initial letter, the letter to Belford, M. asks Belford "to interfere in the affair depending between him [Lovelace] and the most accomplished of women [Clarissa]" because he realizes that, for all his status and wealth, he cannot influence Lovelace: "I am sure he has no reason to slight me as he does. He may and will be the better for me if he outlives me; though he once told me to my face that I might do as I would with my estate; for that he, for his part, loved his liberty as much as he despised money" (606). Powerless over Lovelace, the one weak threat that M. can muster is to engender a son himself: "You may throw in, too, as his friend, that should he provoke me, it may not be too late for me to marry . . . in spite of this gout, I might have a child or two still." But M. himself counters this possibility with one of his proverbs: *"the children of very young and very old men . . . last not long"* (607).

In his first letter to Lovelace—a letter that mistakenly celebrates his nephew's engagement to Clarissa—M. pleads, "Do not despise me for my proverbs" (664), indicates that he no longer can walk, "I am still very bad with my gout; but will come in a litter, as soon as the day is fixed," describes himself as "but a slow writer" (665), and, after charting Lovelace's domestic and political future, concludes, "I could say a great deal more, and all equally to the purpose. But really I am tired" (667). James Harlowe Sr.'s physical impairment, while not as extreme as M.'s, is of the same order; Clarissa reports on one of their confrontations, "he supported himself because of his gout on the back of a chair" (64). James Sr., after all, has produced a son and has brought his family to the verge of a title, but, as Clarissa notes, "my father was soured by the cruel distemper [gout] . . . which seized him all at once in the very prime of life, in so violent a manner as to take from the most active of minds as his was all power of activity, and that, in all appearance, for life. It imprisoned . . . his lively spirits in himself" (55). During the early stages of the Solmes controversy, James Sr. musters considerable "vehemence" and a "terrible voice" (60), but he soon is replaced by his son and becomes, like Lord M., a "tired" figure who has lost "power of activity."

In their respective impairments, James Harlowe Sr. and Lord M. illustrate the powerful effects of the "demographic slump." Both men are tormented by the demands of patrilinear succession: James Sr. must give way to James Jr.; M. must submit to Lovelace's "slights." Perhaps even more notable is that, with the admittedly important exception of six months in James Harlowe Sr.'s life, both of these patriarchs are on, to use Castle's term, Clarissa's "side." M.'s letters are unwavering in their praise of Clarissa's "extraordinary share of wisdom and goodness" (606). He is ready to settle upon her "a thousand pounds a year" and warns Lovelace that "if you do not make the best of husbands to so good a young lady . . . I will renounce you; and settle all I can upon her and hers by you, and leave you out of the question" (605). Until misled by "the instigations" (112, 125, and 137) of James Jr., James Sr., at least in Clarissa's view, has treated her with consummate goodness.

The character in Clarissa who most suggests a viable and powerful father figure is Clarissa's grandfather Harlowe, who points proudly to "my three sons" and to their being "uncommonly prosperous, and . . . very rich" (53). He, of course, favors Clarissa in ways both manifest and, at least for James Jr. and Bella, problematic. In his will, Clarissa's grandfather makes a bequest to Clarissa that he realizes is "not strictly conformable to law, or the forms thereof" (53–54).[8] He, unsuccessfully as events prove, attempts to enforce the bequest through a patriarchal "commandment" to his sons and his other grandchildren. As the conflict over Solmes intensifies, the family regularly will remind

Clarissa that they can overturn the provisions of the will (107), her uncle Anthony at one point telling her the family did not immediately challenge it only "because it was our father's doing" (157). The treatment Clarissa receives from her grandfather and would receive from Lord M. shows clearly that she is not the victim of "patriarchal power." Rather, she is the victim of the fictive versions of kinship that her brother and then Robert Lovelace would impose upon her—those fictive versions of kinship operating only because the patriarch is either dead (her grandfather), severely impaired (Lord M.), or at risk (her father, who must submit to James Jr.'s various depredations because on him "the name depends" (157).

In one of her last conversations with Belford, Clarissa claims, "I have my grandfather's will almost by heart" (1329), and it is fitting that she does, for that will is the great single source of all action and conflict in *Clarissa*—a far more significant event than the duel between James Jr. and Lovelace. When she receives special attention and reward from her grandfather, Clarissa becomes a threat to James Jr.'s plan to raise the status of the family by placing all its property in his hands: "My brother . . . as the only son, thought . . . that all the real estates in the family, to wit, my grandfather's, father's, and two uncles', and the remainder of their respective personal estates, together with what he had an expectancy of from his godmother, would make such a noble fortune and give him such an interest as might entitle him to hope for a peerage" (77). James bases his insatiable ambition not upon "patriarchal power" but upon its reproductive failures. He will become an earl not through rewards for heroic military service (his swordsmanship is suspect anyway) but rather through shrewdly piecing together vacant estates.

James Jr.'s opportunities greatly resemble Lovelace's, but while the latter would distance himself from "extinct" titles,[9] the former eagerly seeks them. Clarissa quotes her uncle Anthony's description of Lovelace's possible inheritances in the same letter in which she describes James Jr.'s ambition leading to an inversion of roles in the Harlowe household; James Jr. she complains, has reduced his uncles to "*his stewards*" and his sister to his "slave" (95). In an earlier letter, she casts herself in the role of defender of the status quo and accuses her brother of overturning the relationship between "superior" and "inferior" in her family (48). When Lovelace expresses interest in Clarissa, particularly with the precedent of the grandfather's will in place, the uncles contemplate building the family name through Clarissa and Lovelace, rather than through James Jr., who panics: "'See, sister Bella,' said he, in an indecent passion before my uncles. . . . 'See how it is!—You and I ought to look about us!—This little siren is in a fair way to *out-uncle* as well as *out-grandfather* us both'" (80).

Threatened by the power Clarissa can wield over the Harlowe family patriarchs, James Jr. (at least in Clarissa's take upon events) hits upon the strategy of making marriage to Solmes a test of his father's power and of isolating Clarissa from her parents. He also makes Lovelace's "morals" an issue—an issue, Clarissa never tires of reminding her family, that did not surface when Lovelace courted Bella. While James Jr. and Lovelace do share a "college-begun antipathy" (77), their mutual dislike is more the repulsion between similars than the misunderstanding of opposites; differences in their "class" are difficult to define, particularly when we note that Lord M. comes to Harlowe Place to propose "in his nephew's name" a marriage to Clarissa, claiming that "it was the ambition of all his family to be related" to the Harlowes (46). Christopher Hill reads Clarissa as a rebel who falls victim to "the feudal-patriarchal family,"[10] but this hardly conforms to her sense of her situation. In a typical response to one of James Jr.'s commands that she meet with Solmes, she asserts, "I will receive, as becomes me, any of my papa's commands; yet as this significa-tion is made me by a brother . . . I think myself entitled to conclude that such a letter as you have sent me is all your own—And of course to declare, that while I so think it, I will not willingly, nor even without violence, go to any place avowedly to receive Mr. Solmes's visits" (219). Clarissa wants to be commanded by the patriarch, not by some fictive version of him, for she always has received both praise and power from him.[11] In its complex, even prolix unfolding, her sentence reflects the complicated rhetorical task she sets herself (and the threat she holds for James Jr.). She wants to separate her brother from her father and thus to reveal how fictive are the son's claims to authority.

Once we understand that Clarissa is victimized by the absence rather than the presence of the patriarch, we also can outline the significance of her possible pregnancy. Here Castle's reading, despite its contestable premise about "patriarchal power," is central. Writing in the wake of various postmodern commentaries (most notably Jacques Derrida's) upon "the sign," Castle takes Clarissa as an example of, also a victim of, the "dissolution of natural signification" (Castle 1982, 59). Castle sees Clarissa as being forced to learn the great lesson of postmodernism: all signs are arbitrarily constructed; there is no "natural" correlation between words and feelings, between words and character ("This signification is made me by a brother"). In a passage that Castle does not cite but that speaks directly to her thesis, Clarissa claims, "What are *words* but the *body* and *dress* of *thought*? And is not the mind indicated by its outward dress?" (543). Clarissa here not only reveals her semiological naiveté, she also assures her destruction by Lovelace, for whom all life is a theater in which he skillfully directs actors to use words and gestures such that they can pretend to be what they are not. In one of his earliest substitutions, Lovelace has an acquaintance named Newcomb pretend to be Captain Mennell, an agent who purportedly will help Clarissa find suitable lodging. The ruse having worked, Lovelace crows to Belford:

> And have I changed his name by virtue of my own single authority. Knowest thou not that I am a great *name-father?* Preferments I bestow both military and civil. I give estates and I take them away at my pleasure. *Quality too I create.* ... What a poor thing is a monarch to me! (569, my italics)

Lovelace celebrates a version of paternity different from the patriarchal. Rather than place identity and inheritance within the seemingly solid constraints of biology and land, he makes fatherhood a matter of "naming," of words detached from any corporeal reality. He invents social status, "Quality" rather than earning or inheriting it; he confers "authority" upon himself but only through the power of his "contrivances."

In his last and greatest deception—the deception that lures Clarissa back to London and to her rape—Lovelace fictionalizes kinship, substituting prostitutes for his cousin and his aunt, noting of the prostitutes that "both are accustomed to ape quality. ... And in their own conceit, when assuming top parts, [become] the very quality they ape" (875). As Lovelace describes himself directing the prostitutes in their parts, he is at his most excited, his happiest in the entire narrative:

> Your common assumed dignity won't do for me now. Airs of superiority, as if born to rank—but no overdo! A little *graver,* Lady Betty. More significance, less bridling, in your dignity.

That's the air! Charmingly hit—Again—You have it.

Devil take you!—Less arrogance. You are got into airs of *young quality*. Be less sensible of your new condition. . . .

Study that air in the pier glass. (876)

As his description continues, Lovelace teaches his prostitutes how to curtsy and how to "guard" their "eyes." Having already taken care of the details of their accoutrements and dress (he invents a story to account for their not riding in a carriage with Lady Betty's coat of arms), Lovelace never pauses to ask: What is this "quality" that it can be "aped"? Enjoying the power that his ability to create images gives him, Lovelace unwittingly dooms any claims to status he might wish to make, not recognizing his potential victimization by the pun implicit in his "pier glass," the mirror that can help prostitutes to act like ladies because in its reflections, disembodied and superficial, all women (and all men) can be "peers."

Clarissa's victimization by Lovelace is of the same order as her victimization by her brother. She, who wants only to address directly her father and her uncles, finds herself cut off from them. To the physical barriers built by James Jr., Lovelace adds the barrier of the "name-father," the fictive version of the father. His most successful and long-enduring "contrivance," the presentation of the smuggler Patrick McDonald as Captain Tomlinson, works so powerfully upon Clarissa because Tomlinson offers Clarissa her most important end: reunification first with her uncle (whose neighbor Tomlinson claims to be), then with her father. If we preface it with a reminder that Clarissa is victimized not by the father but by the "name-father," Castle's summary of the course of that victimization achieves considerable power and admirable conciseness:

Her sense of "Nature" is repeatedly disrupted, through a long process of humiliation, during which her ability to read what is going on around her is thwarted and parodied by others. Clarissa is tricked by actual letters . . . which turn out to be forgeries . . . but she is also tricked by the world of signs itself, which is equally denatured and open to manipulation by the unscrupulous.

The violation she experiences is simultaneously a violation of her body and a violation of her sense of the meaningful. . . . A gap is opened up in her vision of the world: sign and "Nature" split apart. (Castle 1982, 58–59)

Lovelace, who creates "Quality," does denature the most basic family identities. As Clarissa tries to "read" his behavior in terms of her assumptions about family, "Lady Bab Wallis" and "Little Johanetta Golding," with Lovelace directing the "significance" of their gestures, lure her back to Mrs. Sinclair's and to her rape. From the opening of their correspondence, Clarissa and Anna assume that in details there is truth. Lovelace, classically educated and used to his own way, might appear to be their opposite, might appear to be above small details. In fact, he, like Clarissa, cares intensely about particulars, not because they certify his sincerity but because they perfect his deceptions.[12]

An obvious but important question follows once Castle notes the violation of Clarissa's "sense of the meaningful": Why, in the first place, should Clarissa believe that "sign and 'Nature'" are as one? The answer lies in her privileged upbringing.[13] Clarissa has grown up in an extended family, one in which her special virtue has been acknowledged by her uncles (45) and her grandfather (53). Her male relatives consider and "call" her their "own" child. Clarissa can believe that, at least prior to her grandfather's bequest, "everyone loved me" (78) because her own version of virtuous behavior conformed so totally with the version of her relatives. Even in the midst of an argument about Solmes, Clarissa does not dispute her mother's claim that "no child was ever more favoured" (96), but the greatest favor Clarissa received—beyond more household duties and her "Dairy House"—was the unanimity with which the family defined her role and understood her achievements. In his will, her grandfather summarizes the family's pre-Solmes view of her: "From infancy a matchless creature in her duty to me and admired by all . . . as a very extraordinary child. . . . [She has been] the delight of my old age; and I verily think has contributed by her amiable duty and kind and tender regards to prolong my life" (53).

Clarissa's "amiable duty" not only has won her special praise, it also has helped to keep the patriarch alive. In the early stages of the Solmes crisis, Clarissa's mother reports that her father "had pleaded that his frequent gouty paroxysms (every fit more threatening than the former) gave him no extraordinary prospects . . . of long days: that he hoped, that I, who had . . . contributed to the lengthening of his father's life, would not, by my disobedience, shorten his." The patriarch pleads to Clarissa, "Keep me alive," and she gladly would. Her mother has saved this argument, hoping it will end the division in her family, and it almost does: "This was a most affecting plea . . . I wept in silence upon it; I could not speak to it" (109). Only the perfect ugliness of Solmes stands between Clarissa's doing for her father what she did for her grandfather. But Solmes's ugliness is not merely a matter of his physical characteristics. It is largely constituted by Clarissa's contempt for the role that James Jr. has found for him.

By making Solmes central to "a plan that," Clarissa's mother reports, "captivates us all" (101), James Jr. has split the meaning of "duty" in the Harlowe family and made it difficult for Clarissa to be what, all agree, she "hitherto" has been: "such a dutiful young creature" (107). In Clarissa's view, "the world is one great family; originally it was so; what then is this narrow selfishness that reigns in us, but relationship remembered against relationship forgot?" (62). She seeks continually to remind her parents, her uncles, even her siblings of "relationship," of who she is. She accounts for her fall from grace—from the life in which her version of "duty" and that of her family's corresponded exactly— by blaming James Jr. and Bella: "How happy might I have been with any other brother in the world but Mr. James Harlowe; and any other sister but *his* sister" (65–66). James and Bella set up the Solmes proposal such that "between them the family unity was broken" (80).

Clarissa cannot do for her father what she did for her grandfather because James Jr. has placed Solmes, "the upstart man" (81), between them. Clarissa is praised by her mother as "a dutiful, a prudent, and a wise child," is admitted by her mother to be "best beloved of my heart . . . a face ever so amiable to me" (89). However, in the situation that James Jr. and Bella have created, Clarissa cannot defend herself through her emotional ties to her parents. For in this situation, the power of the patriarch has been replaced, even for the much-favored Clarissa, with calculations of family "interest" (51). Clarissa's faith that "duty" is single and uniform and that various household tasks provide "signification" of it—this faith is the first casualty in her brother's campaign to save his inheritances. Clarissa, like characters in *bildungsromane* from David Copperfield to Stephen Dedalus, is asked to learn, to accept that words hold more than one meaning.

What makes Clarissa Harlowe such a remarkable, fearsome, and, finally, proleptic figure is that she refuses to enter the *bildung*.

Barely two days before she flees with Lovelace, Clarissa receives a letter in which Anna Howe assumes the event and urges her friend to recognize that "punctilio is out of doors the moment you are out of *your father's house*" (355, my italics). The sentence stays with Clarissa; she repeats it mere hours before the event, sees its implications as ominous and as good reason not to take "the rash step" (365).[14] Having spirited Clarissa away from "her father's house," Lovelace wants to read the event as Anna does: "she has crossed the Rubicon" (387). On the basis of that analogy, he then boasts to Belford: "Is she not IN MY POWER?" (401).

She's not, however. As Lovelace much later and ruefully will note, "Never knew I what fear of man was—nor fear of woman neither, till I became acquainted with Miss Clarissa Harlowe; nay, what is most surprising, till I came to have her in my power" (959). Clarissa can "surprise" Lovelace because although he tricks her into fleeing her "father's house," she never accepts that "punctilio is out of doors," never cedes her loyalty to the patriarch, whom, in her view, she neither willingly nor consciously has defied. Lovelace's analogy between Clarissa and Julius Caesar—a historical figure to whom he earlier and elaborately compares himself (74)—adumbrates a crucial and only on its surface paradoxical truth about Clarissa's departure: her flight from Harlowe Place, rather than subverting patriarchy, reflects her continuing loyalty to it as a basis for political and social authority. She is rightly, if fatally for Lovelace, compared to the greatest Roman general. She has left home, but her sense of civic virtue, of "duty" and "punctilio," will not waver. In her persistent loyalty to her father and in her subsequent construction of a patriarch for herself, she destroys the version of "POWER" from which Lovelace, the "great name-father," would operate.

In a letter shortly after Clarissa's flight, Bella writes that her father has "imprecated . . . a fearful curse upon you: . . . that you may meet your punishment both *here* and *hereafter*, by means of the very wretch in whom you have chosen to place your wicked confidence" (509). While we might read this curse as the patriarch's last attempt both to suppress the female voice and to coerce the female will, by accepting the curse and devoting the rest of her brief life to winning its remission, Clarissa effectively places herself "above" (646) Lovelace's various "contrivances." Shortly after he gains his "POWER" over Clarissa, Lovelace writes, "Was there ever known to be a daughter who had higher notions of the filial duty, of the parental authority?" (427). He errs only in his verb tense, for, as her response to the curse reveals, Clarissa's high "notions of filial duty" are not altered by her departure. Clarissa will not rush to marry Lovelace, despite the repeated and forceful urgings of Anna, because "I wanted somebody to act for me" (423). Contra Anna's admonition, she increases her "punctilio" because "I have no guardian now; no father, no mother!" (462). By making the lifting of her father's curse her only goal, Clarissa effectively gives her otherwise absent parents a central role in her relationship with Lovelace: "Oh Mr. Lovelace, how happy shall I be, when my heart is lightened from the all-sinking weight of a father's curse" (695).

Although vulnerable to Lovelace in almost any way he might envision, Clarissa defeats his "POWER" in a basic way: she forces him to make his various fictions celebrate the paterfamilias that he otherwise would "slight." Lovelace continues to "create" quality, but for his fictions to work upon Clarissa, they must appeal to her need for reconciliation with her family. The Tomlinson deception—Lovelace's most enduringly successful—is most telling in this regard. Lovelace knows Clarissa (who, in effect, is his audience) well, but he is largely blind to the implications of what he knows. Thus he, who frequently speaks of his hatred for the Harlowes (634) and boasts of making "the whole stupid family . . . do my business for me" (387), invents the Tomlinson character to prey upon Clarissa's desire to be directed once again by "patriarchal power." The deception inscribes the figure of the father, the very "authority" that Lovelace would "slight."

Tomlinson quickly wins the suspicious Clarissa's trust by emphasizing his own paternal role: "Mr. Harlowe [Clarissa's uncle John] sought me to undertake this office [of ascertaining Clarissa's status with Lovelace]. I have daughters and nieces of my own. I thought it a good office, or I, who have many considerable affairs upon my hands, had not accepted of it" (683). Tomlinson then details those affairs. After his retirement from the military, "All my delight . . . for some years past, has been in cultivating my paternal estate." While Anthony is Tomlinson's given name (763), he always is "Captain" Tomlinson, an ex-soldier, a patriarch only recently domesticated: "I love a brave man . . . as well as ever I did in my life" (684). His roughness caps his appeal for Clarissa. He is a male figure—a father, a master of his paternal estate, a former soldier—with whom she is comfortable. Beyond his personal attributes, he offers himself as a means of "general reconciliation" (686), claiming that the key to this end is marriage (692) between Clarissa and Lovelace. Lovelace's strategy is to assert his "POWER" over Clarissa by making reconciliation depend upon his willingness to marry her. But the deception places him—the would-be rake, the advocate of polygamy and of annually renewable marriages—in the position of needing the marriage to occur by Thursday, June 29, for otherwise "it will be impossible that my contrivances and stratagems should be much longer concealed" (959).

As Clarissa resists the fictional equation that Lovelace constructs for her—marriage to him equals reconciliation to her family—she is positioned (largely by Lovelace but also by her family) such that she must celebrate the patriarch in his absence. Once she escapes Lovelace's physical control—an act that occurs almost simultaneously with her discovering his various impostures—Clarissa does not return to Harlowe Place. Rather, she constructs a foster family at the Smith's and finally, in her "my father's house" letter (1233), invents a new and improved version of the patriarch.[15] As Belford sees, the people who surround Clarissa in her final days replace her family. Clarissa is "highly pleased" with the doctor and the apothecary who minister to her because "their behaviour . . . was perfectly paternal." Belford glosses her comment:

> Paternal, poor lady! Never having been, till very lately, from under her parents' wings, and now abandoned by all her friends, she is for finding out something *paternal* and *maternal* in everyone (the latter qualities in Mrs Lovick and Mrs Smith), to supply to herself the father and mother her dutiful heart pants after. (1082)

This recreation of family becomes particularly intense in the case of her nurse, Mrs. Lovick, who puts "her left arm around her neck," Belford reports, "for it seems the lady had bid her do so, saying she had been a mother to her, and she would delight herself in thinking she was in her mamma's arms" (1351).

Anticipating Burney's Cecelia, Lennox's Arabella, and the "Orphan Heiress of Sir Gregory," Clarissa orphans herself. Belford may describe her as "abandoned," but, in the days before her death, she chooses to stand apart, writing to her childhood nurse, Mrs. Norton, "I wish not now . . . to see even my cousin Morden. . . . Neither do I want to see even *you*, my dear Mrs. Norton. . . . I do not wish to see objects so dear to me [her mother and Miss Howe], which might . . . rival my *supreme* love" (1338).

Having been disappointed by the stupidity and venality of her family, Clarissa constructs a better home for herself; the doctor and apothecary are "perfectly" paternal. In converting James Harlowe Sr.'s "house" to God's "house,"[16] Clarissa only takes the last and boldest step in her reconstruction of the patriarch, inventing a "father" who is above the infirmity that characterizes both her father and Lord M. In one of his last references to the latter, Lovelace describes him as "such an old Trojan . . . just dropping into the grave . . . crying out with pain, and grunting with weakness" (1024). This weakened patriarch Lovelace can "slight" and master; just as he has made Harlowe Sr., however unwittingly, do his bidding. But the "father" that Clarissa invents in her "my father's house" letter, whether the "allegory" be "innocent" or not (1297), defends Clarissa from the physical assault that Lovelace intends.

Is Clarissa pregnant? We cannot be sure. But a pregnancy would threaten her construction of a new family and an improved patriarch. Lovelace exults in the possibility because he believes the child will give life to, even vindicate, his contrivances. He assumes she is pregnant on the basis of two lines in a meditation she has written:[17] "The arrows of the Almighty are within me . . . the thing which I greatly feared is come upon me" (1125). Lovelace translates this to mean "in plain English, that the dear creature is in the way to be a mamma" (1147), and he connects the pregnancy with his return to power: "The dear creature unexpectedly finds herself in the way I have so ardently wished her to be in, and . . . this makes her at last incline to favour me, that she may set the better face upon her gestation when at her father's." "All her grievous distresses," he excitedly supposes, "shall end in a man-child" (1239). Clarissa's mother, while hardly exultant, sees similarly the ramifications of a pregnancy. Fearful that "my once darling daughter unmarried . . . may be with child!" she assesses the situation as one in which, as he always has wanted, choice resides with Lovelace: "That he would now marry her, or that she would refuse him if she believed him in earnest, as she has circumstanced herself is not at all probable" (1156).

We should not misunderstand what Clarissa's accession to the "probable" would mean. As indicated by his performance during his family's "trial for all my sins" (1026) and by his even more triumphant encounter with Anna Howe (1133–37), Lovelace has neither his reputation nor his social standing hanging upon a marriage. Clarissa's unwillingness to prosecute him is another sign that his "contrivances," however ineffective with her, have spared him social obloquy. Fine ladies, Anna notes with disgust (1136), continue to find him fascinating. And Clarissa, although admitting to "resentments, strong resentments," claims they do not govern her refusal—despite the pleas of Anna Howe and Mrs. Norton—to marry Lovelace. Clarissa gives "one reason" beyond her "resentment and disappointment" (1115) for her decision. In what might be one of Richardson's most complicated passages, Clarissa, who speaks immediately and repeatedly after her viola-tion about the "pride" (891, 1375) that brought her to it, here bases her refusal upon "my pride." As she describes it, that pride "although a great deal mortified, is not *sufficiently* mortified if it be necessary for me to submit to make that man my choice, whose actions are, and ought to be my abhorrence" (1116). What can this reference to "pride" mean in light of her later claim (in her farewell letter to her uncles) that "I had a secret pride to be punished for, which I had not fathomed: and it was necessary perhaps that some sore and terrible misfortunes should befall me in order to mortify my pride and my vanity" (1375)? By the logic of this last statement, Clarissa might perfect her "mortification" *by* marrying Lovelace.

The "pride" that Clarissa will not "mortify" is her pride in her ability to distinguish between truth and fiction. By forcing Clarissa to marry him, Lovelace will vindicate his various fictive versions of kinship—his substitution of prostitutes for his aunts, his creation of the paternal Tomlinson. This vindication Clarissa must deny him if she is to maintain her version of "patriarchal power." In her rejection of Lovelace, Clarissa's "pride" becomes the coun-terpart of her semiological naiveté. She will mortify her flesh, but she will not give up her faith that "the mind [is] indicated by its outward dress." As she describes to Anna her reasons for rejecting Lovelace, she links her pride with her contempt for false signification:

> Can I vow duty to one so wicked, and hazard my salvation to so great a profligate, now I *know* him to be so? Do you think your Clarissa Harlowe so lost, so sunk at least, as that she could for the sake of patching up in the world's eye a broken reputation, meanly appear indebted to the generosity or *compassion* perhaps, of a man who has, by means so inhuman, robbed her of it. . . . I should not think my penitence for the rash step I took anything better than a specious delusion, if I had not got above the least wish to have Mr. Lovelace for my husband. (1116)

Because she "now ... *know*[s] him," and in order to prevent herself from becoming part of "a specious delusion," Clarissa rejects marriage to Lovelace. The "world" here is a party to all manner of fakery; it is built upon disguise and allows for the "patching up" of reputations, the dressing "up" of whores. Clarissa will not allow Lovelace's blurring of fact and fiction, his creation of "quality," to triumph over her definitions of truth and virtue. She cannot permit the "name-father" to become a biological father lest she destroy her own essentialist definition of paternity: "Supposing I were to have children by such a husband, must it not ... cut a thoughtful person to the heart, to look round upon her little family and think she had given them a father destined, without a miracle, to perdition; and whose immoralities, propagated among them by his vile example, might too probably bring down a curse upon them ... for who *can touch pitch*, and *not be defiled?* (1116)

Clarissa sees her relationship with Lovelace in "black and white" terms, but the very triteness of the cliché warns us that more is at stake here than basic distinctions between virtuous and vicious behavior. Clarissa sets herself against "appearances" that confuse the truth. She concludes her rejection of marriage by recalling her visits to "my poor neighbours" and the "lessons" and "cautions" she gave their children. She then tries to envision herself, after a marriage to Lovelace, teaching the girls: "How should I be able, unconscious and without pain, to say. . . . Fly the delusions of men, who had been supposed to have run away with one?" (1117). Clarissa does not want her "reputation" back, for its restoration would empower the "patching," the disguise that Lovelace has used against her. Instead, she wants to "fly" from "delusion," to set herself apart from Lovelace's ability to create fictions so detailed that they confuse even a reader as astute as herself. Clarissa will not risk what "I know" with all the "suppositions" that her marriage to Lovelace would create. Her children would live under a "curse"—not the curse of Clarissa's father, the curse that Clarissa makes the center of her dying. Rather, their "curse" will be the "vile example" that lies behind Lovelace's appearance as a father; their "curse" will be the irremediable blurring of truth and "delusion" that led to their "propagation."[18]

Clarissa's "pregnancy," then, points to the most basic dichotomy in Richardson's novel, the dichotomy that he does not subvert or muddle. Lovelace and Clarissa respond in fatally different ways to the demographic crisis they confront. Both of their lives are shaped by the demise of the patriarch. Both of them refer to themselves as "fatherless" (1176, 1188). Both of them believe (although in Lovelace's case, the belief is long in coming) that only a father or a father figure could have saved them: Clarissa claims that "nothing less than the intervention of paternal authority . . . could have saved me from . . . his [Lovelace's] deep machinations" (989); Lovelace, near his life's end, complains that Belford should have warned Clarissa: "I believe I should have killed thee at the time. . . . But I am sure now, that I would have thanked thee for it, and thought thee more a father . . . than my real father" (1441).

Though Lovelace and Clarissa both are orphaned, their responses to the impairment/death of the patriarch divide them in ways that adumbrate recent and major developments in literary theory. To go on "*proleptically,* as a rhetorician might say" (1031), Lovelace is easy to recognize as the "deconstructive angel."[19] Freed by the death of his father and the weakness of Lord M. from the burdens of "phallogocentrism," he is the master of "differance." Playing with "signification," he turns prostitutes into great ladies, smugglers into good family men, Anna Howe's writing into his own. He celebrates his independence by declaring himself the "great name-father." Of course, Adam was a great "name-father" too, but the differences between his naming in Genesis I: 27 and Lovelace's throughout *Clarissa* are definitive. As Robert South pointed out in a sermon to the "Lord Mayor and Aldermen of the City of London" on 9 November 1662—a sermon celebrating the Restoration of Charles II—the first patriarch named the things in his world from "notions, not descending from us, but born with us." It was Adam's great "happiness in the state of innocence," South continues, to write "the nature of things upon their names; he could view essences in themselves."[20] For Adam, as South describes him, "words" truly are "the body and dress of thought." They directly express "nature" and thus require no comment. In his naming, Lovelace does not discover "Quality" but rather "creates" it; in the case of social status, he uses all its conventions and signs only to bend them to his own purposes.

Richardson's proleptic characterization of Lovelace perhaps is not as impressive to us as it should be. We are long familiar with postmodern "denaturings" of status, gender, and power, and thus may know this "name-father" too well. But once we heed her response to her victimization, Clarissa achieves striking proleptic force, setting a central question in recent feminist criticism—that of the relationship between generalizations about patriarchy and specific instances, both literary and historical, of male impotence. Spurning Anna Howe's warning that "you are too punctilious" (353), perhaps realizing the "POWER" that this conclusion would grant to Lovelace, Clarissa resists Lovelace by constructing—first through her submission to her father's curse, then through her family at the Smiths, and finally through her redefinition of her "father's house"—a patriarch who both satisfies her needs and gives her power over her oppressors.

The father created by Clarissa bears no relation to James Harlowe Sr. or Lord M., men immobilized by "gouty paroxysms" and reduced to offering banal clichés as their "proverbs." Victims of the demographic crisis described by the Stones, both Lord M. and Harlowe Sr. offer evidence to support Armstrong's critique of Gilbert and Gubar:

> They argue that women authors . . . had to manage the difficult task of simultaneously subverting and conforming to patriarchal standards. But when understood within this gendered frame of reference, the conditions for women's writing appear to remain relatively constant throughout history because the authors in question were women and because the conditions under which they wrote were largely determined by men. Thus . . . Gilbert and Gubar virtually ignore the historical conditions that women have confronted as writers, and in so doing they ignore the place of women's writing in history. (7–8)

In short, the patriarch constructed by Gilbert and Gubar—and by Clarissa Harlowe—has great imaginative power precisely because it pays so little attention to "historical conditions." [21]

Clarissa's father does try to lock her in his version of an attic, but his attempt is foredoomed by Clarissa's place of confinement being a room, then a closet, of her own. Even in her worst moments at Harlowe Place, Clarissa never loses her private space. Her family also tries to take her voice from her (or at least her pens and papers), but this attempt also is foredoomed—and not just by Clarissa's facility at hiding her supplies. Clarissa's father finally cannot control her, indeed, increasingly must be protected from direct confrontations with her, lest he realize that it is in her perfect "duty," not in the fictions of his son, that he can find life. Bonfield, Hollingsworth, the Stones, Wrigley, and Schofield all show that the patriarch, rather than being the oppressive "power" assumed by Castle, was plagued, at least from 1650 to 1740, by an even more debilitating problem than gout. In large numbers, patriarchs were unable to perform the most basic of biological functions: the production of male offspring. This failing powerfully effects fictional characters as diverse as Lennox's "Female Quixote," Inchbald's Miss Milner, and Burney's Cecelia. James Harlowe Jr. says many cruel and stupid things, but readers of the Stones, of Armstrong, or of eighteenth-century fiction, might contend that his stupidest remark comes when he claims "that daughters were but encumbrances and drawbacks upon a family," for in eighteenth-century life and fiction (we only need mention Fielding's Sophia Western and Amelia Booth, Inchbald's Mathilda), families typically were saved by their daughters. The patriarch needed the daughter, as Clarissa's grandfather and father need her, to extend his life. James Jr. cavalierly claims "that a man who has sons brings up chickens for his own table . . . whereas daughters are chickens brought up for the tables of other men," but this statement of male supremacy receives little support either in Richardson or in eighteenth-century fiction in general. Clarissa easily and promptly defeats her complacent brother: "I made his comparison stagger him by asking him, if the sons to make it hold were to have their necks wrung off?" (77).

If Lovelace adumbrates the academic Derridian, Clarissa, silent about her condition, eludes labels. Her pregnancy points to "historical conditions" that bring the "simple abstraction" of "patriarchal power" into question.[22] But as she responds to the death of her grandfather and the impairment of her father by creating a better, even a perfect father, she reveals, at least for a Lacanian, how profoundly she has been "marked" by the phallus (or her lack thereof), how inescapable, even in a time of widespread male impotence, is patriarchy.[23] In Clarissa's reticence about her pregnancy, Richardson places her such that she need endorse neither a historical nor a Lacanian take on the patriarch. Were she to admit herself to be with child, she would vindicate Lovelace's replacement of the biological father with the "name-father"; she would become his accomplice in declaring the superannuation of James Harlowe Sr. and Lord M. She would become a perfect example for the Stones and a perfect argument for Armstrong. Were she to declare herself to be without child, she would open the way for a rapprochement with her family (after a brief exile to the New World). She would submit again to the power of weak men whose only strength lies in their tie to the phallus. She would become the perfect Lacanian case. Remaining silent, Clarissa dies in a "father's house" that is irrevocably and unbreachably her "own."

Clarissa, like Garbo, wants only to be left alone, but demographic crisis makes her potentially a source of great wealth and status (here James Jr.'s anxieties belie his chicken analogy). With "patriarchal power" greatly diminished, Clarissa finds herself in a situation over which her virtue cannot triumph. She rebuilds her "father's house," but what that "house" means finally is as impossible for us to say, as it is for Lovelace. It testifies both to the demise of patriarchy in eighteenth-century England and to the enduring power that men, even gout-stricken and disabled men, derive from Lacan's "phallus," from the mark of sexual difference, from their association with, in Zora Neale Hurston's phrase, "Gawd and a couple of other men."[24] Rather than accept the "dissolution of natural signification," Clarissa will not respond to direct, crucial, and basic questions: "Where do you live?" "Are you pregnant?" Her silence protects her words from being distorted by and thus conferring advantage upon the "name-father," the false father. Yet, it also leaves her understanding of the relationship between individual patriarchs and "patriarchal power" ab ovo. While she predicts the controversies of postmodern feminist criticism, she will not resolve them.[25]

Writing to Belford immediately after Clarissa's second (and final) escape from him, Lovelace claims that Clarissa was safe as long as she remained *within* the domain of the patriarch:

> However ungenerous an appearance what I am going to say may have from *my* pen, let me tell thee that if such a lady as Miss Harlowe chose to enter into the matrimonial state . . . and, according to the old patriarchal system, to go on contributing to get sons and daughters with no other view than to bring them up piously . . . what a devil had she to do to let her fancy run a gadding after a rake? (970).

Amidst all the self-delusion and self-vindication that motivate Lovelace here (and which render his tone problematic), we can see clearly that he casts himself as the opponent of "the old patriarchal system" and accuses Clarissa of complicity in his rebellion—a complicity she ever denies. Similarly, whatever our uncertainties about her "father's house," we can say with confidence that Clarissa's difficulties follow hard upon the death of her grandfather (a patriarch) and the demographic crisis that ensued—that stoked the ambitions of weak and selfish men like her brother.

7

Demographic Crisis and Simple Stories: Burney, Inchbald, Lennox, and the Nature of Incest

These Laws of Nature are 1. *Unalterable;* and that is, where the nature of our persons, and of the objects, which are the foundations of them are unalterable, or still the same: 2. Or mutable, when the *Nature* of the things which are its foundation, is *mutable.* As it is the immutable Law of immutable nature, that we love God as God, and that we do all the good we can, etc. because the *foundation* of it is immutable: But *e.g.* the law against Incest was mutable in nature: For nature bound Adams [*sic*] children to marry each other; and nature bindeth us since (ordinarily) to the contrary.

—Richard Baxter, *The Life of Faith,* 1670

Failures in patrilinear succession play a central role in works by women writers of the last half of the eighteenth century. Much recent criticism of novels by Burney, Inchbald, and Lennox has been based on the assumptions about "patriarchal power" that Castle makes in her reading of *Clarissa.* Castle's development as a critic is particularly instructive in this regard. In her book *Masquerade and Civilization,* which appeared four years after *Clarissa's Ciphers,* she departs slightly but significantly from the Gilbert and Gubar model by applying Mikhail Bakhtin's study of the "carnivalesque" to eighteenth-century fiction.[1] In a passage basic to Castle's argument in the later book, Bakhtin describes "carnivalistic life" as

life drawn out of its *usual* rut, it is to some extent "life turned inside out," "the reverse of the world" ("*monde à l'envers*"). . . . The laws,

141

prohibitions, and restrictions that determine the structure and order of ordinary, that is noncarnival, life are suspended during carnival: what is suspended first of all is hierarchical structure and all the forms of terror, revenge, piety, and etiquette connected with it—that is, every-thing resulting from the sociohierarchical inequality or any other form of inequality among people (including age). All *distance* between people is suspended, and a special carnival category goes into effect: *free and familiar contact* among people. (122–23)

As Castle studies the carnivalesque in eighteenth-century fiction, particularly the "masquerades" that play a central role in novels by Henry Fielding, Frances Burney, and Elizabeth Inchbald, she sees the suspension of "sociohierarchical inequality" serving the "will to liberty" of female protagonists. In her chapter on Inch-bald's *A Simple Story*, she claims that Miss Milner's "desires repeatedly triumph . . . over masculine prerogative" (*Masquerade and Civilization*, 292) and that "the patriarchal realm metamor-phoses" (319) in response to the heroine's needs. While Castle reads Richardson's *Clarissa* as the victim of "patriarchal power," she accords to the heroines of Burney and Inchbald greater poten-tial to act upon their needs and desires.

This brought Castle sharp criticism from Patricia Meyer Spacks and, more recently, Catherine Craft-Fairchild and Eleanor Ty.[2] Spacks and Craft-Fairchild challenge Castle because they both see "patriarchal control firmly in place" (Craft-Fairchild, 77) in Inch-bald's story. Spacks asserts that "the female 'freedom' Castle cele-brates has found little scope" and describes Lord Elmwood, the central male figure in *A Simple Story*, as embodying "a traditional male constellation of authority and apparent rationality" (Spacks 1990, 199). The sharpness of the attacks upon Castle becomes particularly revealing when we note that her differences with her critics actually are not as great as they might seem. Throughout her analysis, Castle refers repeatedly to "entrenched masculine authority" (*Masquerade and Civilization*, 308), "the patriarchal household" (314), and "patriarchal taboo" (324). Castle reads the novel as "a story of law and its violation . . . the crossing of boundaries, the reversal of prohibitions" (294). Miss Milner's "female energy" conflicts with Dorriforth/Elmwood's "repressive masculine logic" (295). Castle, Spacks, and Ty disagree only as they assess the extent to which Miss Milner's "transgressions" are validated in the story. But the basic dynamic that they see driving *A Simple Story* is much the same that Castle sees driving *Clarissa*:

Elmwood, a "tyrannical patriarch" (Ty, 96), contends with (and finally destroys) Miss Milner's version of female desire and will.

While Spacks and Craft-Fairchild would deny her claim,[3] Castle sees that relationships between and amongst characters in *A Simple Story* are remarkably fluid. Sandford, the crotchety Jesuit priest, goes from being Miss Milner's antagonist to being her advocate; the change is both total and unexplained. Castle places this fluidity *inside* the conflict between patriarchal power and female transgression. However, the case is quite different: the fluidity follows from an impairment of the patriarch that precedes the courtship of Elmwood and Miss Milner, the novel's central event. Spacks's criticism of Castle is instructive here because it depends upon our accepting that Elmwood is "a traditional male . . . authority." Certainly in his sporadic anger and his penchant for making rules, Elmwood may seem such. But Elmwood becomes angry and feels compelled to make rules only because, throughout the story, he must cope with changes in his life that he neither expects nor wants. These changes take from him his name (Is he Dorriforth or is he Elmwood?) and his profession (To save his family estate, he must give up his membership in the Society of Jesus). All these changes come to Dorriforth/Elmwood because patriarchs fail to replicate themselves. Rather than offering a dour version of "patriarchal power," Dorriforth/Elmwood offers a recalcitrant, sometimes angry response to its demise.

Central to *A Simple Story* and to other recently much-discussed novels by women in the last half of the eighteenth century—my other examples will be Lennox's *The Female Quixote* and Burney's *Evelina* and *Cecelia*—are the arrangements that men and women must make to overcome the patriarch's failure to produce male progeny. Burney, Inchbald, and Lennox proceed more directly than their male counterparts to these questions of inheritance. While it is difficult to define specifically female plots or techniques in eighteenth-century fiction,[4] Burney, Inchbald, and Lennox do share an opening situation; a beautiful orphan heiress comes to an estate through the demise of her father and must decide how she will live. Lennox's Arabella Wilmot, Inchbald's Miss Milner, and Burney's Cecelia Beverley all find themselves in positions of considerable wealth and potential power. They are so placed because of the patriarch's reproductive failures, and they must invent fictive kin to save their estates. The price of status—witness Burney's Delvile family—can be very high, but it is a price that these female protagonists have it in their power to pay.

In the aftermath of the reproductive failures of their fathers, the actions of these heroines confirm the acuity of James B. Twitchell's study of the "incest taboo."[5] Twitchell reprints the "last page" of the 1761 edition of the *Book of Common Prayer*, which offers "A TABLE of KINDRED and AFFINITY, wherein whosoever are related, are forbidden in Scripture, and our Laws, to marry together" (129). He observes:

> Most of the list makes no *biologic* sense whatsoever. Almost fifty percent of those named bear no genetic linkage to the individual; even more intriguing there is absolutely no mention made of first and second cousins. It may be that these cousins are not only tolerated but accepted as mates because they provide the necessary knots that prevent family wealth from slipping away. (128)[6]

By marrying their first cousins, Inchbald's Mathilda and Lennox's Arabella both will maintain estates and "prevent family wealth from slipping away." In defining the "incest taboo" such that it does not debar certain useful consanguineous marriages, Inchbald and Lennox reveal the logic behind the Prayer Book's "*biologic*" nonsense. While a woman and her grandfather were unlikely (by Lord M.'s logic) to produce a child (and, thus, their coupling is easily banned), a woman and her cousin well might. Amidst a demographic crisis, the need of the elite to produce children shapes the strictures of the Prayer Book as well as the fictions of female authors. Twitchell observes a universal truth about humans: "If we have to be incestuous to breed, we will" (247).

Having discovered Chancery Court records that refer to "some sort of shocking erotic experimentation with his youngest sister" by the "barely twelve" year old Henry Fielding, Martin C. Battestin makes an important point about Fielding's life at the time of his "indecent actions."[7] They occur "when his father was away, completing the rejection of his [recently deceased] mother by marrying again" (23). The recurrence of the incest motif in Fielding's novels (Joseph Andrews, it seems, is ready to marry his sister; Tom Jones, apparently, has bedded his mother) reveals, according to Battestin, Fielding's "fascination" (25, 27) with the idea. In those novels, incest is always both a "dreadful" and a definitive "sin." It also is a sin that, at least in the comic novels, is avoided by the discovery of paternity. Having evoked "dread," Fielding, through the good offices of the birth mystery, purges it, but the recurrence of the possibility in his fictions perhaps indicates that closure was not so easily to be found in his life—his father ever-erratic, his sister Sarah his co-adjutor. For heroines like Lennox's Arabella and Inchbald's Mathilda, incest presents a different but perhaps no less dreadful problem. In the absence of the father, they not only are free but are called upon to define incest and to determine what sorts of fictions they will write with reference to it. Whereas for Defoe's heroines incest looms as a last barrier to fictionalizing, for these later heroines incest becomes fiction's occasion.

As their heroines contemplate the "metamorphosis" of cousins into husbands, Inchbald and Lennox also give point to the great if unspoken lesson of Burney's conclusion to *Evelina*: fictive kin, however unattractive and ungifted in comparison to natural, still must be treated as kin. In the denouement of *Evelina*, all the characters conspire to protect the fictive daughter, who has been foisted upon Belmont by a serving lady. Burney's *anagnorisis*—the scene in which Belmont sees Evelina's mother's face in hers—is one of the most powerful in eighteenth-century fiction. But this anamnestic birth-mystery plot does not place the perpetrators of deception outside its comic resolution. As Baxter denatures incest in his discussion of the first patriarch, so Burney denatures kinship in her resolution of a series of events that begin in Sir John Belmont's failings as a father and a husband.

I

Published to great acclaim and large sales in 1778, *Evelina* offers a subtle but powerful vindication of fictive versions of kinship, and looks toward, although it does not establish, incest as an outcome of the impairment of the patriarch.[8] Burney varies the birth mystery such that she can question whether paternity is, to use Baxter's terms, an "*Unalterable*" or a "*mutable*" condition. Unlike characters in Fielding and Smollett, Evelina knows who her father is, but she must overcome Belmont's refusal to recognize her. Belmont's behavior mystifies Evelina only because she is unaware of the deception under which he labors (Dame Green, the wet nurse, having substituted her daughter for Evelina). As a result, Evelina feels at least two basic uncertainties about fatherhood. First, believing Belmont to be her father, she is shaken by "the strange indifference, that must occasion a father never to make the least enquiry after the health, the welfare, or even the life of his child" (122). If paternity establishes a "natural" bond between father and child, then "nature" has become attenuated in Evelina's case. Second, the virtues of Evelina's foster father, Reverend Villars, confuse, even more than Belmont's failings, the "nature" of paternity. Near the story's end, Villars sends his blessings to Evelina as he commits her to Belmont's care. Evelina quotes him as she responds:

> You *commit me to my real parent*,—Ah, Guardian, Friend, Protector of my youth!—by whom my helpless infancy was cherished, my mind formed, my very life preserved,—*you* are the Parent my heart acknowledges, and to you do I vow eternal duty, gratitude, and affection. (350)

Evelina here redacts comically Clarissa's "my father's house" letter, for she asserts the superiority of the constructed father to the natural.

Evelina's paternity matters because she, once legitimized, can claim the power that demographic crisis conferred upon eighteenth-century women of her lineage; she is the key to the transmission of great estates. In an early letter to Lady Howard, Villars states the case with both precision and anxiety:

> Consider, Madam, the peculiar cruelty of her situation; only child of a wealthy baronet, whose person she has never seen . . . entitled as she is to lawfully inherit his fortune and estate, is there any probability that he will *properly* own her? . . . And as to Mr. Evelyn's estate, I have no doubt but that Madame Duval and her relations will dispose of it among themselves . . . this deserted child, though legally heiress to two large fortunes, must owe all her rational expectations to adoption and friendship. (18–19)

Patrilinear succession, which should empower and enrich Evelina, has failed her. Her only protection for eighteen years has been her "adoption" by Villars; her only "rational" hope for an inheritance lies with her fictive father (who has no other issue).

Evelina, who has been raised in rural isolation, is beautiful, virtuous, and unworldly; Burney generates great comedy from the anxieties and *faux pas* Evelina suffers as she enters the social scene at both London and Bath.[9] But for all her discomfort—for all her expressions of affection for Villars—Evelina chooses to enter this larger world and thus to test the limits of her "good nature."

Throughout her various social misadventures, Evelina struggles to act properly and fairly, but she learns, as Clarissa never will, that words and gestures can mislead, even betray. There is no "natural signification" even in the most basic scenes of family life. This truth appears most startlingly in Evelina's remarkable recognition scene with Belmont. While the scene at first appears to be a triumphant vindication of Evelina's "nature," both Belmont's response to the discovery of his "biological"[10] daughter and the subsequent treatment by all of his fictive daughter reveal Burney's "denaturing" of kinship.

Upon entering Belmont's presence, an overwrought Evelina sinks to the floor and covers her face with her hands. Belmont, however, has "seen" her and, "in a voice scarcely articulate," exclaims, "My God! does Caroline Evelyn still live!" (372). He thus vindicates a claim made earlier by Villars: "Without any other certificate of your birth, that which you carry in your countenance, as it could not be effected by artifice, so it cannot admit of a doubt" (337). Belmont sees in Evelina the "image of my long-lost Caroline." In the daughter, the mother "lives . . . breathes . . . is present to my view!" (372). Belmont takes Evelina as a perfect instance of "natural signification"; she, through what we would call her genetic inheritance, makes the absent Caroline Evelyn "present." In a narrative that includes false signs—Colonel Mirvan's several ruses, Willoughby's forging of Orville's letter, and, greatest of all, Dame Green's substitution of her "bantling" for Evelina—Evelina's face is a birth "certificate" that stands beyond "artifice" and thus beyond "doubt."

Having brought her story to this perfect recognition, Burney makes a remarkable anamnestic turn, a move that recurs, though not as brilliantly, in novels by Inchbald, Lennox, and Burney herself. The *anagnorisis* is perfect, but Belmont, having seen the truth, almost immediately turns away from it. Indeed, his relationship to Evelina from the recognition scene onward will be defined by his *not* seeing her: "'Go, child, go' added he, wildly starting, and pushing me from him, 'take her away, Madam [Mrs. Selwyn],—I cannot bear to look at her!' And then, breaking hastily from me, he rushed out of the room" (372). Why should Belmont respond "with violence almost frantic" to the perfect "presence" that Evelina embodies? Why should he feel both suicidal ("tell her I would plunge a dagger in my heart to serve her") and gravely wounded ("she has set my brain on fire, and I can see her no more!") in this at least potentially joyous moment (373)? That

Roderick Random's sudden illness follows almost immediately upon his discovery of his father tells us much about Smollett's desire to subvert both the literary and the social conventions of mid-eighteenth-century England. Burney, in her "wonderfully melodramatic"[11] scene, gives the trauma to the parent. Belmont immediately suspects Dame Green's fraud and summons her for questioning. She "persisted in affirming that she had really brought him the daughter of Lady Belmont"; not until Mrs. Selwyn joins in the interrogation is "a confession . . . extorted from her" (374).[12] Belmont's response reveals a basic change in the attitude toward paternity, even from Fielding's time. The revelation of sham—the great goal of Fielding's comedy—has occurred, but Belmont derives neither joy nor purpose from it.

While Belmont will not see Evelina, he almost immediately begins to make plans for her. These plans will give her a title and will transform her from Evelina Anville to Lady Orville, with only a brief, single reference to Evelina Belmont (404). Mrs. Selwyn describes Evelina "becoming at once the wife of the man you adore,—and a Countess!" (376). Belmont's plans also protect his fictive daughter; indeed, since Orville already wants to marry Evelina, Belmont's plans are motivated primarily by his need to take care of "poor Polly Green." Like all virtuous eighteenth-century heroines, Evelina is reluctant to wed, asking, "Why all this haste? why may we not be allowed a little longer time?" (378). But her "punctilio" must be sacrificed to the fictive child's well-being. In a rich phrase, Mrs. Selwyn reports that she and Belmont "agreed, that the most eligible scheme for all parties, would be to have the real and the fictitious daughter married without delay" (377). As Evelina and Polly become syntactical equivalents here, so they move toward becoming social equivalents. Of course, Evelina marries the titled Orville, Polly the illegitimate son of Belmont, Macartney; Evelina also has (but eventually gives up) a better financial settlement from Belmont than Polly's. However, the distance between "the bantling of Dame Green, wash-woman and wet nurse of Berry Hill" (378), and Evelina, daughter of Sir John Belmont, is being hidden with the complicity of all the novel's major characters. Evelina herself contributes to this end by announcing that she "must already call, and always consider" Polly to be her "sister" (382). After their respective marriages, Evelina returns to Berry-Hill and Villars, while Macartney and Evelina's "sister," who have no house, "go to one of Sir John's" (377).

Given the perfect proof of her parentage that Evelina offers, her reward is surprisingly incomplete. Her intended, Orville, insists that "the so-long-supposed Miss Belmont should be considered *indeed* as my sister, and as the co-heiress of my father! though not in *law*, in *justice*, he says, she ought ever to be treated as the daughter of Sir John Belmont" (387). But Orville, whatever measures he takes to help "the bantling of Dame Green," still loves Evelina and enjoys her physical presence. At her second (and last) meeting with Belmont, he repeats the truth he announced during the first: "Never was likeness more striking!— the eye,—the face,—the form,—O my child, my child! . . . Oh dear resemblance of thy murdered mother. . . . O . . . thou representa- tive of my departed wife" (387). Even as he wishes God's blessing upon his "dear child," however, he emphasizes that he will see her no more: "Adieu, my child;—be not angry,—I cannot stay with thee—oh Evelina! thy countenance is a dagger to my heart!— just so, thy mother looked, just so—." Evelina does not beg Belmont for money or for a title; she only asks that he not "abandon" her. "Am I again an orphan?" she laments, but Belmont claims that her presence creates in him "emotions which . . . rend my soul" and asks her only to "think of me as well as thou canst" (386).

Early in this second meeting, an overwrought Belmont falls to his knees. Evelina responds, "I cannot bear to see you thus;— reverse not the law of nature" (386). She would restore patriarchal decorums; daughters, in her view, should kneel to their fathers, not vice versa. Evelina is ready to forgive Belmont's treatment of her mother and to defer to him. For all her passivity, however, she brings "horror" to Belmont—the horror of a man whose fiction has been revealed by the indisputable evidence offered in Evelina's "countenance." The fiction is not only or primarily Dame Green's, although it is important to note the steps that Orville and Belmont take to protect instead of punish her deception. Rather, the great fiction, the fiction upon which Belmont has built his life, is that he could end his marriage to Caroline Evelyn by merely burning a piece of paper. Evelina, who explicitly asserts the power of "nature" in this scene, also embodies it. In her very purity, she sends "a dagger" to her father's "heart" (386) because her "presence" destroys his "denial" that he ever was married to Caroline Evelyn. In the hurry that concludes *Evelina*, Mrs. Selwyn, who takes Evelina's marriage to Orville as a great end, and Sir John, who struggles to protect his fictive version of kinship, become unlikely allies. The quick marriages—Evelina to Orville and Macartney to Polly—cover up the confusion created by Belmont as a "very profligate young man" (15). The marriages normalize the offspring of his youthful rakishness.

In a 1991 collection of essays on Burney,[13] all of the contributors assume that the conclusion of *Evelina* depicts her victimization by the patriarch. Susan C. Greenfield notes that Evelina, previously an active and fluid writer, cannot describe the scenes relating to her marriage and claims, "Appropriated by the patriarchy, the heroine loses her voice, and the novel she has constructed must come to an end" (315). Gina Campbell concurs, adding that Evelina's "wedding . . . heals the patriarchal order as well as the figure of the daughter in that order" (336). But who might this patriarch be? Belmont, the principal candidate, is wounded rather than healed by events. Evelina, however unwillingly and unwittingly, is repeatedly described by him as sending "a dagger" to his heart. We also may wonder how Evelina is "appropriated" by a father who cannot bear to be in her presence and who acts promptly to forestall her carrying his name. And Belmont hardly qualifies as a patriarch, at least in the vein of Dryden's David in *Absalom and Achitophel*. Belmont feels guilty about his infidelity, and he takes care to legitimate his illegitimate children (Macartney, the biological illegitimate child, and Polly Green, the fictive illegitimate child). He is an impaired patriarch, a superannuated rake. When Evelina raises him from his knees, she reveals that his authority, however weak, is a product of her need rather than his nature.

In the issue of *Eighteenth-Century Fiction* devoted to Burney, all of the writers assume that, through Evelina, Burney fights her own battle with "patriarchal constraints"; in her descriptions of Evelina's dealings with her several father figures, Burney represents her father's attempts to direct her own career. Charles Burney stands as a powerful and demanding figure, but if we return to Austin Dobson's now largely unheeded account of the daughter's career (or to Margaret Doody's more recent), we see that Charles was more a feckless social gadfly than a tyrant. He lived by his wits and his charm, not by any claim to estate or title. Moreover, he disappointed his children in his second marriage. Gina Campbell sees in portions of *Evelina* "the daughter's contempt for the oversusceptible father" (327), and with Dobson's work in place, we can begin to see that *Evelina* is not about patriarchal constraint but rather about patriarchal weakness.

In this regard, Evelina comically summarizes the basic situation in works by female novelists as diverse as Lennox, Inchbald, Austen, and Radcliffe. The action of *The Female Quixote* begins with the failure at court, then the death, of Arabella's father. In Inchbald's *A Simple Story*, Miss Milner's father is dead, Mathilda's father is absent. Austen's Emma always has had too much "her own way" because her father is a lifelong "valetudinarian."[14] Radcliffe's Emily St. Aubert only becomes prey to Montoni's depredations after the death of her father. In Burney's later and darker *Cecelia*, the heroine loses not only her father but her uncle as well, and she is left in the care of three guardians who are, to put it mildly, incompetent. Evelina concludes her first letter, a letter to Villars: "Your Evelina ____ ____ I cannot to *you* sign *Anville*, and what other name may I claim?" (24). She thus defines her pursuit of identity not as a matter of "constraint" but of "lack."[15] She takes her fictive name, "Anville," to be both unsatisfying and false, yet she, at her story's opening, can see no alternative to it.

Evelina's "ambivalence" is not, as the critics in the Burney volume would have it, "towards the literary patriarchy" (Campbell, 323). Rather, it is a more encompassing ambivalence about the nature of signs, an ambivalence largely owing to the impairment of the patriarch. Evelina becomes a writer when she leaves Villars and Berry-Hill and sets out upon what proves to be a quest after her natural father. Greenfield has noted that Evelina, as she approaches her marriage, no longer writes. But Evelina suffers a similar silencing when she, at roughly the novel's center, returns to Berry-Hill: "You complain of my silence, my dear Miss Mirvan,—but what have I to write? Narrative does not offer, nor does a lively imagination supply the deficiency" (262). Evelina only has something to say when she is between Villars and Belmont, when she mediates between fictive and biological versions of kinship.

Burney places Evelina such that she works between the versions of signification that divide Clarissa and Lovelace and lead to their respective tragic ends. In her very being, Evelina is a perfect case of "natural signification"; Lady Howard writes in an early letter, "She [Evelina] has the same gentleness in her manners, the same *natural grace* in her motions, that I formerly so much admired in her mother" (21, my italics). However, long separated from her father, brought up by an "invented" parent, Evelina learns the lesson that Clarissa finally will not accept: "The real and the fictitious daughter" both have claims upon the father and, more tellingly, upon the larger society. Evelina can so graciously acknowledge Polly as her "sister" because she herself is a "fictitious daughter" (in Villars's case) as well as a natural one (in Belmont's).[16] In her own life, she has learned that fictive kin can be superior to biological.

Burney's comedy depends upon the adroitness with which she places Evelina between fictive and natural understandings of the sign. Just days before her marriage, Evelina says of a letter she has written to Sir Clement Willoughby (a would-be Lovelace, who has admitted that he has written to Evelina "in Orville's name"): "Not knowing what name to sign, I was obliged to send it without any" (389). Namelessness here is not the frightening burden it is at the story's start. Rather, it testifies to Evelina's ability to make herself, to become, as she almost immediately does, "Lady Orville." Having achieved Roxana's great goal—a "title"—Evelina stops writing and *Evelina* ends. But marriage here is a state at which Evelina arrives by writing herself between Villars's name for her and Belmont's. Greenfield makes a helpful observation about Burney's presentation of Evelina: "Although silenced by Orville and Willoughby when she is with them, Evelina regains linguistic mastery by describing these men in prose. In her letters she does all the talking—she controls the representation of both Orville and Willoughby" (309). In her prose, Evelina perfects a "written" signification to accompany her already perfect "natural" signification. She thus wins Orville, who has both great social status and great natural grace. Evelina's various embarrassments as she enters the London social scene reveal that "natural signification" cannot make her fully or even partially understood. Her most open and honest gestures are misread and distorted by characters like Willoughby and Lovel. *Clarissa* ends tragically because, once "sign and 'Nature' split apart," Clarissa cannot be made whole, except in her own unyielding construction/rehabilitation of the patriarch. Evelina loses the tragic stature of Clarissa because she is both a perfect natural sign (her body proving beyond question that she is her mother's daughter) and a writer whose prose both compensates for her failings as a conversationalist and corrects the misimpressions with which villains seek to ruin her.

Evelina is silent—unable to write—when she resides with Villars, the fictive father. And she is silent—apparently too busy to write—as she nears the marriage that will right the confusions caused by her natural father's sexual license. At the extremes of the dialectic between fictive and biological kinship, she cannot write, but her story comes to life as she—beautiful, gracious, and intelligent—mediates between the versions of kinship that Clarissa and Lovelace divide. Broadly stated, Burney's genius resides in her transcending the conflict between deconstructive and essentialist epistemologies. But the splendid reconciliation she achieves between "the real and the fictitious daughter" is not easy to duplicate. In novels by Burney herself and by Inchbald and Lennox, female protagonists, in the absence of a patriarch, must decide how much of their beauty and wealth they will devote to fictive versions of kinship.[17] Like Evelina, these heroines are not ready to dispense with long-enduring notions of the "natural," particularly since those notions privilege them socially and financially; they are all heiresses. But also like Evelina, these heroines quickly learn how tenuous is the distinction between the "natural" and the "fictive." Indeed, their commitment to convincing fictions finally will take them beyond any "natural" aversion they might feel to marrying a first cousin.[18] Consanguineous marriage becomes useful to these heroines because they realize (with Robert Lovelace) that the most powerful fictions are those that come closest to the truth. The cousin is "of" the family although descended from the female line. These heroines neither subvert nor submit to patriarchal "authority." Rather, in the absence of a viable patriarch, they struggle to reconcile (as Evelina so brilliantly does) fictive and natural versions of kinship. As a group, they do not reach Evelina's grand mediation.

II

In her Introduction to the World's Classics edition of *The Female Quixote*,[19] Margaret Doody argues that, as Arabella renounces the romance tradition and marries Glanville, she "forgoes her own control of the world, renounces narrative power, and submits to the role of object of the paternal authority which also claims the name of reason" (xxxii). Having earlier noted Arabella's "dauntless self-fashioning" (xxvi) and the "powers" that Arabella derives from "the romances," Doody centers her interpretation upon the simple abstraction "paternal authority." Writing after Doody, Catherine Gallagher admits the "persistence of patriarchal assumptions" in the eighteenth century but argues that "the remnants of patriarchy" cannot explain the "dispossession" to which both female authors and their protagonists are subjected.[20] While Doody sees Arabella's renunciation of her romances as a total defeat, Gallagher sees the renunciation as opening Arabella to "invention," to "fiction." To read Arabella's story in this way, Gallagher argues that the problem with Arabella's romances is not their fictiveness; rather it is their claim to be history, the claim Arabella honors in her several naive attempts to apply their precedents.

Gallagher thus moves beyond the "patriarchal etiology" that drives most recent readings of The Female Quixote and prompts the question of who is the "paternal authority"? The obvious candidate is the "Marquis of _____," Arabella's father. The novel opens, however, by describing his fall from the position of "first and most distinguished Favourite at Court." While he once "in a manner governed the whole Kingdom," the marquis is victimized by his "extensive Authority [which] could not fail of making him many Enemies." He not only loses his "Employments" but is "banished the Court forever." In "Pain" because of "his undeserved Disgrace," he turns to a still-popular fiction and behaves "rather like a man who had resigned than been dismissed." "For the Place of his *Retreat*" (my italics) he chooses a "small Village" in a "remote" Province (Lennox, 5). Before he enters this world apart, he marries "a young lady greatly inferior to himself in Quality, but whose Beauty and good Sense promised him an agreeable Companion." Having suffered a defeat in the public world, the marquis defies conventions of status in his marriage, a defiance that is not problematic or revolutionary only because it is so private: "His Pride and extreme Reserve rendered him . . . wholly inaccessible to the Country Gentry about him" (6).

Doody might well argue that the marquis's loss of political and social "Authority" in no way impugns or weakens his power within his family. And the marquis does attempt to direct his daughter's education, bringing "the best Masters . . . to attend her" and instructing her in French and Italian himself. But even in this most private of situations, the marquis suffers a defeat that recapitulates his public disgrace: "It is not to be doubted, but she would have made a great Proficiency in all useful Knowledge, had not her whole Time been taken up by another Study." Departing from her father's plan for her education, Arabella gives herself over to reading "Romances . . . not in the original *French*, but very bad Translations." The romances belonged to her late mother:

"The deceased Marchioness had purchased these Books to soften a solitude which she found disagreeable" (7).

Arabella takes the romances for "real Pictures of Life, from them she drew *all her* Notions and Expectations" (my italics). So it is important to place the "authority" of these books. They are her mother's addition to her father's collection: "After her Death, the Marquis removed them from her Closet into his Library, where Arabella found them" (7). The books embody her mother's protest ("found disagreeable") against the "Solitude" that her husband's "Quality" imposed upon her. But while Arabella's mother may be the sad woman in the castle, Arabella, by making her mother's books the center of her life, confers considerable power upon herself. Doody notes: "It is through assuming the powers the romances offer that Arabella can command a space, assert a woman's right to 'a room of one's own,' and take upon herself the power to control the movements and behaviour of others" (Lennox, xxv). Because of these romances, the marquis cannot direct Arabella's "Fondness for Reading," a fondness which, at first, "extremely delighted" him (7).

That the marquis's power is partial, even impaired, appears most clearly in his attempt to marry Arabella to Glanville, the son of his sister. While the marquis could exert unquestioned authority in making his own marriage, he struggles to arrange one for his daughter, who not only has read her mother's books but who also possesses her mother's "Nature" (6). Arabella's "native Charms" make her a likely prospect for marriage, but her reading leads her to find Glanville inadequate. He has not offered the "Service" nor gone through the "Sufferings" of the lovers in Arabella's fictions. The marquis describes Arabella's expectations as "foolish and ridiculous Objections," as "Stuff" (42). At one point he becomes so frustrated by her resistance that he is ready to burn the "foolish Books" that "have turned her Brain!" (55). Of course, we might read this scene in Doody's vein: the father asserts his "natural" right to marry his daughter; the daughter, who represents individual consciousness and female "otherness," has her voice (her books) taken from her by a male hegemony that cannot risk having its own "constructedness" revealed. Arabella's fictions "denature" her father's authority and, thus, he must burn her books.[21] However, he doesn't. The romances are rescued by Glanville (Arabella having left the room), and it is in Glanville's peculiar status that Lennox complicates any attempt to place a patriarch at the novel's center.

As the marquis describes Glanville's virtues, he undercuts his attempts to control Arabella's marriage (and to dismiss her fictions): "I may with reason expect you will conform to my will in the Choice I have made of a Husband for you, since it is impossible to make any Objection either to his Person or Mind; and, being the Son of my Sister, he is certainly not unworthy of you, tho' he has not a Title" (41). The marquis gets off to a strong start here, demanding conformity to his "will" and assuming that his "will" and "reason" are the same. However, by the end of his sentence, he finds himself in the position described by the Stones—that is, he offers a "pious fiction" of kinship to make up for his (and his family's) failure to produce a male heir. While he opens by asserting his will, he concludes by weakening the distinction between "worth" and "Title." Indeed, the lukewarm double negative "not unworthy" emphasizes how equivocal his authority is. The first cousin seems to the marquis a fine choice because he is "family." But in attributing, however negatively, "worth" to Glanville, the marquis relies upon his sister's fecundity rather than his potency. Had Arabella a brother, her dotty fascination with romances would be a tolerable eccentricity. Lacking a brother, she must carry on the family name, the title to the family estates. The marquis would hide the extent of his failure, but, in casting upon Glanville, he relies upon a woman.

In the terms of his "will," the marquis reveals that both his power and his desire to direct Arabella's choice are limited. As Sir Charles Glanville, who is named her "Guardian," explains to his son, "her father has bequeathed you one Third of the Estate, provided she don't marry you" (64). But Arabella otherwise is free to make her own choice. Glanville Sr. continues, "Tho' her father has left me her Guardian, till she is of Age, yet it is with such Restriction that my Niece is quite her own Mistress . . . for tho' she is directed to consult me in her Choice of an Husband, yet my Consent is not absolutely necessary" (64–65). Arabella is free *not* to marry. Upon hearing the will read, she immediately responds by "wishing him [Glanville Jr.] Joy of the Estate that was bequeathed to him" (66). She is both financially and, apparently, emotionally free of any need to treat with him. Both Glanvilles recognize that "Constraint" and "Compulsion" (64) cannot be applied to Arabella; indeed, "restriction" (65) lies upon them in this case, not upon her. We only can wonder what the fate of Clarissa Harlowe might have been with a will such as this in place.[22]

At issue between Arabella and Glanville, both before and after the death of the marquis, is not legal, financial, or even social power. Arabella's status as the only child of a great peer frees her from such considerations. Rather, she and Glanville disagree about how gestures and words are to be understood; they are separated by their different versions of the "sign." Since Arabella has both social and economic power, we should not be surprised that Glanville must enter, however uncomfortably, her sign system. Anticipating the tenets of postmodernism, he "gets the girl" through his skill as a semiotician rather than through his skill as a swordsman.[23] In his earliest meetings with Arabella, Glanville repeatedly violates "the laws of Gallantry and Respect" (32) that she has derived from her mother's romances. This hardly makes him a villain, for no one has read these books as Arabella has. He, long before Arabella undergoes her conversion, must learn to "read" her and, most importantly, to mediate between her narrow and idiosyncratic semiology and the very different system that holds in the larger community.

In a break between class sessions, a student once suggested to me (the thought seemingly too risible to mention in public) that Glanville might be best understood as the prototype for Jack Tripper, the character played by John Ritter in the long-running, now happily even-out-of-syndication situation comedy *Three's Company*. The comedy of *Three's Company* (such as it was) derived from Tripper's attempts either 1) to understand the unique if somewhat dim perspective of Suzanne Sommers's Chrissie or 2) to work himself out of (with considerable mugging and gasping) confusions created by Chrissie in her dealings with their various neighbors. Chrissie-as-naïf creates for Tripper (as does Arabella for Glanville) situations fraught with potentially humorous misunderstandings. The analogy to *Three's Company* breaks down (as I tried to indicate when we discussed it in class) with Chrissie and Arabella. While Doody may wish to see the latter as a victim of "paternal authority," her social status confers great power upon her. Living in supposedly more enlightened times, Chrissie has power only because of her anatomy. Glanville and Tripper, however, do share a frantic nebbishness as they run from one misunderstanding to another, events invariably working out for them not because of their physical or intellectual prowess but rather because of their eager affability, their quickness to translate between Arabella/Chrissie and the "other."

Signs misread, signs partially comprehended, signs almost fully understood—signs are central to Glanville's courtship of his cousin. Consider this excerpt from one of their early meetings: "She made a Sign for him to retire; for he had walked up with her to her Chamber: But, finding he did not obey her, for he really was quite unacquainted with these Sorts of dumb Commands, she hastily retired to her Closet" (36–37). Glanville not only misreads Arabella's "Sign for him to retire," he also misreads her abrupt departure: "He concluded the Affront he had received, proceeded from her Disdain to admit the Addresses of any Person whose Quality was inferior to hers" (37). Raised more conventionally than Arabella, Glanville reads class bias in her actions when, in fact, her impatience with him is owing to his failure to follow the precedents of romance. Because he has "no Notion of his Cousin's heroic Sentiments," Glanville wrongly supposes that "the Scorn she . . . expressed for him was founded upon the Difference of their Rank and Fortune" (33). To court Arabella successfully, Glanville must learn to read her better; no similar accommodation, at least throughout most of the story, is required of her. When Arabella claims, "You have given me no Signs of Repentance for the Fault you committed," Glanville only can respond, "What greater Signs of Repentance can you desire, than this Reformation of my Behaviour" (47). Having offended by being too open in his expressions of love, Glanville must learn both patience and reticence.

Glanville's training by Arabella continues even after he rescues her romances from the fire. She thanks him but then "made a Sign to him to be gone, fearing the Extravagance of his Joy would make him throw himself at her Feet to thank her . . . but, finding he seemed disposed to stay longer, she called one of her Women into the Closet; and by some very significant Frowns, gave *Glanville* to understand his Stay was displeasing" (57). Glanville, a slow but diligent learner, here does slightly better as a reader of Arabella. When she later claims to have saved him from illness and offers him hope of her favor, she ends her "Speech, with a Solemnity of Accent, that gave Mr. *Glanville* to understand, any Reply would offend her, he silently kissed her fair Hand, which she held out to him" (137). Not only is Glanville reading Arabella's gestures here; he also is being properly submissive ("silently") in response to them. Glanville's is no small accomplishment, for Lennox sets numerous scenes in which Arabella's signs are unintelligible. For only one example, in a meeting she has relatively late in the story with a messenger from Sir George Bellmour, a fortune hunter who has tried to win Arabella by cynically using the romances, the messenger awaits her response to a letter he has brought from Sir George:

> Arabella . . . made a Sign with her Hand, very majestically, for him to be gone; but he, not able to comprehend her Meaning, stood still, with an Air of Perplexity, not daring to beg her to explain herself; supposing, she, by that Sign, required something of him.
>
> Why dost thou not obey my Commands? said *Arabella*, finding he did not go.
>
> I will, to be sure, Madam, replied he; wishing at the same time secretly, she would let him know what they were. (256)

Characters from Glanville to this messenger move at Arabella's bidding, once they figure out what that bidding is.

In the course of *The Female Quixote*, Glanville becomes equally adept at understanding Arabella and at protecting her from the judgments of others who do not understand her and, thus, assume, with the beau Tinsel, that "if she is not mad, she is certainly a little out of her senses" (302). While she risks a dangling participle in the sentence, Lennox portrays Glanville's growth quite clearly when she writes, "Then making a Sign to them to leave her alone, Mr. *Glanville* who understood her, took his Father and Sister downstairs, leaving Arabella" (304). Glanville achieves his greatest perceptiveness at what threatens to be his lowest point in the novel: a dialogue with Arabella after an actress hired by Bellmour has pretended to be a princess wronged by Glanville. Appalled and angered by Glanville's purported "treacheries," Arabella astounds him with her accusations and then makes "a Sign to him to be gone." Glanville, "who understood her perfectly well," will not leave until he "know[s] how I have been so unfortunate as to offend you" (352). By pursuing his questioning of Arabella, Glanville begins to see the outlines of Bellmour's fiction, in which he has been aspersed under the name "Ariamnes." Bellmour has used the conventions of romance to discredit his rival. But Glanville, although he avoids reading the romances (33, 49), has learned to read Arabella, and thus he both can detect (although at this point he is not ready to prove) Bellmour's "villainous artifice" and challenge the fictional equivalence that Bellmour has created and by which Arabella would judge him: "Is it me you mean by *Ariamnes*? For so your last Words seem'd to hint—." The scene ends with Arabella, well-deceived by

Bellmour, pushing away from Glanville, who "submissively dropt her Hand" (353). But Glanville's eventual triumph over Bellmour's deception is possible because he, who once "had no Notion of the exact Obedience which was expected of him" (the situation of Bellmour's messenger) now "underst[ands] her perfectly well" and uses that understanding to protect both of them from vice and its fictions.

At story's end, Glanville becomes a figure of considerable decisiveness (an end Jack Tripper never achieves). His sword fight with Bellmour follows hard upon his discovery of his rival's "artifice." This fight occurs almost simultaneously with Arabella's plunge into the Thames (363), an event that Doody, summarizing recent scholarship on Lennox, reads as the most important event in the narrative. Arabella believes that she is fleeing, as Clelia did, men who will ravish her; she attributes evil motives to "three or four Horsemen" by whom none of the other women in her party feel threatened (362). As throughout her story, Arabella acts on "a Precedent" from romance, but here her behavior is both so dangerous and so foolish that it discredits the romances. This matters greatly to Doody because she reads the romances as offering "power" to Arabella. For Arabella to give up the romances is to give up her freedom, to submit to "paternal authority," and to dwindle into a mere wife. Without denying the importance of the change in Arabella to which her misadventure leads, I am arguing that her power resides not in the romances per se but instead in her beauty, wit, and wealth—in all those attributes that lead Glanville and others to submit to her version of the "Sign."

Arabella's near drowning occurs at the same time as Glanville's near murder of his rival. It bears noting that Glanville is both frightened and changed by his experience as well. Dueling is a vestige of patriarchal order, an aristocratic custom under attack at least since Steele's essays in *The Tatler* and *The Spectator*.[24] By granting him superior swordsmanship, Richardson characterizes Lovelace as a would-be chevalier lost in a time when such behavior is as far from military use as the Stuart pretenders are from the British throne. That Glanville's swordplay does not conform to the rules of dueling reveals the custom to be both superannuated and supererogatory.[25] Glanville has, after all, quickly figured out Bellmour's fiction, and it is his perceptiveness, developed during his long internship reading Arabella's signs, that empowers him—not his sword. While Glanville wounds Bellmour, he otherwise botches what only can be loosely called the duel. He labors under a misperception, having mistaken his sister, who is flirting with Bellmour, for Arabella. He enters into the combat "Transported with Rage . . . running like a Madman." In his "irresistible Fury," he observes no decorums: he "cry'd out to Sir *George* to defend himself, who had but just Time to draw his Sword and make an ineffectual Pass at Mr. *Glanville*, when he receiv'd his into his Body, and fell to the Ground" (357).

Having barely given Bellmour time to defend himself, Glanville views the result with fear and remorse: "Losing his Resentment insensibly at the Sight of his Rival's Blood, [he] threw down his Sword . . . with a Heart throbbing with Remorse for what he had done" (357). Before fainting away, Bellmour confesses to his "base . . . practice," but since Glanville already has surmised this, Bellmour's confession offers him neither revelation nor vindication, "tho' now convinc'd of his Treachery, [Glanville] was extremely shock'd at the Condition he saw him in." As Glanville runs for a physician, he meets the steward, Mr. Roberts, who brings news of Arabella's illness subsequent to her rash action, and warns "that her life had been in danger." Glanville, having directed Roberts to care for Bellmour, "flew to Lady *Bella*'s Apartment" and finds her "raving as in a strong Delirium." Again, he sends for physicians and also sends a messenger to his father, who arrives on the scene "amaz'd to the last Degree at two such terrible Accidents" (358). And he is not alone in his linking what the narrator calls "these Two extraordinary Incidents" (360).

By establishing this equivalence between Glanville's sword fight and Arabella's leap, Lennox broadens and refines her criticism of the romances. In his "Rage," Glanville almost kills another man, a man whom, it turns out, his sister loves. In her folly, Arabella almost kills herself. The romance tradition, as Arabella repeatedly describes it, valorizes combat. Lennox, in Glanville's case, shows the duel to be no more than mad violence done by a sword, violence that is needless. The Old Testament patriarchs, from David through Nimrod, are great warriors and use physical combat to resolve their disputes, but Glanville fights rather than duels. Lennox positions him just outside the patriarchal tradition and proves him a worthy husband for Arabella through his learning to read her signs, not through his physical power.

The lesson Arabella must learn is similar but more complicated. Doody rightly observes that Arabella uses the romances to express her power, but she fails to add that women in romances achieve power only as the objects of competition between men.[26] Trapped in rural isolation (in this they very much resemble the maidens of romances) and surrounded by the power of the marquis, Arabella and her mother must find consolation/empowerment where they can, and the romances serve them well in this regard. However, the heroines of La Calpranede, de Scudery, and Gueret all are objects and/or victims of the "gaze" of men.[27] Lennox calls upon Arabella to learn that her models cannot bring her the independence that she seeks. But this is not the same as learning to submit to "paternal authority."

"These Two extraordinary Incidents" reveal the decline of patriarchy in a social (dueling) and a literary (the romance tradition) manifestation. This should not surprise us, as the action of *The Female Quixote* is both initiated and shaped by first the political, then the reproductive failure of the marquis. We also should not be surprised that the decline of the patriarch affects differently Glanville and Arabella. Glanville, although frightened by the result of his actions, metes out physical punishment rather than suffering it. Glanville's "shock" at Sir George's condition, while sincere, quickly is replaced by his "Agonies" about Arabella. The combat recedes into insignificance for him because he stands outside patriarchal custom, at least as characters as grand as the marquis embody it. His father only an ex-soldier, Glanville has no claim to the "Quality" that an heiress like Arabella ("one of the best Matches in England" [202]) might expect. He always is in the position of a nephew/cousin, considered as a possible husband for Arabella only because no heir exists in the male line. Patrilinear succession holds little opportunity for him, and Lennox, thus, has him mishandle the circumstances of (and find no satisfaction in) his combat.

Arabella's case is very different from Glanville's. Because of her wealth and status, she can read people as she pleases, converting gardeners into princes, thieves into cavaliers. She repeatedly relies upon her "Quality" (105, 111, 114) to extricate her from any confusion or difficulty created by her idiosyncratic reading of signs. But her Thames leap is so excessive that it removes her from the protection offered by her status. Her conversion by the virtuous clergyman follows the leap, but only because she is ready for it to occur. Her explanation of why she is ready places her conversion outside the simple abstraction "paternal authority":

> Having been so lately on the Brink of that State, in which all Distinctions but that of Goodness are destroy'd, I have not yet recover'd so

much levity, but that I would yet rather hear Instruction than Compliments . . . I expect you will exert the *Authority of your Function*, and I promise you on my Part, *Sincerity and Submission*. (370, my italics)

Having nearly killed herself, Arabella is ready to change, but her physical distress—"Fever," "fainting"—figures the rapidity and intensity of this event. Glanville has been changing throughout the book, and his physical and emotional distress during his crisis are correspondingly diminished. For Arabella, who is ready to defend her leap as "exactly conformable to the Rules of Heroick Virtue" (368), the "Instruction," however eagerly sought, will not come easily.

The lesson, however, is the same in both "extraordinary Incidents": "the Rules of Heroick Virtue" no longer fit the lives of characters like Glanville and Arabella. They approach the truth very differently, but their differences are social rather than gender specific. In his discussion with Arabella, "the good Divine" maintains "the severity of the Sacerdotal Character" (369) and rings all the obvious changes upon the topic of the romances. They are dismissed, not because they are fictions but because they are "senseless Fictions" (374). They are "senseless Fictions," "empty Fictions," because, as Arabella herself observes, they encourage "the Crime of deliberate unnecessary Bloodshed" (381)—that is, they encourage Glanville's crime, the physical combat to which Arabella urges her suitors.[28]

As the "good Divine" distinguishes for Arabella between virtuous and "senseless Fictions," he refers to Johnson's *Rambler* No. 4 and to Richardson's achievement in *Clarissa*. As the divine rehabilitates fiction from the disrepute into which the romances bring it, he points to Arabella's achievement in her marriage to Glanville. Cured of her obsession with the romances in the novel's penultimate chapter, in its final chapter Arabella weds Glanville. Doody rightly sees the two events as interrelated. Arabella must drop her romance expectations and standards before she will find any suitor suitable. She must give up not, as Gallagher would have it, her resistance to fiction (175), but rather her resistance to her father's fictionalization of kinship. Because Glanville was the choice of Arabella's father, Doody also claims that Arabella's disavowal of the romances prefaces her submission to "paternal authority." But the point of the divine's "Instruction" is that other fictions are available, other fictions can teach "the Passions to move at the Command of Virtue" (377).

By the standards that held among the elite in eighteenth-century England, the marquis, when he first proposes a marriage between Glanville and Arabella, is not exerting "paternal authority" as much as he is attempting to compensate for its failings. In finally agreeing to the marriage, Arabella stands not as her father's victim but as his coadjutor. Two-thirds of the estate already hers, she completes the story that her father started. In his long-suffering, Jack Tripperesque interpreting of Arabella to the world, Glanville has proven himself worthy of this fiction. And thus Lennox concludes the story by emphasizing that Glanville and Arabella transcend both biological and social imperatives. Sir George marries Miss Glanville, but it is a marriage of convenience: "They were privileged to join Fortunes, Equipages, Titles, and Expence; while Mr. *Glanville* and *Arabella* were united, as well in these, as in every Virtue and laudable Affection of the Mind" (383). Glanville has learned to share a sign system with Arabella, and, in this last action, this marriage, he shares a fiction.

The marquis might wish to burn Arabella's books, but he does not; he might wish to control her choice of a husband, but he cannot. The great scenes in *The Female Quixote* take place outside the presence of the marquis. Whether in Arabella's "Day at the Races" or her appearance at Bath, these scenes generate comedy from Glanville's frantic attempts to hide Arabella's "Madness" by mediating between her and the people whom she alternately amuses and astounds. The most commonplace events can require tortuous physical and mental accommodations from Glanville. Even before the "Races (or, as Arabella called them, the [Olympic] Games)," Glanville interrupts a conversation between his sister and Arabella: "Fearing his Sister would make some absurd Answer, and thereby disoblige his Cousin, [he] took up the Discourse: And turning it upon *Grecian* History, engrossed her [Arabella's] Conversation, for two Hours, wholly to himself" (83). Glanville must find a topic that Arabella likes, lest she reveal how different she is and come into conflict with his sister. At the "Races," he must work between Arabella's unique take on the event ("who fancied the Jockeys were Persons of great Distinction") and his sister's "malicious" and "impertinent" responses to Arabella. In this role he adumbrates John Ritter's version of physical comedy, "filled with Confusion and Spite, [he] sat biting his Lips" (84). The situation both elicits and, since it is comic, absorbs Glanville's anxiety. At times Arabella is "so wholly taken up with . . . the Races" that she misses Miss Glanville's "sarcastic

Answer[s]"; at times Miss Glanville and Sir George (who comes upon the scene here) are so involved in the former's "little Coquetries" that they fail to hear Arabella's "odd Speech." But Glanville hears it all. Having fallen in love with Arabella, his sensibility has become both broad and acute enough to see her beauty and the potential for conflict that resides within it. For Arabella, the jockey who wins the first two courses is a "gallant Man" (85), "a very extraordinary Person" in disguise, a hero who eventually will be "obliged to fight a single Combat with one of those Persons whom he had worsted at those Games" (86). Bellmour does not bother to learn the jockey's name (85), and Miss Glanville tries to correct Arabella's misunderstanding: "As for the Heroes, or Jockeys, call them what you please, I believe they have very little Share either of the Profit or Glory: For their Masters have the one, and the Horses the other" (83).

Striving to prevent Arabella's idiosyncrasy from appearing mad or creating conflict, Glanville proposes "returning to the Castle." He wants to move the company away from the events upon which Arabella has such an odd take. But the arrangements for their leave-taking become complicated, frustrating, and, finally, comical. Miss Glanville does not wish "to part so soon" with Sir George; Sir George, "surprised" by the invitation to visit the castle, must make arrangements for his horse. Even as the company proceeds to the castle, Arabella continues to "talk of the Games, *as she called them*" (my italics), so Glanville's purpose is defeated even as he barely achieves what he took to be the means to it. As the scene concludes, he finds himself in a position quite typical for him. He is not defeated, but he has exhausted his patience, used up all his devices in his attempt to contain Arabella's daftness:

> Poor Glanville, who was excessively confused, endeavoured to change the Discourse, not without Apprehension, that every Subject he could think of, would afford *Arabella* an Occasion of shewing her Foible; which notwithstanding the Pain it gave him, could not lessen his Love. (86)

In the course of the narrative, Glanville's position does not change. When Arabella confuses highwaymen for cavaliers, "Mr. *Glanville*, to avoid a longer Dispute, changed the Discourse; having observed with Confusion that Sir *Charles*, and his Sister seemed to look upon his beloved Cousin as one that was out of her Senses" (259). When the fop Tinsel claims that Arabella is "certainly a little out of her Senses," Glanville tries unsuccessfully to direct Arabella away from romance history and warns Tinsel not to sneer at her "or I'll despoil it [Tinsel's face] of a nose" (303). When Glanville makes the mistake of taking Arabella to Vauxhall, she reads masquerade appearance as reality and, in an astonishing scene, confuses an intoxicated prostitute, "disguis'd in a Suit of . . . Boy's Cloaths" (334), for a fine lady in distress. Arabella demands the prostitute be treated as a lady. Her oddity draws a crowd, whose members at first play along with her demands but then begin to offer her "Whispers and Scoffs." A near riot ensues when Arabella threatens to take the "Fair Maid" away from the "Sea-Officer" who has purchased her favors. Again Glanville, while "almost mad with Vexation" (336), tries simultaneously to "pacify" Arabella and to remove her from the scene.

While this last incident leaves Glanville "groaning aloud thro' Impatience at her Absurdities" (338), it leads his father to conclude that "she was absolutely mad" and to "debate . . . whether he ought to bring a Commission of Lunacy against her." Glanville will not let his father pursue this option, quickly exacting from him a promise "he would do nothing in relation to his Niece that he [Glanville Jr.] would not approve of." But his father does "expostulate" with Glanville Jr. "on the Absurdity of her Behaviour and the Ridicule to which she expos'd herself wherever she went." He asks his son "whether in a Wife he could think those Follies supportable, which in a Mistress occasion'd him so much Confusion." Glanville Jr. acknowledges that Arabella must change before he can marry her—"the Whims her Romances had put into her Head" must be "eraz'd" (339). He expects her to bring her fictions into line with "a better Knowledge of Life and Manners" (339–40), but he does not dismiss fiction entirely. He seeks from her the mediation that he has made, however comically and unsuccessfully, as he alternately has striven to "pacify" her and to protect her from the "scorn" of those around her. That Glanville incurs considerable risk in thus protecting Arabella perhaps appears most clearly in the judgment of Tinsel, who asserts of her that "the wisest Thing a Man can do is to keep out of her Way" (303).

In his capacity both to understand and to value Arabella's "Follies," despite her tendency to drive him "almost mad with Vexation" (336), Glanville passes great tests to win her. The tests are not the heroic jousts and sword battles for which Arabella

yearns, but they are difficult nonetheless: Tinsel and Selvin, intimidated by both Arabella's oddity and her strength, will not take on
the challenge that Glanville faces; Bellmour, in assuming that he
need only give the romances "back to" Arabella, misunderstands
the test. One hardly can chastise writers who make much of
volume 9, chapter 11, the dialogue between "the good Divine"
and Arabella, in which she is "cured." The text claims that this is
the *"best Chapter in this History"* (368). The Reverend John
Mitford's theory that Samuel Johnson wrote the chapter,[29] the
suggestion that Mrs. Lennox needed Dr. Johnson to finish her
book—these become inflammatory claims at a time when
"patriarchal power" operates as a compelling simple abstraction.
Both Arabella and her creator, for all their brilliance and beauty,
finally are co-opted, it seems, by men. But Arabella's cure, as we
have seen, only comes when she is ready to "submit" to it. It only
comes after Glanville has shown himself tolerant enough to read
her "Signs" and strong enough, during the dangerous confusion
created by the masquerading prostitute, to challenge them; in the
midst of the confusion at Vauxhall, he will "Whisper" to her, "Are
you mad, Madam . . . to make all this Rout about a Prostitute? Do
you see how every body stares at you?" (336).

   Glanville is Arabella's comic foil throughout the narrative—
much as Jack Tripper is Chrissie's—feeling "Vexation" and
"Confusion" and repeatedly bearing the full brunt of Arabella's
"Absurdities." As he submits, however uneasily and comically, to
the authority of her "Signs," he counterweighs her submission to
the "good Divine" and helps to define the book's great action.
Most critics are rightly chary of allowing authors to be the sole
judges of their own works; most authors are loath to single out
one chapter as their "best." We should be skeptical of Lennox's
chapter heading (if it is Lennox's) just as we should move beyond
interpretations that center upon that chapter. *The Female Quixote*
cannot be summarized or concluded by a single late chapter, for
Lennox is a master of "situation comedy," comedy that may
exhaust itself but that can never end. "Arabella visits the Races,"
"Arabella visits Vauxhall," "Arabella visits Richmond"—the
episodes unfold with brilliant ease once Lennox in her early
scenes ("Arabella and Mr. Hervey," "Arabella and the Gardener,"
"Arabella and Mrs. Morris") sets the formula.

   The novel transcends the sitcom, however, in its presentation of
Glanville Jr., who finally becomes more than a Jack Tripper
nebbish, but who is overlooked by interpreters as different as

Doody and Gallagher. In the early episodes, the episodes prior to the death of the marquis, the comedy follows from Arabella's misperceptions; Lennox has a "one-joke" book. But the later comedy derives from Glanville's attempt to work between Arabella's "Whimsy" and "a better Knowledge of Life and Manners." As he attempts to win Arabella's love, Glanville initiates a comedy of courtship, a comedy in which both parties must submit, after inevitable confusion and misunderstanding, to each other's "Authority," to each other's "Signs." While it may be the "best" chapter in *The Female Quixote*, volume 9, chapter 11, is neither typical nor definitive of the novel as a whole.

The important work of the book is done in those chapters that place Glanville and Arabella in their basic "situation." When Glanville marries Arabella, he neither vindicates nor embodies "paternal authority"; after all, he has defeated his father's attempts to incarcerate this very odd girl. Rather, his marriage to Arabella brings the two of them together in a fiction that has broad social relevance. This fiction originates with Arabella's father, as he attempts to compensate for the impairment of "paternal authority" and to keep intact an estate that otherwise would be broken by his failure to father a son. In the fiction, the marquis's nephew becomes his son, becomes a legitimate male heir. But the fiction can work only with Arabella's consent, and Glanville can become a partner in the fiction only after long practice reading, if not the romances themselves, then Arabella's version of them.

In elevating Glanville, the marriage normalizes the otherwise revolutionary version of status that Arabella's imaginings create; she turns gardeners into princes, prostitutes into ladies. However admirable her concern for these characters (particularly the prostitute) Arabella's masquerade—her turning class distinctions upside down—finally cannot be vindicated by Lennox, who also has Arabella rely continually upon her "Quality" to defend her "Absurdities." The elevation of Glanville is not at such a great distance and, given the tests he passes, hardly subverts Arabella's claims to status. The masquerade at Vauxhall stimulates Arabella's maddest spasm of romancing and almost lands her in an asylum. It reveals that she must temper her fictionalizing, direct it to both more conventional and more "useful" purposes. That she suffers physical trauma in the change only reveals how much careful treatment by Glanville she required before the divine could complete her transformation.

The fiction created by Arabella and Glanville discountenances the incest taboo—a taboo that elsewhere is in force. Midway through the narrative, Arabella begins "to entertain Suspicions, that never would have entered any Imagination but hers" (161). These are that her uncle and guardian "was become the Rival of his own Son." Arabella, as always, finds "precedents in her Romances of Passions full as strange and unjustifiable," but these precedents only enforce the moral taint of this "unlawful Love," "this impious Flame" (164). Even in her baseless suspicion of Glanville Sr., Arabella's moral compass is steady; incestuous relations are improper. She is afraid to speak "in private" with her guardian and blames Glanville Jr. for not staying with her during a brief interview with her uncle. Even at the moment Glanville Jr. brings Arabella to understand that his father proposes for his son, not for himself, Arabella persists in believing that Glanville Sr. once risked "the most unjustifiable conduct imaginable" (203). Yet, in line with the standards of the 1761 Prayer Book, she expresses no anxiety about marriage to her first cousin. The fiction upon which Arabella and her father collaborate is protean in the identities it confers upon Glanville; the nephew becomes the son, the cousin becomes the suitor, then husband. Glanville's adaptability, as evidenced in various comic episodes with Arabella, qualifies him for these metamorphoses.

As Twitchell has shown, the English elite shifted the terms of the incest taboo in the eighteenth century (even as they enforced strictures against consanguineous marriages upon their lessers).[30] Royal families became notoriously inbred; Lord Byron feared revelations about his homosexual relationships but gloried in his physical bond with his half sister. The Stones' history and Lennox's fiction show why the "nature" of incest had to change. Family continuity, even in the case of a girl as "whimsical" as Arabella, outweighed old compunctions. Arabella's marriage to her first cousin gives "use" to her imaginings—to her ability to make people into what they are not. To marry Glanville, Arabella must end her romancing, but her fictionalizing continues, for to join their "Fortunes, Equipages, Titles," she and Glanville "unite" every "laudable Affection of the Mind"—that is, they learn (most of the learning done by the socially disadvantaged Glanville) each other's signs. That Arabella participates in what was becoming a conventional response to demographic crisis in no way impugns her imaginativeness or her beauty, in no way lessens her—at least in Glanville's eyes.

III

Lennox's is an early and comic portrayal of consanguineous marriage as a strategy for dealing with failure in patrilinear succession; Inchbald's *A Simple Story* comes later, near century's end, and broods upon the topic, works over it with disturbing, even haunting ambivalence.[31] Inchbald adds up the cost of the fictionalizing that Lennox celebrates and suggests that it finally may be too much to pay. Unlike Lennox and Burney (at least the Burney of *Evelina*), Inchbald, an actress before she was a novelist, sees the danger in theatricality to which Robert Lovelace is blind: in fictionalizing kinship relations, both authors and the social elite may deprive them of substance. Inchbald understands that once the "fictive" daughter becomes the equal of the "real" daughter, then kinship becomes part of a process rather than a truth fixed by a (phal)logos. As kinship loses its essence, Inchbald, writing at the end of the eighteenth century, asks whether marriage to a cousin is a necessary or attractive means to maintain the fiction of patrilinear succession. She thus follows Burney's treatment of the Delviles in *Cecelia*, that poor but proud family, in their unbending preservation of their "name," appearing at best foolish, at worst satanic.

Castle, Spacks, Craft-Fairchild, and Ty read the two parts of *A Simple Story* as Inchbald's means to question but then submit to, in Jane Spencer's phrase, "patriarchal tyranny."[32] While their estimations of tone differ, they agree that the second half of the novel apologizes for the boldness of the first: Miss Milner's wit and sexuality—her self-assertiveness—are replaced by her daughter's passivity and reticence. This reading has at least one great virtue; it shows that the seventeen-year gap between Miss Milner's story and her daughter's is not owing to some failure in narrative skill on Inchbald's part. But Mathilda, for all her much-discussed weakness, is free, at the story's end, to decide if she will sustain, via marriage to her first cousin Harry Rushbrook, a fictive version of patrilinear succession. Whether she does so is left to the reader to imagine, not to the father to control. While critics who operate from within the simple abstraction "patriarchal authority" emphasize the disparity between the book's two halves—the different personalities of Miss Milner and Mathilda—Dorriforth, the guardian, then husband, then father, appears in both parts. He is present but, revealingly enough, not constant because his life is distorted by the failures of other men to produce heirs. In his erratic, sometimes violent course, Inchbald reveals, as she does in Miss Milner's unhappy end, the cost of those "pious fictions" of kinship practiced by the eighteenth-century elite.

The claim that *A Simple Story* is about "patriarchal tyranny" leads to the question of who the patriarch is. The answer seems clear enough: Dorriforth, the rule maker, the dueler, the erstwhile priest is the patriarch. But once we identify Dorriforth as the patriarch, the story stops being "simple." For if Dorriforth tyrannizes over Miss Milner and Mathilda (a claim that deserves scrutiny), he is no less the victim of the requirements of patrilinear succession, having to give up both his priestly calling and his name to maintain his family's title and estates. While Miss Milner is ever Miss Milner,[33] and Mathilda always Mathilda, Dorriforth becomes Lord Elmwood. How should we refer to him? This problem with nomenclature only betokens a specific problem that Dorriforth/ Elmwood faces: how to know himself as a man in a time when the patriarch, rather than exerting clear authority, dies without male issue. Dorriforth/Elmwood behaves badly because he would hold to traditional notions of personal honor at a time when kinship relations are becoming "pious fictions," and the words "father," "daughter," "son," "husband," and "wife" are losing their claims to essential and unchanging meanings. Dorriforth/Elmwood does not have the flexibility or the comic potential of Glanville. His sense of personal "honour" manifests itself in startlingly different ways because, while Dorriforth/Elmwood would be ever the same, demographic crisis is changing the world around him.

Spencer, who points out that Dorriforth/Elmwood provides "the necessary link between the first and second halves of the story" (xviii), adds that he does not change between the two parts but rather becomes "a heightened version of the tyrant he always was" (xix). In this she follows Spacks, who claims that the two-part story eliminates Miss Milner and with her "the presence and the possibility of passionate, energetic femaleness." Spacks thus reads Inchbald's portrayal of Dorriforth/Elmwood as "tacitly" endorsing "the necessity of dominant maleness" (1990, 201). Dorriforth/Elmwood does change little in the course of the narrative, but his constancy resides in his inability to exert effectively the authority that Spacks and Spencer attribute to him. By observing the failures in patrilinear succession that victimize Dorriforth/ Elmwood, we can see one basis for Castle's portrayal of Inchbald as an antiauthoritarian writer who offers a carnivalesque rendering of male-female relationships and thus empowers female desire. Castle, however, sees Inchbald's subversiveness ending with Miss Milner; I believe it is "tacit" but even more powerful in Mathilda's contemplation of marriage with her cousin, the feckless Harry Rushbrook.

Should she choose to marry Rushbrook, Mathilda will resolve the conflicting claims of herself and her cousin to the Elmwood estate. All power resides with Mathilda in this instance. In the midst of his proposal, she asks Rushbrook if "Lord Elmwood" knows of his intentions, and Rushbrook replies, "I boldly told him of my presumptuous love, and he has yielded to you alone, the power over my happiness or misery" (337). Dorriforth/Elmwood detaches himself from this courtship for good reason. By the standards of patrilinear succession, neither Rushbrook nor Mathilda has a solid claim to his estate. Rushbrook is "the child of a once beloved sister [of Dorriforth's], who married a young officer against her brother's consent" (34). After the deaths of Rushbrook's parents, Dorriforth "maintained [the child but] would never see him" (34). After the death of Miss Milner, Elmwood will maintain Mathilda but refuse to see her.

Rushbrook provides an early instance of Miss Milner's subverting Dorriforth's authority. She introduces the child into Dorriforth's presence, and he, "highly pleased with his engaging wiles, and applicable replies, took him on his knee and kissed him with affection." When the child reveals his name, Dorriforth's authority is compromised by his physical position, and his attempt to rescue his rule involves him in a scene both comic and pathetic:

> Dorriforth was holding him fondly round the waist as he stood with his feet upon his knees; and at this reply he did not throw him from him—but he removed his hands, which supported him, so suddenly, that the child to prevent falling on the floor, threw himself about his uncle's neck ... his uncle took hold of each hand that had twined around him, and placed him immediately on the ground. (35–36)

As Dorriforth attempts to maintain his power over his sister—to support financially but to avoid seeing her child—he acts ludicrously, even irrationally. The image of Dorriforth "unwrapping" the child from him emphasizes that he struggles against his own "affection" for Rushbrook—against a part of himself.

As Dorriforth/Elmwood becomes Miss Milner's suitor instead of her guardian, his authority, already slight and awkward, diminishes. He reconciles himself to Rushbrook and begins to fictionalize kinship relations. When Miss Milner, after a visit to Rushbrook, tells Dorriforth/Elmwood that it "pain[s]" her "to leave the child behind" (150), he tells her to bring the child "home": "If you desire it, this shall be his home—you shall be a mother, and I will, henceforward, be a father to him." Thereafter "whenever Lord Elmwood wished to shew a kindness to Miss Milner, without directing it immediately to her, he took his nephew upon his knee, talked to him, and told him, he 'Was glad they had become acquainted.'" The narrator describes this episode as one of "the various, though delicate, struggles for power between Miss Milner and her guardian" (151). Miss Milner wins the struggle in Rushbrook's case, and her victory has complex significance. On one hand, she reminds Dorriforth of his duty to family, to his sister's child; on the other, she brings Lord Elmwood to accept, even to actively espouse a "pious fiction": "You will be a mother . . . I . . . a father to him." Miss Milner's triumph, then, is not that she replaces biological versions of kinship with fictive; rather, her triumph resides in her showing the biological and the fictive to be irremediably intertwined. Dorriforth can unwrap himself from the frightened embrace of young Harry Rushbrook, but he cannot absent himself from the exigencies and confusions of family to which the deaths of Mr. Milner and the previous Lord Elmwood expose him.

Mathilda's claim to Elmwood's estate is as confused as Rushbrook's. Because of her mother's liaison with the Duke of Avon, Elmwood forms "the unshaken resolution never to acknowledge Lady Mathilda as his child" (202) and makes Rushbrook his heir. But Rushbrook will inherit only Elmwood's estates and not his name because, as Elmwood points out, "Could any thing but a son have preserved my title?" (214). When Lady Elmwood dies without a "will" (207), choosing to "submit" all decisions about Mathilda's future to Elmwood, she is not behaving as passively as she might seem. As in the first half of the story, she forces Dorriforth/Elmwood to deal with a child whom he would rather pretend does not exist. In a posthumous letter, she asks Dorriforth/Elmwood to "protect" Mathilda "for her grandfather's sake." She writes to Dorriforth/Elmwood as "Miss Milner your ward, to whom you never refused a request" and asks this favor "not now for your nephew Rushbrook, but for one so much more dear [to me]" (211).

Her appeal is both complicated and, at first, only partially successful. On one hand, Miss Milner appeals to her husband's friendship with her father, the bond that brought her to Dorriforth as his ward. She emphasizes the value that she gives to kinship, indicating that her feelings for Mathilda are more powerful than those for Rushbrook and implying that Elmwood's should be as well. But at the heart of the letter lies an assumption that kinship relations can be written (in this case, rewritten). She presents herself to Elmwood not as his wife but as his ward, suggesting that she can move between identities rather than be tied to one. At one point she asks, "Be her host: I remit the tie of being her parent" (211), suggesting that Mathilda's identity is as mutable and writable as her own. Elmwood picks up on this appeal, deciding to give Milner's "grandchild the sanction of my protection" (213). Mathilda moves into his home without being acknowledged by him as his daughter. Elmwood, then, tries to exert his will in this matter by establishing rules; he will "grant" Miss Milner's request that he protect Mathilda, but only "in the strictest sense . . . no farther; and one neglect of my commands, releases my promise totally." Those "commands" require that Mathilda "avoids my sight, or the giving me any remembrance of her . . . if . . . I ever see or hear from her; that moment my compliance to her mother's supplication ceases, and I abandon her once more" (213). When the neighbors learn the terms upon which Mathilda lives in her father's house, they pay her no visits. They suppose he wants there to be "no notice whatever that she lived among them: and as Lord Elmwood's will was law all around, such was the consequence of his will being known or supposed" (221).

As Dorriforth/Elmwood offers his "commands," he does appear both a "patriarch" and a "tyrant." His "will" is "law" but only, we should note, in denying his presence to Mathilda. In his "commands," Dorriforth/Elmwood attempts to remove himself from the intermingling of fictive and natural versions of kinship to which Miss Milner exposes him in her reintroduction of Dorriforth/Elmwood first to his nephew, then to his daughter. For all the formidability that he musters in outlining the conditions of Mathilda's residency with him, Dorriforth/Elmwood's position depends upon a breathtakingly thin fiction: that he can protect his friend's ("a name I reverence," 213) "grandchild" without acknowledging her as his child. He tries, in other words, to act without reference to biological ties. Finally, as Dorriforth/Elmwood offers his "commands," while he may appear a tyrant, he actually has fairly common and not very authoritarian motives. He will not permit Mathilda to be mentioned "in his hearing" because he does not wish "to remind himself of happiness he could never taste again, and of ingratitude that might impel him to hatred." He will not risk forming "another attachment near to his heart; more especially so near as a parent's, which might a second time expose him to all the torments of ingratitude, from one whom he affectionately loved" (202). Dorriforth/Elmwood offers his "commands" not out of strength and confidence but out of fear and hurt.

In her adulterous relationship with Lord Avon (the action that defines Mathilda's status at the opening of the second half of the story) Lady Elmwood also mixes up the versions of kinship that Dorriforth/Elmwood wishes to keep separate. Lord Avon is the erstwhile Lord Frederick Lawnly, "who next to Lord Elmwood, was ever of all her lovers most prevalent in her heart." Lawnly has become Avon because of "the decease of his father and eldest brother" (198). He is in his position because, as they do throughout *A Simple Story*, men fail to produce legitimate male issue; he comes to his estate and title free of paternal constraint, able to pursue liaisons at his pleasure. But Lawnly is not alone in standing outside patriarchal supervision. After four years of "the most perfect enjoyment of happiness, the marriage state could give . . . Lord Elmwood was then under the indispensable necessity of leaving them [his wife and daughter] . . . in order to save from the depredation of his steward, a very large estate in the West Indies" (196). This is not the first time Elmwood has left Miss Milner to her own devices. When they come up to London prior to their marriage, "a lawsuit and some other intricate affairs that came with his title and estate, frequently kept Lord Elmwood from his house part of the day; sometimes the whole evening; and when at home would often closet him for hours with his lawyers." Miss Milner, "to hasten on the tedious hours that intervened . . . varied and diverted them with . . . many recreations her intended husband could not approve" (140)—including the "masquerade" that almost leads to their breaking off their engagement.[34]

The London period is brief, and Sandford watches over Miss Milner during it, but Elmwood's three-year absence in the Indies leads her, "in spite of his injunctions, to divert the melancholy hours his absence caused, by mixing in the gayest circles of London" (196). Eventually she succumbs to Lawnly/Avon's "art and industry" (198). In both instances—one merely dangerous, one finally fatal—Miss Milner is a victim not of Elmwood's tyranny but of his absence. Dorriforth/Elmwood is "detained abroad" in part because of a "severe and dangerous illness," which he does not reveal to his wife. He sends lame if "frequent apologies for not returning," but these only increase his lady's "resentment" (196) and thus her vulnerability. Lady Elmwood's liaison, then, begins in her lord's weakness (illness), which extends his absence: an absence required by the "title and estate" Elmwood has inherited. Whatever suzerainty the patriarch once might have claimed, Elmwood finds himself in the midst of "intricate affairs" managed by lawyers. In the absence of legitimate patrilinear succession, lawyers and "pious fictions" must keep the estate whole.

Dorriforth/Elmwood's refusal to acknowledge his daughter is owing to events that have as much to do with the impairment of his authority—through illness, absence, and inattention—as they have to do with his wife's sexuality. To acknowledge Mathilda as his daughter and heir, he also would have to acknowledge other versions of his lady's story. In a brilliant small touch, Inchbald places a newspaper obituary in her text and thus challenges Dorriforth/Elmwood's sovereignty as the interpreter of the events of his marriage. The newspaper attributes the "separation" of Lord and Lady Elmwood to the "consequences" of Elmwood's going abroad and leaving "a most captivating young woman . . . without a protector" (204).

Mathilda's history not only reveals Dorriforth/Elmwood to be a weak, frequently absent authority; it also emphasizes the pervasiveness of demographic crisis. Mathilda is, her mother notes in her posthumous letter, "the last and only remaining branch of his [Mr. Milner's] family" (211). Like Robert Lovelace, Mathilda conjoins several family lines on the verge of extinction. She not only is the last Milner but also, with the problematic exception of Harry Rushbrook, the last Dorriforth/Elmwood as well. If he truly represented the "extreme of patriarchal tyranny," Dorriforth/Elmwood would negotiate his daughter's marriage. That he stands aside in this instance reveals how little his version of authority has to do with either Rushbrook (who wiggles out of his uncle's several attempts to marry him) or Mathilda, both of whom come into Dorriforth/Elmwood's presence through the good offices of Miss Milner's fictions.

Terry Castle claims that Inchbald brings Dorriforth/Elmwood "to forego austerity and emotional detachment for a new life of passion and adhesiveness."[35] However, if we recall Dorriforth unwrapping himself from young Harry Rushbrook's embrace, we may wonder if this is the case; "adhesiveness" hardly seems a trait of Dorriforth/Elmwood, a man who frequently is *not* present. Called to the bedside of his dying friend and fellow Roman Catholic, Dorriforth receives Milner's "injunctions," one of which "restrained him from all authority to direct his ward in one religious opinion contrary to those her mother professed, and in which she herself had been educated" (5). Dorriforth enters into his guardianship stripped of any "authority" that his priesthood might give him. In a move that initiates his persistent tendency to be absent, he misses Milner's funeral. While Miss Milner, who has been away at Bath and not informed of her father's condition, "flew to pay her last duty to his remains and performed it with the truest filial love ... Dorriforth, upon important business, was obliged to return to town." Even before he meets Miss Milner, Dorriforth fears "he had undertaken a task he was too weak to execute—the protection of a young woman of fashion" (6). During his preparations for his first meeting with her, he goes so far as to claim, "I wish I had never known her father" (10). The same father who gives Dorriforth "authority" over his daughter almost simultaneously deprives him of the means to exert it.

Besides emphasizing Dorriforth/Elmwood's absences, Inchbald also renders problematic his behavior in those instances in which he would assert himself actively. As in *The Female Quixote*, references to dueling in *A Simple Story* reveal both how superannuated and how unhelpful patriarchal traditions have become. Dorriforth participates in two duels and spurns a chance to enter another. The first occurs because he, in the midst of a physical confrontation created by his attempting to stop Lord Frederick Lawnly from visiting Miss Milner, strikes Lawnly "a blow in the face" (61). Even before he receives a formal challenge from Lawnly, Dorriforth feels great "remorse" for having "departed from my character—from the sacred character, and dignity of my profession and sentiments—I have departed from myself.—I am no longer the philosopher, but the ruffian" (62). Castle might note that Miss Milner, who by her own account is only trifling with Lawnly, here causes Dorriforth to lose his "character." In a carnivalesque metamorphosis, he changes from "philosopher" to "ruffian." Dorriforth, however, attempts to resolve this confusion, to escape it, by agreeing to "atone for this outrage in whatever manner he [Lawnly] may choose, and the law of justice and equity (though in this one instance, contrary to the law of religion) enjoins, that if he demands my life in satisfaction for his wounded honour, it is his due" (63). In short, if Lawnly asks for a duel, Dorriforth will grant him one but will not fight.

This episode defines Dorriforth's character in several important ways. First, although he fails to maintain his priestly "character," this does not lead him to doubt the validity or worth of that "character." Rather, he seeks to defend it in a difficult circumstance by absenting himself from the event to which his failure has led. He will be *at* the duel, but he will not be *in* it. Second, Dorriforth acts here upon a notion of personal honor that is powerful but also difficult to define. Sandford, upon hearing of the duel, vehemently argues that Dorriforth, as a priest, cannot participate. Miss Milner, upon learning of it, falsely tells Dorriforth that she is in love with Lawnly, in the hope that he will not fight the man who means so much to her. Dorriforth, however, takes this as only one more reason to show up but not fight. Neither his "character" as priest nor his "character" as Miss Milner's guardian require or even allow Dorriforth to meet Lawnly. But for all his fealty to those two roles, Dorriforth acts outside of them; he refers to a "law of justice and equity" that governs his choice, but the basis for this law is hard to define, principally because Dorriforth's code of personal honor no longer can find a public counterpart.

When Dorriforth returns from the duel, he shows Miss Milner his wounded arm, claiming, "Lord Frederick is safe . . . and the disgrace of his blow washed away entirely, by a few drops of blood from this arm" (77). Dorriforth believes that if he stages the duel appropriately, he can "wash away" the loss of his "character." He wants to bring his life back to moral clarity rather than to mediate between "socioerotic categories" (Castle 1986, 305). Miss Milner faints away because she loves Dorriforth, not Lawnly, a truth that she only has just revealed to Miss Woodly and of which Dorriforth has no inkling. "In the duel . . . Dorriforth . . . received his antagonist's fire, but positively refused to return it; by which he had kept his promise to not endanger his lordship's life" (79). His bravery is indisputable, but as Lovelace needs no ideology to do evil, so here Dorriforth has no basis (other than his private notion of "equity") for doing good. Most revealing and, finally, most destructive about Dorriforth's duel is that he enters it ready to admit that he was wrong, out of "character" to strike Lawnly. Even before it begins, Dorriforth has emptied the duel of its traditional function: determining the truth and/or value of its participants' claims (Kiernan, 126).

In the second duel, the participants are the same, but their names have changed. Dorriforth now is Lord Elmwood; Lawnly is Lord Avon. Elmwood's motives and justifications would appear to be much clearer and more powerful than Dorriforth's. Lawnly/Avon has committed adultery with Elmwood's wife. Lady Elmwood having fled from meeting her returned Lord, Elmwood turns to "an affair of still weightier importance—that of life or death:—he determined upon his own death, or the death of the man who had wounded his honour and his happiness." As Inchbald presents Elmwood's thinking here, "death" and "honour" precede his decision that "a duel with his old antagonist" (198) must occur. Inchbald undercuts the clarity of Elmwood's decision by creating distance between his absolute and inflexible behavior and the social conventions—including the duel—available to him. She employs a vocabulary that is comparative—"weightier," "more prevalent," "short"—to imply disparity between Elmwood's version of "honour" and the social codes through which he will try to express it.

This second duel also differs from the first in that it, apparently, is fought with swords rather than with pistols. The change in weapons manifests the increasing brutality of the means by which Dorriforth/Elmwood defends his honor. Indeed, he is not interested here in honor as abstractly or even socially understood; he is interested only in killing Lawnly/Avon or being killed himself. As V. G. Kiernan points out, the customs of dueling required that "the weapon had to be an 'honourable' one," this so the elite could distinguish their combats from "plebeian buffets or quarterstaff blows" (141). In one sense, by fighting with a sword, Dorriforth/Elmwood returns to the origins of dueling and seeks his revenge in a "purer" form than Lawnly sought his. But Elmwood's conduct in the duel discredits his sword. Kiernan notes that "duels were less often inspired . . . by the desire to kill or maim an opponent"; "satisfaction" was the goal of the duelist (143). Elmwood operates outside such conventions:

> As Lord Elmwood was inexorable to all accommodation; their engagement lasted for some space of time; nor any thing but the steadfast assurance his opponent was slain, could at last have torn his lordship from the field, though he was mortally wounded.

Believing him dead, Elmwood actually leaves Avon "so maimed and defaced with scars, as never again to endanger the honour of a husband" (198).

Inchbald carefully places the equivocations in this description. Elmwood, we are told, is "mortally wounded," but then he lives. Lawnly/Avon, who stopped his duel after his shot wounded Dorriforth, here finds no "accommodation." What seems a clear vindication of Dorriforth/Elmwood's "honour" becomes an ugly and excessive scene. While swordsmen, particularly continental swordsmen, might display their "scars" with some pride (Kiernan, 203), permanently maiming one's opponent was bad form. And this duel, other than maiming Avon for life, brings no closure; even on what he believes to be his deathbed, Elmwood will not "forgive" his wife or offer a "last blessing" upon his daughter. From the medieval period onward, the duel had as one of its ends the reestablishment of a husband's authority over his wife (Kiernan, 127–30). Elmwood wins a ghastly victory and then, as throughout the story, absents himself from its consequences.

Inchbald makes her final reference to dueling in Elmwood's rescue of Mathilda from Lord Margrave. This scene is narrated from Mathilda's point of view, and the physical conflict is outside the reader's range. She hears "the report of a pistol, and a confusion of persons"—all this deterring Margrave, who has kidnapped her and is just ready to violate her. Her father then enters the room, she falls into his arms, and Margrave quits the scene, calling out, "My Lord Elmwood, if you have any demands on me." To which Elmwood responds, "Would you make me an executioner? The law shall be your only antagonist" (329). If we look here for consistency in Elmwood—if we look for some basis on which he decides that he will "execute" his wife's lover but not his daughter's kidnapper—I think we get nowhere. How can the man to whom critics otherwise as diverse as Castle, Spacks, Spencer, and Ty attribute "patriarchal dictate," "patriarchal authority," and "patriarchal tyranny" suddenly leave his vengeance to "the law"? Inchbald provides no evidence that Elmwood is a changed man, no sign that he has undergone the eighteenth-century equivalent of a "consciousness-raising experience." Rather, what we see in Elmwood is a patriarch who has run amok, a man who, because of the accidents of demographic crisis, has become a leader of a family but who cannot find any viable means for linking his personal sense of honor to more public understandings of the term.

Elmwood's turning of Margrave over to "the law" is an abdication of authority that adumbrates his final and greatest abdication—ceding to Mathilda the decision about Rushbrook's proposal. These abdications apparently come easily for Elmwood and are, by today's standards, good choices. But they are of a piece with his earlier absences. They reflect not "patriarchal tyranny" but rather the extent to which the role of patriarch never has suited Dorriforth/Elmwood. Even before Miss Milner became his ward, even before he became Lord Elmwood in order to save an "ancient title" from becoming "extinct," Dorriforth was a priest whom we never see practice any of the duties of his office. His relation to patriarchy—both before and after his transmutation from Dorriforth to Elmwood—is defined by absence.

His "usual tranquillity" taken from him by the death of Mr. Milner, his name taken from him by "the early death of the late Lord Elmwood" (99), Dorriforth/Elmwood can find no viable model for patriarchal authority outside himself. He runs his estates not through direct command but through lawyers and stewards. His "affairs" are "intricate" and not easily explained. In Castle's terms, Dorriforth/Elmwood "internalizes" his notion of "honour," rendering it impossible to read.[36] This internalization makes his behavior impossible to predict. Neither of his duels is "right"; only in his concluding rejection of a duel for the "law" does he, while contradicting his earlier behavior, do well. Dorriforth/Elmwood remains a powerful but finally problematic figure because while "a certain decorum attended all . . . [his] actions" that decorum is one of which others are "ignorant" (280) or read only with great uncertainty.

Upon hearing of Mathilda's kidnapping by Margrave, Elmwood, who only recently has banished her from his home because a chance meeting between them violated his "command," goes to rescue her. He acts with remarkable laconicity, and his motives are unfathomable. Sandford tries to define the event's significance: "Will you then prove yourself a father?" Elmwood "only" responds "yes" and then absents himself (324). Neither the reader nor Sandford is privy to the internal calculations Elmwood makes of where "honour" now lies. A mere chapter earlier, he is offering commandments about his daughter's exile, "'I solemnly swear,'—he was proceeding with violence" (319)—an "oath" that Sandford barely interrupts. For all the happiness of Mathilda's reunion with her father, a fate like her mother's may await her. With his "honour" "internalized" and his "decorum" unfathomable, Dorriforth/Elmwood can be angered in ways difficult to predict, and his anger will take him outside social conventions that govern dueling or parenting.

Spacks, Spencer, and even Castle emphasize the differences between the two parts of *A Simple Story* in order to establish an omnicompetent "patriarchal power." But while Mathilda may lack her mother's feistiness, Inchbald is at pains to emphasize the continuity between her character and her mother's: "Mathilda's person, shape, and complection were . . . extremely like what her mother's once were." And she returns to her father's house "in her seventeenth year—of the same age, within a year and a few months, of her mother when she became the ward of Dorriforth" (220). Margrave compares his "proposals" for a liaison with Mathilda to those "the Duke of Avon made to her mother" (301). Like her mother before her, Mathilda's life is shaped more by her father's absences than by his dictates. She returns "home" only to encounter a man who, even when he acts for good, neither can explain nor justify his motives. Human relationships become remarkably, even frighteningly unstable in *A Simple Story* (the dynamic of banishment-reconciliation-banishment is unceasing) because *both* the patriarch and the female figure of antiauthoritarianism have "internalized" their motives, thus making them difficult to read.

Inchbald's sympathy with this "interiorization"—her sense that it confers freedom upon both men and women—is obvious.[37] Rescued by her father in "the middle of November," all becomes "green" for Mathilda (331). Inchbald's onomastics are not particularly subtle here: Dorriforth is opened to life and sensuality by Miss Milner, and he becomes Elmwood; the villainous character of social cultivation is Lawnly; the sere voice of religious convention is Sandford; the crucial if finally vacant mediator of misunderstandings is Woodley; before we learn of Rushbrook's love for Mathilda, Elmwood wants him to marry "a rich heiress" and "only child" named "Miss Winterton" (314). With Mathilda's reconciliation to her father, spring comes to her: "The fields to her delighted eye appeared green; the trees in their bloom" (331). But farmers, even incompetent landscapers like myself know well the dangers of spring weather in late autumn, the "false" spring that can fool plants into blossoming, seeds into germinating such that they will freeze and die when winter's cold returns. According to Mrs. Inchbald's nineteenth-century biographer, *A Simple Story* is modeled upon Shakespeare's *The Winter's Tale*, a play which also includes a seventeen-year gap, a play in which Inchbald acted.[38] The fields "appear" green; Rushbrook seems to be rescued from "winter"; Elmwood seems to have come alive. But who is responsible for this appearance, this fiction? And who can be sure this spring will last? Given the hard and obscure "decorum" upon which Dorriforth/Elmwood acts, the tale easily could become "wintry" again.

As the inventor of this fictional "spring," Mathilda finally must decide what value she will give to it—and to fiction in general. In the novel's final scene, the cycle of banishment and reconciliation continues, although a reversal of roles has occurred; Elmwood is ready to banish Rushbrook for his love of Mathilda. She, not knowing of Rushbrook's proposal, defends him as "my relation . . . my companion, my friend" (335–36). Elmwood sends her to meet Rushbrook, to learn "what he has asked of me." He sends her off with the words, "On your will his fate will depend" (336). Attempting to comfort Rushbrook even before she knows what he wants, Mathilda tells him, "His lordship has told me it *shall* be in my power; and has desired me to give, or refuse it to you, at my own pleasure" (337). In the absence of patriarchal mandate (Elmwood, before Rushbrook confesses his love for Mathilda, still plans to give his nephew his estate and to marry him profitably), "power" resides with Mathilda.

During the early stages of Miss Milner's discovery of her love for Dorriforth, the narrator warns against incest, claiming that proper education "would have given such a prohibition to her love, that she had been precluded from it, as by that barrier which divides a brother from a sister" (74). Miss Milner should not love a priest, and only the accidents of demographic crisis finally allow her to love him without breaking a "prohibition." Still, Miss Milner once promises Dorriforth "ever to obey him as her father" (13), and the taint of incest, the sense of violation of taboo, shadows their relationship, particularly in its sad end. Unlike her mother, Mathilda must decide if she will accept the freedom from the incest taboo afforded her by her family's need for a fictive version of kinship. She must decide how much power and hope she will give to rewriting her relationship with her father and with her cousin. Bred in the "school of prudence—though of adversity" (338), Mathilda may have the advantage of her mother, may sense that fictionalized false springs can lead to harsh "Winter's Tales." With the patriarch absent and the "power" in her hands, Mathilda also must decide if she wants a consanguineous marriage that will transform Rushbrook from a "relation" and "companion" into a husband.

In the brilliant reticence of her conclusion, Inchbald suggests that fictive versions of kinship do not serve the heroine's needs and desires. With her future in her "power," Mathilda receives Rushbrook's proposal with surprise: "She started and cried, 'Could Lord Elmwood know for what he sent me?'" (337). She seems to wish for a patriarchal injunction, a category in the Prayer Book that would rescue her from the choice now hers. In the midst of a demographic crisis, must she now prop up the family with a "pious fiction"? Might she have another version of a husband in mind? We cannot know because motive has become internalized in this not-so-simple story. We can say, however, that Inchbald refuses to have Mathilda answer Rushbrook's proposal and, in so doing, suggests that the submission of men and women to fictive versions of kinship—the day for such fictions—has passed. Rushbrook pleads with Mathilda, who has "the power over my happiness or misery," not to "doom me to the latter." Inchbald writes:

> Whether the heart of Mathilda . . . *could* sentence him to misery, the reader is left to surmise—and if he suppose that it did not, he has every reason to suppose their wedded life was a life of happiness. (337)

A consanguineous marriage remains possible here but, Inchbald coyly suggests, not particularly exciting. The compulsion to care for a "fictional" daughter that we witness in Burney, the happiness with a marriage between cousins that we witness in Lennox, the praise of inbreeding as it maintains elite families in the eighteenth century—none of these appear in Inchbald's concluding offer of the story to the reader. "He" may write the story and end it as he pleases. But Inchbald, as she silences Mathilda, does not enforce "patriarchal tyranny." Nor does she anticipate the language of Lacan's *école freudienne.* Unlike Clarissa's silence about her condition, Mathilda's reticence begins in her freedom rather than being a requirement of it. In Mathilda's silence, Inchbald suggests that a more gratifying fiction—for her, for Mathilda—is possible.

Conclusion:
From the Birth Mystery to
the Family Romance: Peter Brooks, Fathers,
and the Motives for Fictions

In *Reading for the Plot*, Peter Brooks claims: "The question of fathers and sons [is] perhaps the dominant thematic and structural concern and shaping force in the nineteenth-century novel, ultimately perhaps constituting a theme and structure incorporate with the very nature of the novel as we know it" (307). Written in the midst of a demographic crisis that only began to ease in the 1750s, eighteenth-century novels stand apart from Brooks's conclusion because they are as likely to raise the question of fathers and daughters as of fathers and sons. As Brooks describes how nineteenth-century novelists deal with "the question of fathers and sons," he suggests an even more important difference between fiction of the eighteenth and nineteenth centuries. Using Freud's essay on "Family Romances" as one basis for his study, Brooks shows how much novels by Dickens, Stendhal, Sue, and others rely upon their characters' "phantas[ies] of being an adopted child whose parents are more exalted creatures than . . . [their] actual parents." Nineteenth-century writers make the "uncertainty of fatherhood" (64) both a great motive and a great theme; insofar as fathers in fictions are inadequate, boring, or absent, their weakness suggests broader questions about political and social authority during the revolutionary decades from 1790 to 1830.

The case of Julien Sorel is particularly telling. Having won Mathilda de la Mole's love, he receives from her father a new name, a commission in the army, and, finally, a large sum of money. All this comes with one important "stipulation," finely summarized by Brooks. The Marquis de la Mole requires Julien

> to consider this a gift from his real (that is natural, illegitimate) father and will donate some of it to his legal father, Sorel the carpenter, who took care of him in childhood. Julien wonders if this fiction of the illegitimate aristocratic father might not be the truth after all: "Might it really be possible, he said to himself, that I am the natural son of some great noble exiled in our mountains by the terrible Napoleon? With every moment the idea seemed less improbable to him. . . . My hatred for my father would be a proof . . . I would no longer be a monster!" (66–67)

The story Julien imagines here is in its broad outline very much like the stories of Tom Jones, Roderick Random, even, in her own way, Clarissa Harlowe—that is, the story of a child who discovers his/her parentage to be both different and better than all had supposed. As Brooks himself points out, Julien's fiction is "an eighteenth-century novel—by a writer such as Fielding or Marivaux—where the hero is a foundling [or, I would add, an orphan heiress] whose aristocratic origins eventually will out . . . Julien's plot could simply be a *nostos*, a homecoming, the least transgressive, the least monstrous of narratives" (67). But *The Red and the Black is* a "Chronicle of 1830," *not* an eighteenth-century novel because Julien's story is a family romance rather than a birth mystery. This is to say that Julien's is a fiction of his own invention and a fiction that he directs to his emotional and social needs. He will use the fiction to prove that he is not a "monster": it "will offer a complete retrospective motivation—and absolution—for his desire to rise in the world" (67). However angry and mistreated they may be, protagonists in eighteenth-century fiction, both male and female, do not think like this.

Their newfound status "happens" to Tom Jones, Joseph Andrews, even to Roderick Random and Humphry Clinker. They do not seek it. Burney's Evelina and Inchbald's Mathilda are even more apposite to Julien. They will win status if they can get their "real" fathers to acknowledge them; that accomplished, they need imagine no others. Julien, whatever guilt he may feel, wants "to rise in the world." In this he departs from the eighteenth-century model as Fielding establishes it in an early scene between Parson Adams and Joseph Andrews:

> The Curate, surprized to find such Instances of Industry and Application in a young Man, who had never met with the least Encourage-

ment, asked him, if he did not extremely regret the want of a liberal Education, and the not having been born of Parents, who might have indulged his Talents and Desire of Knowledge? To which he answered, "he hoped he had profited somewhat better from the Books he had read, than to lament his Condition in this World. That for his part, he was perfectly content with the State to which he was called, that he should endeavour to improve his Talent, which was all required of him, but not repine at his own Lot, nor envy those of his Betters." (24–25)

Not yet identified as Wilson's son, Joseph carries within him the problem of status inconsistency. He has come to Adams's attention because he answers questions about the Scriptures, Adams "privately" admits, "better than Sir *Thomas* [Booby], or two other neighbouring Justices of the Peace could probably have done" (23). He will come to Lady Booby's attention because he is handsomer, more well made, than the gentlemen with whom she consorts; near the story's end, clothes "rather too large for the Squire [Booby]" fit Joseph "exactly" (291).

These are only brief examples of the status inconsistency—the sense that servants are superior to their masters—that pervades *Joseph Andrews*. From Defoe to Smollett, status inconsistency recurs. The orphan Moll has more talent and beauty than the daughters in her guardian's family. Humphry Clinker, a penniless and disheveled (to put it kindly) servant, wins his argument about grace and faith with the gentleman Matthew Bramble. But these eighteenth-century novels attempt to place their virtuous, talented, and beautiful servants. This is not to say that the novels are monolithic. Smollett's anamnesis is much less reassuring than Fielding's mimesis; even in Fielding, the carnivalesque subversion of social and gender categories is a powerful threat that must be set (as in the adventures at Upton) carefully in place. Defoe's heroines flirt with the destruction of the social categories "lady," "princess," "countess," but finally, if tragically, they vindicate the power of those words in their need to be named by them.

When Julien Sorel receives his new name and his military title from the marquis, he thinks "*mon roman est fini.*"[1] But it's not. In eleven additional chapters, Julien will go from his perfect ending to death at the guillotine. His ambition and pride (he also thinks at this moment, "*et à moi seul tout le merite*") will find their punishment, a punishment with almost no precedent in eighteenth-century fiction other than Roxana's elliptically reported "Misery."

Julien's story, for all its precedents in the eighteenth century, is "transgressive" (and, thus, it continues on to his demise) because he is "guilty," in Patricia Meyer Spacks's fine phrase, of "imagining a self."[2] The birth-mystery plot of the eighteenth-century novel undergoes a profound transformation in the case of Julien Sorel. From the books he reads, Joseph Andrews learns submission. And while Lennox's Arabella derives an exalted, if finally dangerous and violent, sense of herself from her mother's romances, she is largely protected from transgressiveness by Glanville's good offices and her status as the daughter of a marquis. But from his books—the books he memorizes and then recites to the wonder of his social superiors—Julien learns a story of social advancement, a story that he takes as a model for his own self-made and self-willed rise ("*et a moi seul tout le merite*").

To clarify the difference between Julien and his eighteenth-century forebears, we can begin with Terry Castle's history of the masquerade in England, particularly with her analysis of why the masquerade, having been a hugely popular entertainment at mid-century, disappears at century's end. The masquerade, at its peak, belonged to a "traditional domain of collective drama and social ritual." It entailed a public acting out of "subversive desire." But Inchbald, writing near the century's end, reveals such "transgressive modes" to have become private and domestic rather than public.[3] Miss Milner's visit to a masquerade is not a definitive event, but only because the terms of her antiauthoritarianism already have been so well defined—in dinner table dialogues with Sandford, in her rescue of young Harry Rushbrook, in her excitement at the sexual opportunity that Lawnly presents. With the "internalization" of its antiauthoritarianism, the masquerade loses its function and, thus, its appeal: "For the nineteenth-century novelist, unlike his or her eighteenth-century counterpart, transgression no longer has the shape of a discontinuous or naive diversion. It has become . . . the central, self-conscious concern of the fictional enterprise itself."[4]

In the nineteenth century, characters no longer need masquerades to set in motion plots in which they rebel against conventions of class, age, and gender. Julien Sorel, in willing himself to become the beloved of Mathilda de la Mole, transgresses the safe bounds set by the "naive" plots of the eighteenth-century novel. He internalizes the birth mystery, turning it into a family romance. While this gives him freedom to change his name, it also opens him to all the bad passion that Freud locates in the family scene. No matter how detached from the father male characters may be, no matter how badly treated by him female characters may be, characters in eighteenth-century fiction—including Smollett's much knocked-about Peregrine Pickle—do not feel or express to themselves, as Julien does, "hatred for my father." Instead, characters in eighteenth-century novels by men and women alike devote them-selves to maintaining "pious fictions" that preserve the patriarch's claims to authority. Consanguineous marriage becomes a virtue rather than a "monstrous" transgression, even as variations upon the birth mystery enable authors to deal with the problems created by the impairment of the patriarch, most notably the problem of status inconsistency.

Characters in nineteenth-century novels define themselves by imagining their parents; Philip Pirrip runs his fingers over the letters on his parents' gravestones and from his touch upon the stones invents a version of them. Brooks points out that Philip Pirrip's status as an orphan allows his narrative to begin with an act of "self-naming" (he is Pip). In setting up his narrative, Dickens offers a "gift" to Pip: the "occulting [of] the biological father." From the opening of his story, Pip faces the task to which Julien Sorel only gradually comes: "Julien's fictional scenarios make him not only the actor, the feigning self, but also the stage manager of his own destiny, constantly projecting the self into the future on the basis of hypothetical plots" (Brooks, 72). Brooks links this projection of the self via "fictional scenarios" to "questions of authority, legitimacy, and paternity" (71); by "occulting the biological father," Dickens and Stendhal envision other figures of authority than the patriarch, or, perhaps more precisely, they envision different versions of paternity than biological. The invention of the self is fostered by, even depends upon, the absence of the father.[5]

This helps to explain why, in the eighteenth century, "imagin-ing a self," as Spacks observes, is much more likely to occur in autobiographies and histories, even in periodical essays, than in novels. Spacks expresses some bemusement, even frustration, with this, by modern standards, odd truth: to find even partially realized selves in eighteenth-century literature, we have to wait for the novelists to catch up with Rousseau, Gibbon, even Addison and Steele. Spacks describes the eighteenth-century novel mani-festing a "profound ambivalence" towards the "energy of impulse as well as of repression." She sees this ambivalence manifesting itself most powerfully in "female novelists," but as she describes it, its relevance to male novelists is clear (*Roderick Random* offers the "energy of impulse as well as of repression" writ large, Fielding's scene at Upton offers it writ small):

> Even in its more amateurish manifestations, it seems, the novel can contain and express through its patterns of action complexities of feeling that it nowhere directly acknowledges: complexities, indeed, often contradicted by its explicit, moralistic statements. Even the most conventional fictions find ways to convey the personal. Most eighteenth-century novels by women emphatically communicate the world's impingement upon the personal, while expressing also the fantasies through which women combat impingements—enthusiastic endorsement of the system at the same time comprising a subtle mode of combat.[6]

In Spacks's analysis the fictions of eighteenth-century women are shaped by the various social and cultural "impingements" that women faced. The woman writer must practice anamnesis, must couch her subversion in conventional terms. But Spacks's finest, most suggestive comment is not gender specific: "Even the most conventional fictions find ways to convey the personal."

In studying the "pious fictions" by which eighteenth-century families maintained a version of patrilinear succession, we can see why the selves imagined in eighteenth-century novels seem stunted, much "impinged" upon. These eighteenth-century selves precede the internalization of the birth-mystery plot in the nineteenth-century novel—that is, they precede Freud's discovery of the "family romance."[7] In eighteenth-century novels, by men and women alike, art imitated life, but life, particularly among the elite, already depended greatly upon fiction. As the patriarchy declined, families (and then writers) used name changes and men from the female line—Tom Jones, Glanville Jr., Walpole's Theodore, and perhaps Harry Rushbrook—to maintain unimpaired their claims to estates. Fiction's power, while real, was problematic. For one hardly has to be as villainous as Robert Lovelace to see that if the real daughter and the fictive daughter receive equal favor, then daughterhood no longer is an essence. How important can patriarchal succession be if aunts, cousins, and daughters all, with some theatrical work, can be "aped"? The marquis wants to find a husband for Arabella from within his immediate family and thus typifies the attempts by families to limit the extent of their fictionalizing. But Moll Flanders and Roxana both reveal that the appetite for fiction may not be so easily or happily sated. Once families could create an heir from a Glanville or a Harry Rushbrook, what was to stop heiresses like Arabella and Mathilda from making a man of their choice—a man without the pale of family but within the pale of desire—into an heir?

The transition from Fielding, Smollett, and Lennox to Stendhal, the Brontës and Dickens centers in a basic change in the social role of fiction. When England's demographic crisis eased in the 1750s, fiction no longer needed to prop up an impaired patriarchy. Nor could the patriarchy, having relied upon fictive versions of kinship for a century, dismiss or constrain fiction's power. The novel could do more than finesse the problem of status inconsistency—do more than find appropriate places for virtuous servants by reuniting fathers and sons, do more than marry wealthy and willful heiresses to their cousins. The novel could find other functions, most notably the exploration of the wishes and dreams, the developing inner lives of its characters. What Spacks identifies as "repression" in the eighteenth-century novel actually might be seen more positively as a legitimate social function: the preservation of a centuries-old tradition of patrilinear succession. But whether viewed with regret or with exultation, the patriarch's failure was manifest to the eighteenth century. From Fielding's Squire Booby to Lennox's marquis, gentlemen do not provide legitimate male heirs for their titles and estates. Clarissa's grandfather is a remarkable (and bourgeoisie) exception to the rule. Roxana's mobility only testifies to the fluidity of social categories in the wake of the patriarch's decline. But Defoe's protagonists also define a paradoxical attitude toward status that will endure at least through Inchbald and the late eighteenth century. Having fictionalized kinship, having pretended to be gentleladies and princesses, Defoe's heroines still yearn for the stable identity that they assume kinship confers. They want their fictional titles to hold clear and certain meaning. Their memorable equivocalness lies in their valuing so highly the very categories that they seem to break; they, too, prop up the social conventions they seem to defeat. Even in Smollett's anamnestic fictions, the quest for status (witness Matthew Bramble) remains a dominant—if now problematic—motive.

Defoe's heroines and Smollett's picaros reveal that the "divided impulse," which Spacks attributes to fiction by women, actually is present in all major eighteenth-century fiction,[8] if we attend to the details of family and property in which those stories begin. While the question of when the novel begins is moot, we can say that during the eighteenth century, during an early stage, the British novel finds its plots in a social crisis—the failure of patrilinear succession. Novelists, like elite families, direct their fictions to reinventing the lost leader. They attempt, as Sir Robert Filmer did, to "re-nature" the family, to adhere to "God's plot" by grounding political society in the family and adhering to the scriptural model of family life.[9] However, "even the most conventional fictions find ways to convey the personal," for even the most conventional fictions begin with impaired patriarchs. As novelists move from recording the fall of the patriarch to attempting to put him "back together again" via a fictive version of kinship, their efforts, however comically and energetically pursued, inevitably lead to "profound ambivalence" about the "established system." Once fictionalized, the family no longer can constrain the fiction that sustains it. In the second half of the eighteenth century, virtuous heiresses (and Sterne's great antihero) threaten to take fiction out of its public role. Consanguinity becomes less attractive as a marital option; the discovery of paternity no longer holds the power it does in Fielding or, to a lesser degree, in Smollett.[10] Fiction stands ready to assume its great nineteenth-century role—self-study and self-creation—and to free itself from the task of reinventing the family.

Inchbald brilliantly adumbrates this change. Harry Rushbrook is a decent enough fellow, but he typically is sick or ordered elsewhere when Mathilda needs him. He is a good "friend" but an unexciting lover. Her marriage within her power, Mathilda listens to Rushbrook's proposal but does not respond. The conventional response is for her to marry her closest male relative, to serve the "pious fiction" of patrilinear succession. Inchbald allows her readers to write this conclusion, but she will not pen it herself. In Mathilda's silence, Inchbald stands just beyond the "impingements" that her readers and her society would place upon her. She allows us to imagine an ending different from Evelina's or Arabella's, different from Tom Jones's (or is he Tom Allworthy, Tom Western, or Tom Summer?). Latent in her silence is the possibility that Mathilda may both discover and act upon an "energy of impulse," a personal agenda. Inchbald, in the odd, demanding tone of her conclusion, places her heroine outside her readers' expectations. Mathilda stands between the birth-mystery plot and the family romance. She never invents herself, as Brooks shows Julien and Pip doing. But Inchbald ends Mathilda's story by hinting that she may be thinking of Rushbrook, of her father, in ways that readers might not expect or recognize. Inchbald barely defers to both narrative and social convention; indeed, in her silence she may not defer at all. And in that silence, if we hear it rightly, the imagined selves of Julien, Pip, and the heroines of the Brontës wait to be born.

Notes

Introduction

1. *Desire and Domestic Fiction: A Political History of the Novel* (New York and Oxford: Oxford University Press, 1987), 23.

2. Lawrence and Jeanne C. Fawtier Stone, *An Open Elite? England 1540–1880* (Oxford: Clarendon Press, 1984), 100. The Stones base their generalizations upon legal records in three counties—Hertfordshire, Northamptonshire, and Northumberland—that describe the transfer of country seats. Their study focuses upon the elite. The Stones' description of a "demographic crisis" finds support in E. A. Wrigley and R. S. Schofield's *The Population History of England, 1541–1871: A Reconstruction* (Cambridge, Mass.: Harvard University Press, 1981). Wrigley, Schofield, and their associates base their generalizations upon 404 parish registers and the almost "3.7 million monthly totals of baptisms, burials, and marriages" that those registers provide (11). They offer generalizations relevant to the entire population rather than the elite. But they too notice a "sharp reduction in the rate of population increase" between the "mid seventeenth and mid eighteenth centuries" (1). Offering a yearly breakdown of their data, they show that the eleven most severe mortality crises "all occurred before 1750" (333), and that while a person born in 1701 had a life expectancy of 37.11 years, a person born in 1731 had one of only 27.88 (529). In support of the Stones' narrower sample, then, Wrigley and Schofield show that mortality rates not only remained high in the eighteenth century but actually increased before 1750. For fine reviews of the relevance and applicability of work done by Wrigley and Schofield's Cambridge Group for the History of Population and Social Structure, see J. Paul Hunter, *Before Novels: The Cultural Contexts of Eighteenth Century Fiction* (New York: W. W. Norton, 1990), 63–65, and Michael McKeon, *The Origins of the English Novel 1600–1740* (Baltimore: The Johns Hopkins University Press, 1987), 153–54.

3. E. Leroy Ladurie, "Un Concept: L' Unification Microbienne du Monde (xive–xvlle siecles)," in *Le Territoire De l'Historien* (Paris: Editions Gallimard, 1978), vol. 2. Cited in Stones, 93.

4. See particularly, "English Landownership, 1680–1740," *Economic History Review*, o.s. 10 (1940): 2–17; "Marriage Settlements in the Eighteenth Century," *Transactions of the Royal Historical Society*, 4th ser., 32 (1950): 15–30; "The Rise and Fall of English Landed Families, 1600–1800," *Transactions of the Royal Historical Society*, 5th ser., 29 (1979): 187–207, 30 (1980): 199–221, and 31 (1981): 195–217.

5. Richard M. Smith, "Some issues concerning families and property in rural England 1250–1800," in *Land, Kinship and Life-Cycle*, ed. Richard M. Smith (Cambridge: Cambridge University Press, 1984), 55.

6. "Marriage Settlements and the 'Rise of Great Estates': The Demographic Aspect," *Economic History Review*, 2d ser., 32 (1979): 483–93. Hollingsworth's "Demography of the Peerage" first appeared as a supplement to *Population Studies* 18 (1964): iv–108. Subsequent to his 1979 essay, Bonfield elaborated his argument in *Marriage Settlements, 1601–1740: The Adoption of the Strict Settlement* (Cambridge: Cambridge University Press, 1983).

7. See Lawrence Stone's influential *The Family, Sex and Marriage in England, 1500–1800*, 1977; abridged ed. (New York: Harper and Row, 1979). His chapter on "The Demographic Facts" describes family matters other than property and succession in which high mortality rates had a definitive role. In a famous passage, he claims that "it looks very much as if modern divorce is little more than a functional substitute for death. The decline of the adult mortality rate after the eighteenth century, by prolonging the expected duration of marriage to unprecedented lengths, eventually forced Western society to adopt the institutionalized escape-hatch of divorce" (46).

8. The statistics offered by the Stones and others take on a human face in *The Diary of Ralph Josselin 1616–1683*, ed. Alan Macfarlane (London: The Oxford University Press, 1976). Josselin was vicar of Earls Colne, Essex, from 1641 to 1683, and his diary offers a remarkable and, now, widely cited look at life among gentlemen of his status in seventeenth-century England. Josselin and his wife, who survived him, had ten children, five of whom died during Josselin's lifetime. One son, John, reached maturity and fathered a son named Ralph. Josselin himself was the "only sonne" (1) of his father, who died when Josselin was nineteen. In his helpful *The Family Life of Ralph Josselin: A Seventeenth Century Clergyman* (Cambridge: Cambridge University Press, 1970), 164, Alan Macfarlane summarizes "these many deaths": "His parents both died before he was twenty; his aunts and uncles were dying off when he was between twenty and thirty, his children between his thirtieth and fortieth years." Macfarlane notes that the "incidence of death" in Josselin's family is very unlike the incidence in families in modern industrial society. "The effects of these many deaths on Josselin's mentality can only be guessed," but, I suggest, they also can be studied in fictional responses to the demographic crisis. Josselin, as an "only sonne" who had only one son survive to maturity, that son also engendering only one son, shows how perilous patrilinear succession was at the time of the novel's origins.

9. London: Sampson Low, 1799. *The Orphan Heiress* purportedly is narrated by Sir Gregory's chaplain, who has survived the demise of the entire family. He

promised Sir Gregory that he would write the history of Sir Gregory's "venerable house" (3) and claims to have gone from the Normans through Elizabeth; the reader, however, gets only the history of the Commonwealth period. In the fragment, the narrative is continuous. The text has suffered no depredations and presents no excisions in the manner of Swift or Sterne. The book is dedicated to Henry Temple, Second Viscount Palmerston, the father of the great nineteenth-century foreign secretary who helped create the Quadrilateral Alliance. The earlier Palmerston enjoyed the company of distinguished men. In the 1760s, he spent time in Paris with John Wilkes, time in Lausanne with Edward Gibbon. He was elected to Dr. Johnson's Club in 1784 and was a pallbearer at the funerals of David Garrick and Joshua Reynolds. His life and his son's certainly were inimical to the revolutionary currents at work in 1799. As *The Orphan Heiress* portrays Cromwell as a vile "Usurper," it implicitly speaks against Napoleon's consulship.

10. Charles M. Gray, introduction to Sir Matthew Hale, *The History of the Common Law of England* (Chicago & London: The University of Chicago Press, 1971), xiii.

11. Henry Fielding's library included Hale's two-volume *History of the Pleas of the Crown* and his *Primitive Origination of Mankind*. See Ethel M. Thornbury, *Henry Fielding's Theory of the Comic Prose Epic* (Madison: University of Wisconsin Press, 1931), 173 and 182. For the extent to which Hale's writings influenced Fielding's thinking about society and law, see Malvin R. Zirker's edition of *An Enquiry into the Causes of the Late Increase of Robbers and Related Writings* (Middletown Conn.: Wesleyan University Press, 1988), xxxi–xxxiii and lxxix. Fielding also was familiar with Hale's opinions about witchcraft although less favorably so. See his *The Journal of a Voyage to Lisbon*, in *Complete Works*, ed. W. E. Henley (London: Heineman, 1903), 16:269.

12. Gray, xiii. For one example, Susan Staves, in her fine book *Married Women's Separate Property in England, 1660–1833* (Cambridge, Mass.: Harvard University Press, 1990), does not mention Hale.

13. I will cite the edition of *De Successionibus* edited by Sir Bartholomew Shower and published (London: S.S., 1700). In all subsequent references to *De Succesionibus*, page numbers will be indicated in parentheses.

14. See Norman Moore's article on Hale in the *Dictionary of National Biography*, (Oxford: Humphrey Milford, 1917), 902. Moore's account of Hale's life is accurate, but his history of the publication of *De Succesionibus* is not; he is aware of only one edition published in 1700. Relevant to the theme of demographic crisis, Moore points out that both of Hale's parents died before he was five years old and that Hale's "posterity died out in the male line in 1782" (905). Hale's statistics as a father, while slightly worse than Ralph Josselin's, are slightly better than Sir Gregory's in *The Orphan Heiress*. With his first wife, Hale had ten children, "all of whom, except the eldest daughter and youngest son, died in his lifetime" (904). He might well write with particular concern for successions occurring in "Default of Heirs."

15. *The Compleat Lawyer* (London: John Amery, 1674), 3. Page numbers for all subsequent references to *The Compleat Lawyer* will be given in parentheses in the text.

16. Staves (4) sees property law as the servant of "deeper patriarchal structures" but also points out that "Equitable Jointure," in principle if not in case law, offered a "degree of independence and financial security" (96) to women. In general, Staves bases her argument upon specific cases rather than upon the legal writings of jurists like Sir Matthew Hale. Zomchick's book, *Family and the law in eighteenth-century fiction: The public conscience in the private sphere* (Cambridge: Cambridge University Press, 1993), particularly in its chapters on *Clarissa*, 58–104, attributes power to women in their "contracting" to marry. For examples of important decisions about jointure and free bench that are left to women, see Frances Sheridan, *The Memoirs of Miss Sidney Biddulph*, ed. Patricia Koster and Jean Coates Cleary (Oxford & New York: Oxford University Press, 1995), 65–70, 74–79, 93–95, and 242–55. Sidney Biddulph arrives at financial and personal ruin in part because of bad decisions by her mother.

17. "Widows in preindustrial society: an essay upon their economic functions," in Smith, *Land, Kinship, and Life-Cycle*, 435.

18. Mr. Arnold loses an estate to his infant niece, whose legitimacy is aspersed but whose claim to represent the older brother is accepted—after much legal wrangling (*The Memoirs of Miss Sidney Biddulph*, 113 ff).

19. Jill Campbell, *Natural Masques: Gender and Identity in Fielding's Plays and Novels* (Stanford: Stanford University Press, 1995), 7 and 12. Judith Butler, *Gender Trouble: Feminism and the Subversion of Identity* (New York: Routledge, 1990), 7, argues, "Gender ought not to be conceived merely as the cultural inscription of meaning on a pregiven sex . . . gender must also designate the very apparatus of production whereby the sexes themselves are established. As a result, gender is not to culture as sex is to nature; gender is also the discursive/cultural means by which 'sexed nature' or 'natural sex' is produced and established as 'prediscursive.'" Both Fielding and Hale would disagree, I believe, with Butler's notion that there is no sex prior to gender. But they are ready to write about the ways in which sex roles can be fictionalized. For the role of "gender" in recent feminist criticism, see also Joan Wallach Scott, *Gender and the Politics of History* (New York: Columbia University Press, 1988), 2–7, and Donna J. Harraway, *Simians, Cyborgs, and Women: The Reinvention of Nature* (New York: Routledge, 1991), 129–37.

20. "Michael McKeon and Some Recent Studies of Eighteenth-Century Fiction," *Eighteenth-Century Fiction* 1 (1988): 53–66. In a recent essay, "Reply to David Richter: Ideology and Literary Form in Fielding's *Tom Jones*," *The Eighteenth Century: Theory and Interpretation* 37 (1996): 207, John Richetti, as he discusses "refinements of our understanding of ideology," echoes and confirms Duckworth's summary: "Indeed, something like a rehabilitation of the concept might already be said to be established (if not always articulated) in the current intense re-examination of the origins and meanings of the British eighteenth-

century novel, which in recent crucial re-evaluations such as those of McKeon, Bender, Hunter, Davis, Mullan, Armstrong, and Warner is everywhere understood by these critics as an exploration of questions that are fundamentally socio-cultural."

21. "Manners, Morals, and the Novel," in *The Liberal Imagination* (Garden City, N.Y.: Doubleday, 1957), 215.

22. (New Haven & London: Yale University Press, 1979). In all subsequent references to *The Madwoman in the Attic*, page numbers will be given in parentheses in the text.

23. (Madison: The University of Wisconsin Press, 1989), 227. In all subsequent references to *The Iron Pen*, page numbers will be given in parentheses.

24. See Margaret Anne Doody, *Frances Burney: The Life in the Works* (New Brunswick, N.J.: Rutgers University Press, 1988), 315, 288, 206, and 250, for more detail about these instances of Burney's empowerment by her fiction.

25. As Doody (1988) describes him, Burney's father, Charles, certainly attempted to manage her literary career and succeeded in suppressing her plays. Doody also describes Charles as failing to spare Burney from the rigors of the court. She cites a passage from Burney's journal in which Burney claims, "My dear father's own courage failed him at this moment" (171), a moment when, the journal indicates, she was hoping he would act with some decisiveness. Because of his disadvantages as a Frenchman who would not fight against the English, Burney's husband, Alexander d'Arblay, treated her, Doody claims, "as an equal." She was "in a position where she was not to be passive and where she counted for much" (203). Other than a small pension he eventually received from the French government, d'Arblay could not help his wife financially. Burney's son, also named Alexander, while an "only child . . . [and] much loved," was, as Doody puts it, "never strong." He "made no real place for himself" and led such a vacuous life that he "seems almost to have welcomed death" (380). I would not claim that these traits of the men in Burney's life or these events disprove the "patriarchal etiology," but they can supplement it, offer instructive resistance to it. For a series of essays that use "psychobiography" to trace the "patriarchal etiology" in Burney's writing, particularly the repressive hand of her father, see *Eighteenth-Century Fiction* 3 (1991). For a portrait of Charles Burney as a feckless social gadfly, see Austen Dobson, *Fanny Burney (Madame D'Arblay)* (London: Macmillan and Co., 1903), 3–35.

26. *The Rise of the Novel* (Berkeley & Los Angeles: University of California Press, 1957), 7. In all subsequent references to *The Rise of the Novel*, page numbers will be given in parentheses in the text.

27. *Anatomy of Criticism: Four Essays* (Princeton: Princeton University Press, 1957), 51. In all subsequent references to *Anatomy*, page numbers will be given in parentheses in the text.

28. I take this term from Phillip Harth's *Swift and Anglican Rationalism: The Religious Background of A Tale of A Tub* (Chicago: University of Chicago Press, 1961). Insofar as Sir Gregory's chaplain sets himself against "enthusiasm" and

discounts interventions of the "spirit" in man's life, he becomes a fine example for Harth's argument; he also sets himself against Margaret's version of faith and truth, although the fragment does not develop this conflict.

29. *The Art of the Novel*, ed. R. P. Blackmur (New York: Charles Scribner's Sons, 1934), 129. This comment comes from James's Preface to *The Spoils of Poynton* and is made in reference to Fleda Vetch.

30. I am not proposing that *The Orphan Heiress* be elevated to a place of prominence in the canon; I do not expect it to appear as a title in Oxford's World's Classics series, the series that recently has returned Frances Sheridan, Charlotte Lennox, and Elizabeth Inchbald, as well as the "lesser" novels of Frances Burney, to visibility. Sheridan, Lennox, Inchbald, and Burney not only place their narratives within the consciousnesses of female protagonists, they also deny their characters any retreat from the dialectic between presence and absence. For all the intensity of Margaret's last days and the ensuing visits by her spirit, most of her life is passed in the serene isolation guaranteed by her father's hidden money. The chaplain, unlike guardians in works by Inchbald, Burney, and Lennox, has no need for or worries about her. Her long time apart from the chaplain, placed at the very center of the action, is an absence so complete that it avoids any contest with presence.

Chapter 1: The "Quest for the Proper Name": *Don Quixote* and the Madness of "Fictive Kin"

1. I base my summary of the English translations of *Don Quixote* on the following articles in the *Dictionary of National Biography*, ed. Sir Leslie Stephen and Sir Sidney Lee (London: Humphrey Milford, 1917): Thomas Seccombe, "John Ozell," 15:19–20; Sidney Lee, "John Phillips," 15:1091–93; Sidney Lee, "Thomas Shelton," 28:44–45. For a definitive attribution of the 1755 *Quixote* to Smollett, see Martin C. Battestin, "The Authorship of Smollett's *Don Quixote*," *Studies in Bibliography* 50 (1997), 295–321.

2. See Laurence Sterne, *The Life and Opinions of Tristram Shandy, Gentleman*, ed. Melvyn New (Gainesville: University of Florida Press, 1978), 1:18, 23, and 34.

3. *Don Quixote: An Anatomy of Subversive Discourse* (Newark, Del.: Juan de la Cuesta, 1988), 93. All subsequent references to Parr's study will be noted parenthetically in the text.

4. *Narrative Discourse: An Essay on Method*, trans. Jane E. Lewin (Ithaca & London: Cornell University Press, 1980).

5. Academic critics trained in the 1960s and familiar with Wayne C. Booth's *The Rhetoric of Fiction* (Chicago & London: University of Chicago Press, 1961) also could answer Parr's question by referring to Booth's discussion (71–76) of the "implied author." Whether we talk about Cervantes as a historical figure or as an "implied author," we broaden Parr's focus upon narrative voice. In his *Aspects of the Novel* (New York: Harcourt Brace, 1927), E. M. Forster reminds us that the greatest novelists—Charles Dickens in *Bleak House* is his most telling example—

frequently "bounce" their readers between points of view. Forster concludes, perceptively if somewhat cavalierly: "A novelist can shift his viewpoint if it comes off, and it came off with Dickens and Tolstoy. Indeed this power to expand and contract perception (of which the shifting viewpoint is a symptom) . . . I find . . . one of the great advantages of the novel-form, and it has a parallel in our perception of life. We are stupider at some times than others; we can enter into people's minds occasionally but not always" (81). The best answer to Parr's question is to include Cervantes with Dickens and Tolstoy.

6. See *Aspects of the Novel* 79 for Forster's comment on "technical trouble," 81 for "all to pieces logically."

7. See R. Trevor Davies, *The Golden Century of Spain 1501–1621* (London: Macmillan and Co., 1958), for a summary of the careers of Ferdinand and Isabella (1–33) and for a summary of the treatment of *conversos* and *Moriscos* (227–48).

8. *Don Quixote*, the Ormsby translation revised, ed. Joseph R. Jones and Kenneth Douglas (New York: W. W. Norton, 1981), 441. All subsequent references to *Don Quixote* will be to the Norton edition. Page numbers will be given in parentheses.

9. A corollary to Charles I's attempt to regulate status in Spain was Elizabeth I's attempt to promulgate a national dress code in England. Elizabeth, in a proclamation of 6 July 1597, sought to end "the confusion in all places . . . where the meanest are as richly appareled as their betters." Charles I sought to preclude *conversos* and *Moriscos* from appearing as "Old Christians." See Armstrong, 70, for analysis of the social motives behind Elizabeth's code.

10. See William Byron, *Cervantes: A Biography* (Garden City, N.Y.: Doubleday, 1978), 16–30, for Cervantes' family background and possible ties to the *conversos*.

11. For a fine meditation upon this question as well as helpful summary of its central place in studies of the *Quixote*, see John J. Allen, *Don Quixote: Hero or Fool?* (Gainesville: University of Florida Press, 1971), and *Don Quixote: Hero or Fool? Part II* (Gainesville: University of Florida Press, 1979).

12. Carrol B. Johnson, *Madness and Lust: A Psychological Approach to Don Quixote* (Berkeley: University of California Press, 1983).

13. *Madness and Civilization: A History of Insanity in the Age of Reason*, trans. Richard Howard (New York: Random House, 1965). All further references to *Madness and Civilization* will be to the Howard translation; page numbers will be given in parentheses.

14. *Don Quixote and the Dulcineated World* (Austin: University of Texas Press, 1971).

15. I will use Richard Carew's 1594 translation, *The Examination of Men's Wits;* rpt. (New York: Da Capo Press, 1969). Page numbers will be given in parentheses. Huarte's *Examen* also was translated in the following editions: *Anacrise, ou parfait jugement des esprits propres et naiz aux sciences*, trans. Gabriel Chappuys (Lyon: Estinne Brignol, 1580). *L'examen des esprits pour les sciences*, trans. Charles Vion Dalibray (Paris: Jean le Bouc, 1645). *L'Examen des esprits pour les sciences*, trans. Francois Savinien d'Alquie (Amsterdam: Jean de Ravenstein, 1672). *Essame*

de gli ingegni de gli huomini per apprender la scienza, trans. Camillo Camilli (Venice: Aldo, 1582). *Essamina de gl' ingegni de gli huomini ad apprender qual si volgia*, trans. Salustio Gratii (Venice: Barezzo Barezzi, 1600). *Examen de Ingenios, or the Tryal of Wits*, trans. Edward Bellamy (London: Richard Sare, 1698). *Scrutinium ingeniorum pro iis qui excellere cupiunt*, trans. Aeschacius Major (Leipzig: In Officina Cothoniensi, 1622). *Onderzoek der byzondere Vernuftens Eygentlijkke Abelheen*, trans. Henrik Takama (Amsterdam: Johannes Ravenstein, 1659). *Johann Huarts Prufung der Kopfe zu den Wissenschaften*, trans. Gotthold Ephraim Lessing (Zerbt: Zimmerman, 1752). First published in 1575, the *Examen* appeared in a revised, expanded, and censored version in 1594, five years after Huarte's death. I take the wide and relatively rapid translation of the *Examen* to indicate that Huarte's ideas had wide currency.

16. *Juan Huarte de San Juan* (Boston: G. K. Hall, 1981), 38.

17. Cervantes' father was a physician and trained at Alcala de Henares at roughly the same time that Huarte did. There also is evidence that both Cervantes and Huarte were *conversos*. For a helpful summary of the debate about Huarte's influence on Cervantes, see Read, 110–15.

18. In an influential article, "El 'Ingenioso' Hidalgo," *Hispanic Review* 25 (1957): 175–93, Otis Green linked Huarte's work with the story of "El Ingenioso . . . Don Quixote." Recently, Teresa Scott Soufas, in *Melancholy and the Secular Mind in Spanish Golden Age Literature* (Columbia: University of Missouri Press, 1990), has argued that, "It is . . . erroneous to read Cervantes's novel as a literary espousal of Huarte's *Examen*." (30). She attacks Green by arguing that Don Quixote's dominant humor is melancholia not, as Green argues, choler. She then groups Quixote with other golden age "melancholy characters," whose authors "generally reject the strength and autonomy of the secular intellect which melancholics embody" (163). By attacking the Cervantes-Huarte connection, she would support her thesis that Spanish golden age authors reveal, in "their varied portrayals of melancholia," a "conservative" attitude toward the "reorganization of the structure of thought undertaken in the sixteenth and seventeenth centuries in Europe" (x). Taking a Foucauldian line, she contends that Cervantes and other authors (Tirso de Molina, Lope de Vega, and Calderon de la Barca) disapprove of their "various melancholic characters" and punish their unconventionality. In her eagerness to overturn Green's work, Soufas overlooks that the distinction between choler and "adust melancholy"—the active stage of melancholia that she attributes to Don Quixote—is less important than the humoral imbalance Don Quixote has developed during his long course of solitary reading. That imbalance, be its source in choler or melancholy, leads to his "mad" behavior.

19. *The Chivalric World of Don Quixote: Style, Structure, and Narrative Technique* (Columbia: University of Missouri Press, 1982), 22–41.

20. The term "family romance" comes from Freud's essay "Family Romances" [*Der Familien Roman der Neurotiker*] (1908), *The Standard Edition of the Complete Psychological Works of Sigmund Freud*, ed. and trans. James Strachey (London: Hogarth Press, 1953–74), 9:237–41. In turning to a "family romance" to resolve

status inconsistency, Don Quixote anticipates the imaginings of Julien Sorel and Dickens's Pip as they are analyzed by Peter Brooks in his *Reading for the Plot: Design and Intention in Narrative* (New York: Albert A. Knopf, 1984), 90–143. Christine Van Boheemen, *The Novel as Family Romance: Language, Gender, and Authority from Fielding to Joyce* (Ithaca & London: Cornell University Press, 1987), describes changes in the pursuit of "origin" between eighteenth-century and modern writers. She describes the "family romance" mediating conflicts of gender rather than of class.

21. For a summary of this view, see Maurice Z. Schroder, "The Novel as Genre," *Massachussetts Review* 4 (1963): 291–308.

22. Carroll B. Johnson, "A Gallery of Decadents: Society in *Don Quijote*, Part II," *Indiana Journal of Hispanic Literature* 5 (1994): 195. My discussion of Don Diego de Miranda as a hidalgo in decline is indebted throughout to Johnson's essay.

Chapter 2: Milton's Two Versions of the Patriarch: Mimetic and Anamnestic Plots

All references in this chapter to Milton's poetry and prose will be from John Milton, *Complete Poems and Major Prose*, ed. Merrit Y. Hughes (Indianapolis and New York: Bobbs-Merrill, 1957). In the case of *Paradise Lost*, book and line numbers will be indicated in parentheses. In the cases of "At A Solemn Music," "Ad Patrem," and *Comus*, line numbers will be given in parentheses. References to *Areopagitica* will give page numbers in parentheses.

1. *Milton and Influence: Presence in Literature, History, and Culture* (Pittsburgh: Duquesne University Press, 1991), 43.

2. *The Influence of Milton on English Poetry* (Cambridge, Mass.: Harvard University Press, 1922).

3. Bloom's most influential but hardly lone commentary on Milton comes in his *The Anxiety of Influence* (New York: Oxford University Press, 1973), 10–12 and 19–45, particularly 33.

4. Damrosch Jr., *God's Plot and Man's Stories: Studies in the Fictional Imagination from Milton to Fielding* (Chicago & London: University of Chicago Press, 1985), 78. All subsequent references to *God's Plot* will give page numbers in parentheses in the text.

5. "Clarissa Regained: Richardson's Redemption of Eve," *Eighteenth-Century Life* 13 (1989): 87–99.

6. "The Pilgrimage of the Family: Structure in the Novels of Fielding and Smollett," *Tobias Smollett: Bicentenary Essays to Lewis Knapp*, ed. G. S. Rousseau and P. G. Boucé (New York: Oxford University Press, 1971), 57–78.

7. Henry Fielding, *The History of Tom Jones a Foundling*, ed. Martin C. Battestin and Fredson Bowers (Middletown, Conn.: Wesleyan Universty Press, 1975), 331.

8. On Fielding's conservatism, see John Richetti, "The Old Order and New Novel of the Mid-Eighteenth Century," *Eighteenth-Century Fiction* 2 (1990): 194–96.

9. James G. Basker, *Tobias Smollett: Critic and Journalist* (Newark: University of Delaware Press, 1988), 92.

10. *The Politics of Samuel Johnson* (New Haven: Yale University Press, 1960).

11. For the references to anamnesis by Plato, see the Loeb Classical Library No. 36, trans. Harold N. Fowler (Cambridge, Mass.: Harvard University Press, 1914), 263–65, and No. 165, trans. W. R. M. Lamb (Cambridge, Mass. Harvard University Press, 1924), 267, 307, 313, and 319. Peacham's definition occurs in *The Garden of Eloquence* (London: R.F. and H. Jackson, 1593), 76. The *OED* cites eighteenth and nineteenth definitions from medical textbooks. Feyerabend defines the term in his *Against Method: Outline of an Anarchistic Theory of Knowledge* (London: Verso, 1975), 12, 73, 81, 87–89, and 202–7.

12. For extended criticism of Plato, see Smollett's *The Critical Review* (London: A. Hamilton), 7 (1759):421–27 and 9 (1761):194 and 357.

13. *The Consolation of Philosophy*, trans. R. H. Green (Indianapolis: Bobbs-Merrill, 1962), 117.

14. Smollett's sense that his Scots background kept him out of the English literary and social mainstream perhaps appears most clearly in his attempts to produce his play *The Regicide*. See Howard Swayze Buck, *A Study in Smollett: Chiefly of Peregrine Pickle*, rpt. 1925 (Mamaroneck, N.Y. : Paul P. Appel, Publisher, 1973), ix and 54, and Lewis M. Knapp, *Tobias Smollett: Doctor of Men and Manners* (Princeton: Princeton University Press, 1949), 92. Insofar as he identified Fielding as the leading playwright of the day, Smollett could see himself as the victim of theater managers who always, within the limits imposed by the Licensing Act, seemed to have Fielding's interests at heart. While such psychological generalizations are risky, I suspect that the bitterness of Smollett's newspaper battles with Fielding in large part is owing to Smollett's identification of Fielding as privileged in ways Smollett never could hope to be.

15. See the introduction by Peter Laslett to his edition of *Patriarcha and Other Political Works of Sir Robert Filmer* (Oxford: Basil Blackwell, 1949), 3, 10, and 34, for the publication history of *Patriarcha*. All subsequent references to Filmer's political writings will be to the Oxford edition; page numbers will be indicated in parentheses in the text. References to Laslett's introduction also will be made in parentheses.

16. See John Locke, *An Essay Concerning Human Understanding*, ed. Peter Nidditch (Oxford: Clarendon Press, 1975), 386 and 401. Locke admits that "Men are . . . forward to suppose, that the abstract *Ideas* they have in their Minds, are such, as agree to the Things existing without them . . . and are the same also, to which Names they give them, do by the Use and Propriety of that Language belong." He defines this human attribute as "*double Conformity*" and shows that without it men "should think both amiss of Things in themselves, and talk of them unintelligibly to others." But he devotes book 3 of the *Essay* to considering

"the Nature, Use, and Signification of Language" because he sees "double Conformity" as a human invention rather than as a natural phenomenon.

17. Sterne (1978), 1:54, will have Walter Shandy cite Filmer as Walter defends his decision to force Mrs. Shandy to have her lying-in at Shandy Hall rather than in London. Walter believes "that any such Instance would infallibly throw a balance of power, too great already, into the weaker vessels of the gentry, in his own, or higher stations;—which, with many other usurped rights which that part of the constitution was hourly establishing,—would, in the end, prove fatal to the monarchical sysyem of domestick government established in the first creation of things by God." By describing Walter as "entirely of Sir *Robert Filmer's* opinion," Sterne points out the comedy of Walter's meditation upon the corruption and the urbanization of the British body politic. For Sterne, Filmer is a convenient foil rather than a significant political philosopher, and Tristram Shandy's problems with paternity are intimate rather than public. Walter's meditation upon Filmer and British society runs throughout chap. 18 of vol. 1.

18. Gilbert and Gubar (1979), 188.

19. Ibid., 210.

20. In letters numbers 161 and 233, Lovelace directly invokes Milton. See *Clarissa*, ed. Angus Ross (Harmondsworth, England: Penguin Books, 1985), 545 and 772. All subsequent references to *Clarissa* are to the Penguin edition. For further discussion of the strengths and weaknesses of this edition, see chap. 6, n. 1.

Chapter 3: Dorotea's Daughters: *Moll Flanders, Roxana,* and the Perils of Fictive Kinship

1. The quotation is from the first page of Burney's *Cecelia*, ed. Peter Sabor and Margaret Anne Doody (Oxford & New York: Oxford University Press, 1988). All subsequent references to *Cecelia* will be to the Oxford edition; page numbers will be given in parentheses.

2. Daniel Defoe, *Roxana*, ed. David Blewett (Harmondsworth England: Penguin Books, 1982), 37. All subsequent references to *Roxana* will be to the Penguin edition; pages will be indicated in parentheses.

3. In his 1697 *An Essay on Projects* (rpt., Menston, England: Scolar Press, 1969), 8, for example, Defoe describes a salvage scheme in which Sir William Phipps used a diving bell to remove 200,000 pounds from a sunken Spanish ship as a "Lottery" of 100,000 to 1 odds. If he had failed, Phipps would have been "as much ridicul'd as *Don Quixot's Adventure upon the Windmill.*"

4. Daniel Defoe, *Moll Flanders*, ed. Edward Kelly (New York: W. W. Norton, 1973), 10. All subsequent references to *Moll Flanders* will be to the Norton edition; page numbers will be given in parentheses.

5. See George A. Starr's *Defoe and Casuistry* (Princeton: Princeton University Press, 1971), 111–20, for a perceptive discussion of the ways in which Moll's story

"tends to subvert" traditional moral responses. As Defoe creates "sympathy" for a character like Moll, so he also allows her both to participate in and to justify all manner of criminal behavior. I am arguing that we need to understand why, in the case of incest, Moll will not proceed casuistically.

6. We cannot tell why Susan is so different from her brother and her sister. While Defoe is one of the great figures in the origin of the English novel, he does not differentiate characters on the basis of their life experiences and resultant psychologies.

7. Daniel Defoe, *Robinson Crusoe*, ed. Angus Ross (Harmondsworth, England: Penguin Books, 1965), 298. All subsequent references to *Robinson Crusoe* are to the Penguin edition; page numbers will be given in parentheses.

8. Defoe has a revealing tendency to give to both Moll and Roxana lovers whose wives are disabled, sometimes physically, usually mentally. The tendency is revealing because it encourages characters to develop fictive versions of kinship—not only is the wife not around, she is not going to be around—but also limits the extent of the fictions. Their lovers are not free to marry either Moll or Roxana.

9. The descriptions are taken from the dust jacket of the Penguin edition of *Roxana*. With them, the editors at Penguin summarize a widely held view of *Roxana*.

10. The classic studies by Hunter, *The Reluctant Pilgrim: Defoe's Emblematic Method and the Quest for Form in* Robinson Crusoe (Baltimore: The Johns Hopkins University Press, 1966), and Starr, *Defoe and Spiritual Autobiography* (Princeton: Princeton University Press, 1965), appeared almost simultaneously and argued that Defoe structures his narratives with reference to seventeenth-century devotional literature. Damrosch's study (1985) comes twenty years later and describes Defoe following Milton in psychologizing Christian doctrine, individualizing the great Christian drama of man's Fall and Redemption.

11. See her "Defoe" in *The Common Reader*, 1st ser. (New York: Harcourt, Brace and World, 1925), 89–97.

12. Paula R. Backscheider, *Daniel Defoe: His Life* (Baltimore & London: The Johns Hopkins University Press, 1989), 33 and 55. Backscheider describes (180) Defoe as "haunted" by his loss of his wife's dowry and his "ill husbandry" of their assets in general. My discussion of Defoe's quest for status is based upon Backscheider's biography, although my interpretation of that quest, my connection of it to the motif of fictive kinship in the novels, is my own. References to page numbers in Backscheider's biography will be given in parentheses.

13. *The Letters of Daniel Defoe*, ed. George H. Healey (Oxford: Clarendon Press, 1969), 189 (27 January 1707). Cited in Backscheider (1989), 231–33.

14. See Backscheider, 535, for a summary of recent commentary upon Defoe's turning away from the novel. Backscheider argues that Defoe no longer could see the "use" of fiction. I suggest instead that, in *Roxana*, he reached a *terminus ad quem* in his treatment of status inconsistency.

15. David Blewett, *Defoe's Art of Fiction* (Toronto: University of Toronto Press, 1979), 118.

16. Recent critics have debated at length the question of irony in Defoe's fiction, a debate that goes back at least as far as Ian Watt's chapter on *Moll Flanders*, in which he proposes that Defoe lacks the narrative sophistication to give readers confidence about how they are to judge his characters. In Watt's view, Defoe achieves "realism of presentation" but not "realism of assessment." Critics like Hunter, Starr, and even Damrosch, who wish to claim a spiritual dimension for Defoe's fictions, repeatedly come up hard against the venality of his characters. Without claiming to solve the problem of irony in Defoe, I only note that the problem arises because the characters themselves, whatever their opportunism, whatever their crimes, always seek to define their achievements in conventional terms. The characters are outlaws, but they all seek status.

Chapter 4: Night Moves: Henry Fielding and the Birth-Mystery Plot Under Stress

Throughout this chapter, I will refer to Fielding's fiction as mimetic, as an attempt to represent in human terms and words a divine order. See C. J. Rawson, *Henry Fielding and the Augustan Ideal Under Stress* (London: Routledge and Kegan Paul, 1972), for a version of Fielding's art that emphasizes the difficulty rather than the achievement of mimesis. Rawson's version of Fielding offers a helpful counterpoint to that of Martin C. Battestin, the greatest contemporary authority on Fielding's life and art. References to Fielding's novels are taken from Battestin's editions (Middletown, Conn.: Wesleyan University Press): *Joseph Andrews*, 1967; *Tom Jones*, 1975; *Amelia*, 1983. Page numbers are indicated in parentheses. The letter from Filding to Feilding comes from Manuscripts of the Earl of Denbigh, ed. Mrs. S. C. Lomas (London: Historical Manuscripts Commission, 1911), 14.

1. For the details of the Feilding/Denbigh genealogy, see *The Complete Peerage*, ed. Vicary Gibbs (London: St. Catharine Press, 1916), 4:181, and *Burke's Peerage*, ed. Peter Townend, 99th ed. (London: D. Guinness, 1950), 569.

2. See Frederick T. Blanchard, *Fielding the Novelist* (New Haven: Yale University Press, 1927), 136–38, for a series of Richardsonian complaints about Fielding's topics and his tone.

3. A famous anecdote has Fielding speaking with his cousin, the 5th Earl of Denbigh. In response to the earl's questioning why the spellings of their surname differ, Fielding rejoins, "Why sir, 'tis because my branch of the family knew how to spell." See Wilbur L. Cross, *The History of Henry Fielding* (New Haven: Yale University Press, 1918), 1:83.

4. For the evidence that underlies my claims about the role of Pamela in *Joseph Andrews* and for additional discussion of the social motives that underlie Fielding's birth mystery and his characterization of Adams, see my "Rewriting *Pamela*:

Social Change and Religious Faith in *Joseph Andrews*," *Studies in the Novel* 16 (1984): 137–49. For a discussion of the place of this essay in recent work on eighteenth-century fiction, particularly the "canny criticism" that exposes the once-hidden ideological basis of all writing, see David Richter, "The Closing of Masterpiece Theatre: Henry Fielding and the Valorization of Incoherence," *Eighteenth Century: Theory and Interpretation* 37 (1996): 195–97.

5. Fielding's rehabilitation of the elite is heralded by a caveat that he offers in bk. 3, chap. 2. Having reunited Joseph, Fanny, and Adams and started them on their way home, he writes: "The Reader must excuse me if I am not particular as to the way they took; for as we are now drawing near the Seat of the *Boobies*; and as that is a ticklish Name, which malicious Persons may apply according to their evil Inclinations to several worthy Country 'Squires, a Race of Men whom we look upon as entirely inoffensive, and for whom we have an adequate Regard, we shall lend no assistance to any such malicious Purposes" (191–92). Words like "inoffensive" and "adequate" make the tone here far from lapidary, but Fielding does indicate that he stands ready to protect the Boobies. For additional details about this tendency in the second half of *Joseph Andrews*, see Brian McCrea, "'Had not Joseph Withheld Him': The Portrayal of the Social Elite in *Joseph Andrews*," in *Man, God, and Nature in the Enlightenment*, ed. Donald C. Mell Jr., Theodore E. D. Braun, and Lucia D. Palmer (East Lansing, Mich.: Colleagues Press, 1988), 123–28.

6. For the finest discussion of Adams's latitudinarian version of Anglicanism, see Martin C. Battestin, *The Moral Basis of Fielding's Art* (Middletown, Conn.: Wesleyan University Press, 1959). Frans de Bruyn, "Latitudinarianism and Its Importance as a Precursor of Sensibility," *Journal of English and Germanic Philology* 80 (1981): 349–68, rehearses the critical response to Battestin's book and vindicates Battestin's claim for the importance of latitudinarianism to our understanding of Fielding. I only would add that Adams's sense of his role as a patriarch—the teacher, helper, judge of those in his care—spares him from any conflict between his latitudinarianism and his loyalty to the Anglican communion.

7. "Comic Resolution in Fielding's *Joseph Andrews*," *College English* 15 (1953): 18.

8. *Problems of Dostoevsky's Poetics*, ed. and trans. Caryl Emerson (Minneapolis: University of Minnesota Press, 1984), 122–25. I do not mean to imply here that Bakhtin's work is not helpful in regard to Fielding's several "carnivals." See the references to Terry Castle's work on *Amelia* in chap. 7.

9. Hilles, "Art and Artifice in *Tom Jones*," in *Imagined Worlds: Essays on Some English Novels and Novelists in Honour of John Butt*, eds. Maynard Mack and Ian Gregor (London: Methuen, 1968), 91–110; Battestin, "Fielding's Definition of Wisdom: Some Functions of Ambiguity and Emblem in *Tom Jones*," *ELH* 35 (1968): 188–217.

10. *Amelia* is Fielding's first major literary project subsequent to the rise of Henry Pelham to the First Lordship of the Treasury in 1743. (I accept here Martin C. Battestin's argument that Fielding was at work on *Tom Jones* as early as 1743;

see the Wesleyan edition of *Tom Jones*, xxv–xxix.) Fielding was a Pelhamite and received his magistrateship through Pelham's good offices. But Pelham's political virtues—his founding of his ministry upon a "broad-bottom"—took from Fielding poor administration as an excuse for Britain's ills. Throughout his early political writing, Fielding boasts that the British "live under the *best* Constitution, if *well* administer'd, that has been made known to the World" (*The True Patriot*, ed. Miriam Austin Locke [University: University of Alabama Press, 1964], 161). This commonplace of eighteenth-century political writing held one particularly important use for Fielding. During his years of political opposition to Robert Walpole, he assumed that Walpole's excesses did not reflect upon the British constitution, political and moral. The political venality that he satirized was owing, Fielding reasoned, to a bad administrator, not to a bad society. When corruption of the sort described in *Amelia* persisted after Pelham's rise, Fielding had to consider that the British "Constitution" might be flawed. Thus, *Amelia* opens with an ambivalent meditation upon "Imperfections" in the "Machine" of British "Laws" (18–20) and then moves to a discussion of the British "Constitution." See Brian McCrea, *Henry Fielding and the Politics of Mid-Eighteenth-Century England* (Athens: University of Georgia Press, 1981), 165–96, for Fielding's response to Pelham's political virtue.

11. Michael Irwin, *Henry Fielding: The Tentative Realist* (Oxford: The Clarendon Press, 1967), 21–23, notes equivocations in Fielding's treatment of rank but attributes them to religious rather than political motives.

12. Terry Castle, *Masquerade and Civilization: The Carnivalesque in Eighteenth-Century English Culture and Fiction* (Stanford: Stanford University Press, 1986), 177–252, gives a chapter to the masquerade in *Amelia*. Her essay is rich and difficult to summarize briefly, but she traces the restoration of Amelia's estate to the events of the masquerade. Thus, with some qualification, she sees the masquerade opening a morally dead world, bringing the chance for justice into it. She claims (230) that "Mrs. Atkinson's trick creates a minor disturbance in the fictional world." With this I disagree. Mrs. Atkinson's "trick" leads to basic questions about status that the characters in the novel lack the wherewithal to resolve. Whereas in his earlier novels Fielding uses a birth mystery to straighten out the confusion created by his night moves, here the confusion lingers, resolved only by the good offices of Harrison, a powerful but frequently absent representative of the patriarchy. Masquerade confusion is not seen as positively in *Amelia* as Castle suggests.

13. J. Paul Hunter, "The Lesson of *Amelia*," in *Quick Springs of Sense: Studies in the Eighteenth Century*, ed. Larry S. Champion (Athens: University of Georgia Press, 1974), 159–63, claims that Amelia's temptation in this scene is sexual; he argues that "we are here meant to recall the early seduction scene in *Joseph Andrews*" (160). I find this implausible and am in greater accord with Irwin, *Fielding Tentative Realist*, 121–22, who focuses upon the social categories through which Fielding places the two characters.

14. Rawson, *Augustan Ideal Under Stress*, 4–8.

15. Ibid., 8–9, describes in detail Atkinson's social awkwardness.

16. See Brian McCrea, "Politics and Narrative Technique in Fielding's *Amelia*," *Journal of Narrative Technique* 13 (1983): 138, for explanations of why Fielding's comedy darkens in his final novel and "favourite Child." Morris Golden, "Public Context and the Imagining Self in *Amelia*," *University of Toronto Quarterly* 56 (1987): 377–91, connects the darkening financial and familial circumstances of Fielding's life in the 1750s to his diminished faith in brighter fictive worlds.

17. "The Problem of *Amelia*: Hume, Barrow, and the Conversion of Captain Booth," *ELH* 41 (1974): 613–48.

18. See Blanchard, *Fielding the Novelist*, 84–88, for a summary of satires by Fielding's contemporaries, most notably Smollett, upon Amelia's nose.

19. Hunter, "The Lesson of *Amelia*," 172–73, notes an analogous philosophical problem in the novel: "One trouble with *Amelia* may be that Fielding never made up his mind where he stood on the question of innate human nature, for if there is more harshness toward institutions and classes here, there is also an unwillingness to acquit the individual, on the one hand, and the ultimate order of things on the other."

20. The great example of this tongue biting comes in bk. 11, chap. 2, titled "Matters Political." Here Harrison asks an unnamed lord for a commission for Booth. The lord will not help unless Harrison gives him his vote in an upcoming election; he justifies his demand by offering a long description of corruption in the British body politic. Rather than challenging the lord's easy venality, Harrison accepts his premises and tries to argue within them. The rebuke that we might expect from the novel's figure of moral rectitude never comes. Abraham Adams would not have treated the corrupt lord so suavely.

21. Fielding contrives events such that when Winckworth, a wealthier and greater suitor, comes on the scene, Booth luckily already has a marriage agreement with Mrs. Harris. Fielding thus places the law on the side of the lovers as they thwart Mrs. Harris's scheme to make a greater match for Amelia (80–82).

22. Adams loses an argument about education with Joseph (230–32) and an argument about learning with a virtuous innkeeper (180–84), but he refuses to accept their telling points or to modify his views.

Chapter 5: Roderick Random's "Agreeable Lassitude" and Smollett's Anamnestic Fiction

1. Tuvia Bloch, "Smollett's Quest for Form," *Modern Philology* 65 (1967): 103–13. For responses to Bloch's essay, see Damian Grant, *Tobias Smollett: A Study in Style* (Manchester: Manchester University Press, 1977), ix–46, and Paul-Gabriel Boucé, *The Novels of Tobias Smollett*, trans. Antonia White (London & New York: Longman, 1976), 103–42. The responses of Grant and Boucé are impeded by the issue of "form" even as they try to get beyond it. Grant tries to dismiss the "quest

for form" as a "pseudo-problem" and claims that Smollett's novels are "unamenable to the vocabulary of forms." For him the novels are unified by their "verbal power" (42–44). Boucé also detours around the problem of form, claiming instead that Smollett's novels are structured by the "unity of the moral life" they present. Both these studies, despite their pro-Smollett sentiments, cede the question of form rather than asserting that Smollett's form is of a different sort (what I will call anamnestic) than Fielding's (mimetic). Grant tries to overcome criticism of Smollett's purported formal failings by appealing to linguistic standards, Boucé by appealing to moral.

2. Richetti (1990), 194 and 196.

3. *Uneasy Sensations: Smollett and the Body* (Chicago & London: University of Chicago Press, 1995). Page numbers for all subsequent references to *Uneasy Sensations* will be given in parentheses in the text.

4. Hilles (1968), 91–110, argues that *Tom Jones* is shaped "like a Palladian mansion" specifically imitating Ralph Allen's home at Prior Park; Robert Alter, *Fielding and the Nature of the Novel* (Cambridge, Mass.: Harvard University Press, 1968), finds an "inviolable unity of design" in Tom Jones as well as a "doubleness of irony" (139, 158) that permits Fielding to judge but also to represent the public world in his fictional characters; Battestin (1968), 188–217, describes Fielding using "iconomatic" means to make his scenes and characters stand as emblems for moral values. For Battestin, even ambiguity serves a mimetic function within the novel, revealing how difficult it is to distinguish in our lives true prudence from false, to distinguish wisdom from mere cunning.

5. *Novels of the 1740s* (Athens: University of Georgia Press, 1982), 186–87.

6. Richetti (1990), 196.

7. Smollett's sense that his Scots background kept him out of the English literary and social mainstream does appear clearly in his repeated attempts to produce his play *The Regicide* and his frequent anger at what he took to be the unfair treatment that the play received. See Buck (rpt. 1925; 1973), ix, 54, and 92. After the great success of *Roderick Random* in 1747, Smollett's life in London combined insider and outsider sympathies to a degree that made anamnesis a congenial response for him.

8. I will be citing the following works by Smollett. Page numbers will be included in parentheses in the text: *Roderick Random*, ed. Paul-Gabriel Boucé (Oxford: Oxford University Press, 1979); *Humphry Clinker*, ed. Thomas R. Preston (Athens: University of Georgia Press, 1990); *The Life and Adventures of Sir Launcelot Greaves*, ed. Peter Wagner (London: Penguin Books, 1988).

9. When Dowling reports Bridget's death "at Salisbury," he is, as is frequently the case, considerably agitated (5.8.245). When he later meets Jones at the Bell Inn in Gloucester, he responds "a little eagerly" when Jones is identified, then he sits "silent, biting his Fingers, making Faces, grinning, and looking wonderfully arch" (8.8.433). When Jones next encounters Dowling, both men are waiting for horses on their way to Coventry, they drink a bottle together, and Dowling refers in passing to "your Uncle Allworthy" (12.10.657). This is a revelation that Jones

overlooks and only the most observant of readers will catch. But Fielding does assure that the reader has clues available. As remains the case in his climactic interview with Allworthy, Dowling will reveal the truth only if he is asked the right questions (18.8.948–49).

10. This characterization is John Barth's. See his "Afterword," to *Roderick Random* (New York: New American Library, 1964), 476 and 474. Barth notes Smollett's birth mystery but then dismisses it: "Perhaps the less *said* about that clanking device the better" (471). We can learn much about both the different social motives and the different notions of literary representation held by Fielding and Smollett if we attend more carefully to the sometimes small details that make Smollett's plot "clank." Barth reads Smollett's "resentment" as constitutional, a part of his nature, rather than as owing to his bitterness about the slights he suffered as a Scotsman.

11. Paulson, "Smollett: The Satirist as a Character Type," chap. 5 of *Satire and the Novel in Eighteenth-Century England* (New Haven & London: Yale University Press, 1967), 165–97. Knapp (1949), 308–15. Paulson claims that "in Smollett's novels satire itself is the main aim" (165); Knapp claims that Smollett's intentions, particularly early in his career, "were instruction and reform through satire" (310). Both Paulson and Knapp take a line similar to that of Rufus D. Putney in his influential essay, "The Plan of *Peregrine Pickle*," *PMLA* 60 (1945): 1051–65. Putney responds to the claim that *Peregrine Pickle* "is formless" by arguing that it actually is "carefully planned to promote the ends of satire" (1051, 1053). In other words, Putney seemingly avoids the problem of Smollett's "quest for form" by pointing to a satiric unity in the novels. The problem with this rehabilitation of Smollett via the label "satirist" is that it places him once again within mimetic rather than within anamnestic categories. Satire, as both Putney and Paulson point out, has public ends. Its disturbing or even subversive tendencies are curbed by its moral goals. Smollett, I contend, is exploding the very terms of moral questions as they were being debated in mid-eighteenth-century England. Thus, when Putney claims that *Peregrine Pickle* is "composed of eleven major divisions" (1059) or Paulson claims that "Roderick Random acted as a satirist of society out of both desire for revenge (private) and moral conviction (public)" (269), their arguments are ingenious but, upon review, unconvincing. No reader who struggles through *Peregrine Pickle* can say where those neat divisions are; no reader of *Roderick Random* can say what "moral conviction" might be for Roderick. Anamnesis and satire overlap insofar as they both may subvert the status quo, but anamnesis stands apart from satire as a criticism of the basic assumptions about representation that satirists—writers like Fielding, for one example—make. Knapp, Paulson, Bloch, and Putney all claim that satire diminishes in Smollett's later work, particularly in *Humphry Clinker*. This claim is important for my argument precisely because, while the tone of *Humphry Clinker* may be kinder and gentler, that novel actually intensifies the anamnestic tendencies of *Roderick Random*.

12. See Beasley (1982), 54–55, for a fine analysis of how Fielding's first-person narrators achieve the power both to order and to judge events.

13. Ibid., 124.

14. For a fuller discussion of Fielding's rehabilitation of the elite in *Joseph Andrews*, see McCrea (1988), 124–27.

15. For the best recent discussion of the conservative and traditional nature of Fielding's social attitudes, see Malvin R. Zirker's "General Introduction" (1988), lix–lxxxiii.

16. See Boucé (1976), 344–45, both for this excerpt from the *Critical Review* as well as for the standard interpretation of it.

17. J. Campbell (1995), 12–14, argues that masking becomes more problematic for Fielding as his career advances. His early "hope that the face . . . may survive" as a repository of "authentic identity, feeling, and value" (12) is replaced, in the case of the mask that Amelia wears after her surgery, with the sense that the mask makes no difference. Amelia, however, is a virtuous character; she has nothing to hide. The revelation of Square behind the curtain in Molly Seagrim's bedroom—this is unmasking of the sort that remains viable and vital for Fielding throughout his writing.

18. See Battestin (1968), 189–96, for an extended commentary upon both the nature and the significance of Jones's conversion. Mary Poovey, "Journeys from This World to the Next: The Providential Promise in *Clarissa* and *Tom Jones*," *ELH* 43 (1976): 314, argues that the reward Tom receives as a result of his conversion figures the reward that all virtuous Christians may expect. Prudence in the human realm corresponds with Providence in the divine.

19. Beasley (1982), 118.

20. Battestin (1968), 213.

21. *Sir Launcelot Greaves* opens with a character, Captain Crowe, who has been cheated out of an estate by "two malicious old women [who] docked the entail and left the estate to an alien" (42). Crowe, although "he was heir of blood" (248), could not defeat the women's claims until Ferret reveals that he was clandestinely married to one of them. She "consequently could not transact any deed of alienation without his concurrence; ergo, the docking of the intail of the estate . . . was illegal and of none effect" (249). The estate is worth 12,000 pounds and Crowe uses part of it to help his nephew, Tom Clarke, and Dolly Cowslip begin married life. In his handling of Crowe's estate, Smollett not only redacts comically the anxieties about property in the cases of Launcelot and Aurelia, he also reveals how Hale's "right of Representation" could empower eighteenth-century women. Ferret's maleness finally defeats his clandestine wife's bad purposes, but, for most of the novel, his status has been absent and/or disguised. For references to Ferret as a specifically Hobbesian cynic, see 247 and 248.

22. Douglas (1995), 118–19, notes that Ferret wins arguments with Greaves about law and society, but she does not take this as evidence against her claim that Smollett here gives precedence to the aristocratic body and, by implication, to the traditions of romance.

Chapter 6: Clarissa's Pregnancy
and the Fate of Patriarchal Power

1. In "Scholarly Texts: An Unapologetic Defense," *Theory and Tradition in Eighteenth-Century Studies*, ed. Richard B. Schwartz (Carbondale: Southern Illinois University Press, 1990), 156, John Middendorf attacks Angus Ross's edition of *Clarissa* because it "contains no textual apparatus and simply reprints, with alterations, the first edition." Middendorf is particularly upset by Ross's handling of Richardson's punctuation. All my subsequent references to *Clarissa* will be to Ross's edition, which I use despite Middendorf's criticism of it, because I believe Richardson's portrayal of Lovelace and Clarissa in the first edition—before he set about "blackening" Lovelace's character in the subsequent editions—reveals most clearly the kinship between the two young lovers, the similarity in the problems they face. Also the Ross edition has the advantage of being available in a single volume. Readers interested in Richardson's revisions of *Clarissa* should consult Shirley Van Marter's essays on that topic in *Studies In Bibliography* 26 (1973): 107–32 and 28 (1975): 119–52, as well as Florian Stuber's introduction to the photofacsimile of the third edition of *Clarissa* (New York: AMS Press, Inc., 1990), 20–39. Stuber also, 18–19, gives an evenhanded summary of the strengths and weaknesses of Ross's edition.

2. Judith Wilt, "He Could Go No Farther: A Modest Proposal About Lovelace and Clarissa," *PMLA* 92 (1977): 19–32. Castle's critique of Wilt's essay occurs in her *Clarissa's Ciphers: Meaning and Disruption in Richardson's "Clarissa"* (Ithaca & London: Cornell University Press, 1982), 166 n.

3. For the connection between abortion and infanticide in eighteenth-century canon law, see Eugene R. Quay, "Justifiable Abortion—Medical and Legal Foundations—Part II," *The Georgetown Law Journal* 49 (1961): 395–538. For studies of abortion in common law, particularly the importance of "quickening," see R. Sauer, "Infanticide and Abortion in Nineteenth-Century Britain," *Population Studies* 32 (1978): 83–84, and Colin Francome, *Abortion Practice in Britain and the United States* (London: Allen and Unwin, 1986), 12. Richardson places Clarissa's death twelve weeks and two days after her rape, or just before, were she pregnant, the period when "quickening" might occur. He thus protects her from guilt—at least by the standards of the common law. Clarissa herself anticipates the charge that she commits the sin of self-destruction: "Although I wish not for life, yet I would not like a poor coward desert my post, when I *can*, and when it is my *duty* to maintain it" (1117).

4. Gilbert and Gubar (1979) traced both the fact and the trope of patriarchal dominion over the female voice in authors ranging from Milton to Emily Dickinson. They established for critics of Castle's generation a way of reading both verse and prose fiction—one in which reference to "patriarchal power" defines our understanding of the treatment of female protagonists. In *Clarissa's Ciphers*, Castle responds to William Beatty Warner's *Reading "Clarissa": The Struggles of Interpretation* (New Haven: Yale University Press, 1979), which is an avowedly

deconstructive reading of the novel. Warner emphasizes that Clarissa and Lovelace are equivalent in their love of writing; he thus wins from Castle the accusation of "startling primitive misogyny" (194), and she uses "patriarchal power" to reestablish ethical distance between the two characters. Armstrong (1987), claims that Gilbert and Gubar (and Ian Watt as well) do not attend to the "political" power women invent for themselves in the eighteenth-century "domestic sphere." She finds in conduct books of the period "historical conditions" that, she claims, Gilbert and Gubar ignore. Hers is one of the first major books of the 1980s to spurn "patriarchal power" as a premise of interpretation.

5. For only two examples of critics influenced by Castle, see Linda S. Kauffman, *Discourses of Desire: Gender, Genre, and Epistolary Fictions* (Ithaca & London: Cornell University Press, 1986), and Tassie Gwillym, *Samuel Richardson's Fictions of Gender* (Stanford: Stanford University Press, 1993).

6. See *Feminine Sexuality: Jacques Lacan and the "école freudienne,"* ed. Juliet Mitchell and Jacqueline Rose, trans. Jacqueline Rose (New York: W.W. Norton, 1982), 74–86, for Lacan's distinction between the penis and the phallus, particularly page 82 for his discussion of the phallus as a "male sign" that "marks" both men and women (men being marked with authority, women with "lack"). This marking takes place apart from specific considerations of potency. As Gilbert and Gubar's version of "patriarchal power" came into question in the 1980s, Lacan's vocabulary grew in influence because he justifies references to patriarchy in conjunction with a recognition of the historical vagaries of male impotence. For Lacan, "Meaning is only and ever erected, it is set up and fixed. The phallus symbolises the effects of the signifier in that having no value in itself, it can represent that to which value accrues" (43). For Lacan, the weakness of James Harlowe Sr. and Lord M. would not preclude Clarissa's violation by "patriarchy."

7. *The Rape of Clarissa* (Minneapolis: University of Minnesota Press, 1982), 52–53. Richardson's troubling treatment of the distinction between "masculine" and "feminine" is only one of several in *Clarissa*. For example, the harder we look at the social categories that underlie classic essays on the novel by Christopher Hill and Ian Watt—upwardly mobile middle class versus decaying aristocracy—the more tenuous they become. The same happens with distinctions between Clarissa's sincerity and Lovelace's theatricality, between Clarissa's concern with private feelings and Lovelace's with public image. Lovelace achieves vicious ends by assuming/creating identities for himself and others, but what are we to make of the various pseudonyms under which Clarissa transacts her correspondence? If Clarissa and Anna prove their virtue in their writing, what are we to make of Lovelace's having "always . . . a pen in his fingers" (74)? Lovelace offhandedly assumes his social superiority to the Harlowes, but Clarissa observes that her "family . . . was as good as his own, 'bating that it was not allied to the peerage" (321). If Lovelace is more the social equivalent than the social antithesis of James Harlowe Jr., then how can we use status to decide where virtue or truth resides?

8. For a commentary upon this will that parallels mine, see Zomchick (1993), 62–64. Zomchick does not note the doubts that Clarissa's grandfather himself expresses about the will, but he does see that the patriarch in *Clarissa* is "weakened" (70). Rather than accounting for that weakness, Zomchick places Clarissa between "juridical and patriarchal values" (81), between a view of family that emphasizes interest and a view that emphasizes affection. He writes quite convincingly about the ways in which James Jr. and Arabella use commercial interests to destroy family unity but is less convincing in his discussion of "Lovelace's aristocratic character" (82). He overlooks that Lovelace is (or could be) as much the beneficiary of demographic crisis as James Harlowe Jr. hopes to be.

9. Clarissa's uncle Anthony reports of Lovelace that "besides his paternal estate, he was the immediate heir to very splendid fortunes; that when he [Anthony] was in treaty for his niece Arabella, Lord M. told him what great things he and his two half sisters intended to do for him [Lovelace], in order to qualify him for the title (which would be extinct at his lordship's death) . . . or a still higher, that of these ladies' father, which had been for some time extinct on failure of heirs male." Both Lovelace and James Jr. are spoiled by relatives who see in them their various families' last, best hope for genealogical continuity. But while James Jr. eagerly pursues his opportunities (perhaps in this he does reveal himself an arriviste), Lovelace slights his family. He does so, I am suggesting, because the extinction of lines is a burden for him. Even in his own line, he is, as Belford dolefully reminds him, "the last of thy name" (502), a truth that Lovelace already has announced, referring to himself as the "*last* of the blood of the Lovelaces" (426).

10. "Clarissa Harlowe and Her Times," *Essays in Criticism* 5 (1955): 338. Hill argues that the "greatness" of *Clarissa* "derives" from its being about "social institutions." More specifically, he describes Clarissa falling victim in a conflict between "developing bourgeois society," as represented by the Harlowes, and a cavalier aristocracy, as represented by Lovelace, who "descends from the heroes of Restoration comedy" (315, 322, and 326). In the same vein, in his chapter "Richardson as Novelist: *Clarissa*" (1957), 222, Ian Watt casts Clarissa as a heroic individual set against "the aristocracy, the patriarchal family system."

11. Clarissa repeatedly asserts that her "fight" with her brother only can be "fair" if her father acts on her behalf. When James Jr. urges her to forbid Lovelace's visits, she asks "what authority I had to take such a step in *my father's house*" (49, my italics). Later, as the crisis intensifies, she implores her father, "Transfer not, I beseech you, to a brother and sister, your own authority over your child" (221–22).

12. Anna Howe and Clarissa repeatedly ask each other for "particulars," thus justifying the length of their correspondence. For a brief sample, see 39, 40, 41, 53, and 107. While differently motivated, Lovelace's focus upon "minutiae" is equally intent. See 473, 762, 923, and 961. When Mowbray writes to Belford, "I send by poor Lovelace's desire, for *particulars*. . . . He cannot bear to set pen to paper; yet wants to know every minute passage of Miss Harlowe's departure"

(1359), Lovelace's situation—his inability to write, his reliance upon Belford and Mowbray—reveals his defeat before Clarissa's version of the "particular."

13. That Clarissa *is* privileged in her wealth and status relative to almost any percentage of people living in eighteenth-century England that we might care to name is indisputable. Critics who focus upon "the institutionalized advantages of patriarchal power" (Castle, 193) tend to overlook this. Richardson will not fix her legal and educational disadvantages vis-a-vis men of her class. She gives up her claim to the dairy house because she will not "litigate with my papa" (134). But Anna Howe apparently believes she can win the case, and Zomchick (62–64) shows that she does have viable recourse in this matter. She, at age seventeen, is only now preparing to study Latin (1468), a language the men of her class would have studied from boyhood. But how their exposure to the classics has bettered Lovelace and James Jr. is difficult to say. Without wishing to minimize the discrimination under which women labored in the eighteenth century, I do contend that all cultural deprivation is relative and that Clarissa Harlowe's life, until her brother feels threatened by her, has been one of great privilege.

14. Robert A Erickson, "'Written in the Heart': *Clarissa* and Scripture," *Eighteenth-Century Fiction* 2 (1989): 26, points out that Clarissa's letter to Lovelace rescinding her decision to seek shelter with his family—the letter he is clever enough not to pick up—is an "appeal to Scriptural authority over a father's dealing with a daughter." Clarissa invokes Numbers 30 in her letter and "Richardson the editor appends a note (in all editions) pointing out that 'the vows of a single woman, and of a wife, if the father of one, or the husband of the other, disallow of them, as soon as they know of them, are to be of no force.'" Clarissa would rely upon the authority of the "father" to protect her from Lovelace and from the consequences of her running off with him. But her biological father has been alienated from her, and Lovelace "slights" the patriarch rather than deferring to him. Clarissa would invoke the authority of both the Scripture and her father, but sent amidst various "fictive" versions of kinship, the letter does not reach its intended audience and cannot save her.

15. The text of this, perhaps Clarissa's most famous and most provocative letter, reads in part: "I have good news to tell you. I am setting out with all diligence for my father's house. . . . I am overjoyed with the assurance of a thorough reconciliation through the interposition of a dear blessed friend, whom I have always loved and honoured. . . . You may in time, possibly, see me at my father's, at least if it be not your own fault" (1233). The letter misleads Lovelace, who fails to "read . . . for *my father's house*, Heaven" (1274), but he is hardly alone. Belford is at first "amazed" by the letter (1243), and Morden and Lord M. (1286) also misunderstand it, participating fully in what Belford later refers to as his "stupidity" (1274). Their mistake is easy enough to make, for Clarissa here replaces James Harlowe Sr., her biological father, with a father of her own invention.

16. Lovelace accuses Clarissa of "deception" in the "my father's house" letter and claims that it excuses him "for all his stratagems and attempts against her" (1302). Clarissa anticipates his self-vindication and worries about her behavior.

Belford reports that "she meant only an innocent allegory . . . and . . . was afraid it was not quite right in *her*" (1297). Clarissa's punctilio in this regard—Lovelace, after all, was ready to invade her quarters—reveals how much she needs to maintain her distinction between truth and "delusion," and how fragile she now sees that distinction to be.

17. Erickson (39) notes that Clarissa's various meditations on Scripture make "changes" in the texts; he sees those changes as "nothing less than a revision of patriarchal scripture into her own person and gender." But the meditations also might be read as her attempt to maintain the influence of the patriarch in her greatly altered condition.

18. In her instructions to the children of her "poor neighbours," her warnings against "the delusions of men," Clarissa states the moral of her story much more powerfully than in her somewhat implausible advice to her cousin Dolly that in "a strict observance of filial duty" (1377) lies both security and happiness.

19. I allude here to M. H. Abrams's controversial essay "The Deconstructive Angel," *Critical Inquiry* 3 (1976): 425–38, but not to join in Abrams's attack upon Jacques Derrida and his American adherents for their celebration of "indeterminacy." Rather, I use the phrase to emphasize a resemblance between Lovelace and Derrida as writers who reveal that signs (be they written, spoken, or denotative of class) can be objects of play, of fabrication. Both Derrida and Lovelace begin this free play with the death of the father, the end of "phallogocentrism." Lovelace is not the agent of "patriarchal power" so much as he is, at least in his own mind, its antitype, even its victim. In one of his first letters, he describes his first "love," a "quality-jilt, whose infidelity I have vowed to revenge upon as many of the sex as shall come into my power" (143). Lovelace's adolescent sexuality—he places this affair in "my early manhood"—is shaped by "quality," which he uses synonymously with class: "I could not bear that a woman should prefer a coronet to me" (144). The threat of patriarchal "quality" to Lovelace becomes clear when Lord M. assumes his right to take both Lovelace's name and (if Clarissa is pregnant) his son: "May this marriage be crowned with a great many fine boys (I desire no girls) to build up again a family so ancient. The first boy shall take my name by Act of Parliament" (787). While M.'s dismissal of "girls" reveals "patriarchal power" operating as Castle understands it, his grasping after Lovelace's "first boy" reveals how vitiated that power is. For typical Derridian comments upon the father and the sign, see his *Of Grammatology*, trans. Gayatri Chakravorty Spivak (Baltimore & London: The Johns Hopkins University Press, 1976), 50–63.

20. *Sermons Preached Upon Several Occasions* (Oxford: The Clarendon Press, 1823), 1:37. Erickson (19), describes South as a clergyman "closer to him [Richardson] in temperament than those of his own day."

21. Here I would link the passivity and weakness of Sir Robert Filmer (see chap. 2), as described by Peter Laslett, with the physical impairments of Lord M. and James Harlowe Sr. In Filmer's "real" life and in Richardson's fiction, the "historical condition" of male impotence has considerable impact.

22. See Michael McKeon (1987), 19 and 22, for both a definition and an application of "simple abstraction." McKeon takes the term from Marx's *Grundrisse*, as it is explicated by Louis Althusser. "Simple abstraction" comes at the "end" of a historical process when "the stabilizing of terminology" is possible, as it was not at the "beginning." McKeon's two central examples of "simple abstraction" are the terms "novel" and "middle class," particularly as critics have used them in studies of eighteenth-century fiction. In the twenty years since the publication of Gilbert and Gubar's *The Madwoman in the Attic*, "patriarchal power" and "patriarchal authority" have become, I believe, "simple abstractions." Like many simple abstractions, "patriarchy" has great explanatory power, even though claims based upon it do not always jibe with the "histories" of individual patriarchs.

23. Refusing to answer questions, Clarissa places herself outside Lacan's vocabulary. That vocabulary, as developed by the master, his *école*, and his recent interpreters, is characterized by an epistemological and ontological insistence that is alien to the detailed and domestic world of Clarissa. Consider for one example Ellie Ragland-Sullivan's summary of the Lacanian phallus and female lack: "The Phallus is . . . the signifier or creator of the lack that establishes substitutive Desire as a permanent ontological state and makes adult 'wanting' a shadow pantomime of the primordial dream of Desire between mother and infant," *Jacques Lacan and the Philosophy of Psychoanalysis* (Urbana & Chicago: University of Illinois Press, 1987), 271. I translate this to mean that patriarchal power resides apart from individual men and is expressed in a culture's social, economic, and political arrangements as all of those "mark" the child. In her silence, Clarissa frees herself from this signification.

24. "Sweat," in *I Love Myself When I Am Laughing*, ed. Alice Walker (Old Westbury, N.Y.: The Feminist Press, 1979), 198.

25. Simone de Beauvoir's introduction to *The Second Sex*, trans. H. M. Parshley (New York: Knopf, 1952), offers a potentially helpful guide to Clarissa's status, particularly since de Beauvoir describes "patriarchal power" but does not call it that. In rebuilding her "father's house" on her own terms, Clarissa anticipates de Beauvoir's definition of woman as "other": "She is defined and differentiated with reference to man, not he with reference to her; she is the incidental, the inessential as opposed to the essential. He is the Subject, he is the Absolute—she is the Other. The category of the Other is as primordial as consciousness itself" (11).

Chapter 7: Demographic Crisis and Simple Stories: Burney, Inchbald, Lennox, and the Nature of Incest

1. Castle's *Masquerade and Civilization* was published in 1986. For Bakhtin's work on the "carnivalesque," see his *Problems of Dostoevsky's Poetics* (1984). In

references to *Dostoevsky's Poetics*, page numbers will be given in parentheses in the text.

2. Patricia Meyer Spacks, *Desire and Truth: Functions of Plot in Eighteenth-Century Novels* (Chicago & London: University of Chicago Press, 1990); Catherine Craft-Fairchild, *Masquerade and Gender: Disguise and Female Identity in Eighteenth-Century Fictions by Women* (University Park: The Pennsylvania State University Press, 1993); Eleanor Ty, *Unsex'd Revolutionaries: Five Women Novelists of the 1790s* (Toronto: University of Toronto Press, 1993). All subsequent references to these books are given in the text, with page numbers in parentheses.

3. Ty is a revealing exception here. She is remarkably sensitive to signs of weakness and uncertainty in Dorriforth/Elmwood. She points to cases in which one "patriarchal injunction in fact negates or contradicts" another. She notices instances in which "Dorriforth breaks down and submits to" Miss Milner (93). But the "patriarchal etiology" finally predominates so powerfully in her writing that these "transgressions against the patriarch" (92) do not lead her to reassess the power that she attributes to him.

4. Claims that there are specifically female plots abound in recent criticism, but they frequently are undercut by novels by male authors that share literary techniques with novels by female authors. The result is that the most eminent feminist critics tend to put gender in quotation marks. Paula R. Backscheider in her *Daniel Defoe: Ambition and Innovation* (Lexington: The University of Kentucky Press, 1986) provides one example. Seeking to illustrate Defoe's debts to female novelists, she confronts the problem of asserting that a woman's novel can be written by a man. Her response (182, 183) is to put the woman's novel is quota-tion marks. In her *Desire and Truth*, Patricia Meyer Spacks takes a similar course. Because many male authors share the plots and techniques that she would label female, she puts masculine and feminine in quotation marks (187 and 195). In her afterword, Spacks offers a fine summary of this tendency: "To the 'masculine' realm belong self-love, reason, sublimity, art. Social sentiment, emotion of all kinds, beauty, and nature associate themselves with the 'feminine.' . . . In a crude sense, self-love, reason, and sublimity can be understood as categories of domi-nation, their 'feminine' counterparts as emblems of community" (235). Sentimen-tal fictions by Sterne and Mackenzie provide only the most obvious challenges to Spacks's "crude" generalizations.

5. *Forbidden Partners: The Incest Taboo in Modern Culture* (New York: Columbia University Press, 1987). See particularly 126–41. Page numbers for all subsequent references to Twitchell's study will be given in parentheses in the text.

6. Jack Goody, "A Comparative Approach to Incest and Adultery," *British Journal of Sociology* 7 (1956): 286–305, studies the toleration of incest by families interested in maintaining their wealth. Writing thirty years in advance of the Stones, he does not see the particular relevance of this practice to the eighteenth-century elite.

7. Martin C. Battestin with Ruthe R. Battestin, *Henry Fielding: A Life* (London & New York: Routledge, 1989), 18–24. Page numbers for all subsequent references

to the *Life* will be given in parentheses in the text. Battestin also traces the motif of incest in Fielding's novels in his "Henry Fielding, Sarah Fielding, and the 'dreadful Sin of Incest,'" *Novel: A Forum on Fiction* 13 (1979): 6–18.

8. Ed. Edward A. and Lillian D. Bloom (Oxford & New York: Oxford University Press, 1968). All subsequent references to *Evelina* will be to the Blooms' edition; page numbers will be indicated in parentheses. Burney does not raise the question of consanguineous marriage, but the paternal image of Villars is perhaps awash in a darker tint. His professions of love for Evelina are powerfully impassioned: "She is one . . . for whom I have lately wished to live; and she is one whom to serve I would with transport die" (20). His hopes for her adulthood are to bestow "her on one who may be sensible of her worth, and then sink . . . to eternal rest in her arms" (15). Does he wish to give her away, or does he wish to keep her near him for the rest of his life? Despite being the blushing bride of Lord Orville, Evelina, at the novel's close, returns to Berry Hill and "the arms of the best of men" (406). The arms are not those of Orville, but of Villars. If we can find husbandly tints in Evelina's father, so we can find fatherly tints in her husband. Orville, throughout her various embarrassments in London, is repeatedly described as her protector; he is more guardian than suitor. In Burney's *Cecelia*, Mortimer Delvile is the son of first cousins.

9. Margaret Anne Doody, "Beyond *Evelina*: The Individual Novel and The Community of Literature," *Eighteenth-Century Fiction* 3 (1991): 363–65, offers a helpful reminder that Burney once was celebrated for her comedy rather than, as today, used to test various feminist approaches. Susan C. Greenfield, "'O Dear Resemblance of Thy Murdered Mother': Female Authorship in *Evelina*," *Eighteenth-Century Fiction* 3 (1991): 308, points out that Evelina, despite claiming that it is not her wish, does leave Villars; she chooses to "defy her surrogate father and enter the forbidden public world."

10. The temptation, of course, is to describe Evelina as Belmont's "natural" or his "real" daughter. I use "biological" here to emphasize that Burney brings the "nature" of filial relations into question. Demographic crisis and the turn to fictive versions of kinship make the word "natural" equivocal in discussions of eighteenth-century kinship. Today, the prevalence of divorce has a similar effect, at least in American culture, as parents in blended families, unwilling to imply potentially derogatory distinctions between their "biological" and their stepchildren, also avoid "real."

11. Julia Epstein, "Burney Criticism: Family Romance, Psychobiography, and Social History," *Eighteenth-Century Fiction* 3 (1991): 278, thus characterizes the recognition scene.

12. I would give considerable weight to the verb "extorted" here. As fictive and biological versions of kinship become increasingly intertwined in the eighteenth century, fraud becomes not only more difficult to detect but also more difficult to dismiss. Dame Green, the erstwhile washerwoman, does not crumble before Belmont. Her resistance is stronger than that which Blifil offers to Allworthy in *Tom Jones*. In *Evelina*, the revelation of the birth mystery does not place the characters as rapidly as it does in *Joseph Andrews* or in *Roderick Random*.

13. *Eighteenth-Century Fiction* 3 (1991). Besides the previously cited essays by Julia Epstein, Margaret Anne Doody, and Susan C. Greenfield, the collection includes Amy J. Pawl, "'What Other Name May I Claim?': Names and Their Owners in Frances Burney's *Evelina*," and Gina Campbell, "Bringing Belmont to Justice: Burney's Quest for Paternal Recognition in *Evelina*." References to these essays will give page numbers in parentheses.

14. Jane Austen, *Emma*, ed. David Lodge and James Kinsley (London: Oxford University Press, 1971), 4, 5.

15. Lacan's distinction between the phallus and the penis, his notion that men and women are marked by patriarchy apart from the material circumstances of particular men and women, can help to explain Evelina's "need" for Belmont to be a father to her—just as it can help to explain Clarissa's rebuilding of her "father's house" (see chap. 6).

16. Here we can see one specific way in which Polly is not Evelina's equal. Lacking Evelina's beauty and grace, Polly apparently never learns—at least the text does not tell us—who her natural father is.

17. In *Cecelia*, Burney places her heroine such that the accommodations reached by Evelina are impossible. Cecelia's guardians include the miser Briggs, the spendthrift Harrel, and the supercilious aristocrat Delvile. The diversity that her uncle hoped would protect her actually gives her no place to go when these men cannot speak to each other. Cecelia falls in love with Mortimer Delvile, the son of one of her guardians. Mortimer is the offspring of a marriage between cousins that attempts to save a family "name" from extinction. If his breeding manifests itself in his virtue and grace, it also means that Mortimer cannot meet the one condition for Cecelia's husband set by her uncle's will—that her husband take her name. The Delvile family is unceasing in its praise of Cecelia's beauty and virtue. Because her ancestors were farmers, they take her as a splendid example of lower-class virtue, but they will not sacrifice their name to that virtue. When Mortimer falls in love with Cecelia, he only can propose a clandestine marriage to her; he is unwilling to risk his parents' negative. Cecelia is torn by his proposal, comes to the altar with him, but is driven from it when a mysterious woman objects to the marriage. Cecelia and Mortimer, while in many ways the equals of Evelina and Orville, cannot write themselves free of the conflicts between status and virtue that surround them. Cecelia has money, and Mortimer has a "name," but they lack a fiction to disguise the differences between them. Their marriage occurs only at the cost of Cecelia's wealth and thus of her opportunities to do good.

18. See Twitchell (1987), 246–47, for a summary of the effects of close proximity, particularly from childhood, upon procreation. Twitchell shows that, "Familiarity does not breed contempt; it simply does not breed at all." Interestingly enough, these female novelists say little about the childhood relationships between their protagonists. Twitchell's is a helpful reminder that the cousin, particularly if he were raised near the female, likely would be uninteresting to her—at least as a sexual partner.

19. Ed. Margaret Dalziel (Oxford & New York: Oxford University Press, 1989). All subsequent references to *The Female Quixote* are to this World's Classics edition. Page numbers will be given in parentheses in the text.

20. *Nobody's Story: The Vanishing Acts of Women Writers in the Marketplace, 1670–1820* (Berkeley & Los Angeles: University of California Press, 1994), xx–xxi. Gallagher emphasizes that "the 'nobodies' of my title are not ignored, silenced, erased, or anonymous women" (xiii). Rather, the nobodies are authors, women first but then men as well, who seek to convert paper into property, writing into wealth. These men and women are nobodies because they have no property and no standing in conventional terms—that is, land inherited patrilinearly. But they are important nobodies, nobodies who make livings as writers, because they are part of the transformation of wealth in the eighteenth century. They stand at the beginnings of the novel and at the beginning of an economy that is based upon paper and credit rather than upon land and its products.

21. In Susan C. Greenfield's essay for the *Eighteenth-Century Fiction* volume on Burney, she correlates Belmont's burning of his certificate of marriage to Caroline Evelyn with Burney's burning, to please her father, of a manuscript of the same name (306–7). Whatever Burney's motives for burning her *Caroline Evelyn*, her triumph in *Evelina*, her rising, as it were, from the ashes, proved her comic genius. Her subsequent instances of deference to her father were perhaps gracious but could not be required by him. Doody (1988), 148, claims of *Cecelia*, "Nobody who reads the novel can imagine this was a work ground out to please the author's father. Dr. Burney's deepest and most comforting beliefs are questioned."

22. Gallagher (1994), 195, errs in her summary of the situation in which the will leaves Arabella: "As long as Arabella refuses fiction, resists the suppositional, she owns her estate, but when she capitulates to textuality, she becomes the vehicle through which the estate descends from her father to his chosen male heir, her cousin." Gallagher's notion that Arabella controls her estate as long as she reads life via the romances redacts Doody's reading of the story. But Arabella increases the estate by one-third by marrying Glanville. The distinction between the romances and fiction that Gallagher's interpretation requires her to draw finally is untenable. Arabella, at the story's end, does not enter into fiction; rather she enters into useful fiction.

23. In bk. 9, chap. 8, Glanville does wound Sir George Bellmour with a sword. He acts out of "irresistible Fury" (357), failing to send a challenge or to give Bellmour time to prepare. His triumph is short-lived, and he achieves his final reward through other means. His swordsmanship, then, is even less important than Lovelace's. The day for solving disputes with duels has passed.

24. V. G. Kiernan, *The Duel in European History: Honour and the Reign of Aristocracy* (Oxford: Oxford University Press, 1988), 2–44, describes the social distinctions that dueling maintained. He then, 46–80, describes some of the rules that governed dueling. As his title indicates, dueling was for centuries an aristocratic activity, and its regulations were clear, if not elaborate. The encounter between

Glanville and Bellmour is more a fight than a duel. All subsequent references to Kiernan's book will be made parenthetically in the text.

25. Glanville is a hero of a new order, not a hero out of romance. For an attempt to read him as the latter, see James J. Lynch, "Romance and Realism in Charlotte Lennox's *Female Quixote," Essays on Literature* 14 (1987): 51–63.

26. C. S. Lewis, *The Allegory of Love: A Study in Medieval Tradition* (London: Oxford University Press, 1936), 30–38, discusses the limits placed upon women in the traditions of courtly love, traditions that, at first glance, seem to confer considerable power upon women of rank.

27. See Michel Foucault's discussion of the "gaze" and its power to incarcerate its object in part 3, "Docile Bodies," of his *Discipline and Punish: The Birthplace of the Prison,* trans. Alan Sheridan (New York: Pantheon Books, 1979).

28. Arabella repeatedly associates "Victories over Hearts" with "Quarrels" and "Bloodshed" (86, 110–11). She demands (127) that Glanville fight for her, citing precedents in her romances. In this case, Glanville's sister speaks the truth that is overlooked until the story's conclusion: "If those Persons you have named were Murderers, and made a Practice of killing People, I hope my Brother will be too wise to follow their Examples: A strange kind of Virtue and Courage indeed, to take away the Lives of one's Fellow-Creatures!" (127–28).

29. See the appendix written by Duncan Isles to the Oxford edition of *The Female Quixote* (419–28) for a discussion of the writing of the novel and the roles of both Johnson and Samuel Richardson in Lennox's career.

30. Twitchell (1987), 136–42.

31. Ed. J. M. S. Tompkins (Oxford & New York: Oxford University Press, 1988). All references to *A Simple Story* are taken from this World's Classics edition; page numbers are indicated in parentheses in the text.

32. See Spencer's introduction to the World's Classics edition, xix.

33. In her obituary, Miss Milner is referred to as Lady Elmwood (204), but otherwise references to her by her married name are very few.

34. See Castle (1986), 290–330, for a helpful reading of the function of this masquerade. Castle notes that the masquerade plays a less important role in *A Simple Story* than in earlier fictions; the event and the misunderstanding it creates are quite rapidly handled by Inchbald. I agree with Castle's claim (328) that "*A Simple Story* . . . leaves the masquerade behind, not because its imagery of liberation offends, but because liberation has become the currency of everyday life." In the vacuum created by the impairment of the patriarch, willful and sensuous women like Miss Milner have more exciting ways to challenge social traditions and assumptions about gender. (Characters disagree about whether Miss Milner has attended the masquerade in men's clothing, but the issue finally does not matter very much; she's bored by the event.)

35. Ibid., 305.

36. Ibid., 325–26, observes that, while Miss Milner is bored by the masquerade she attends because she has more exciting ways to challenge social traditions, in

Mathilda's case her world is turned upside down in a "simple meeting" with her father on a staircase. Mathilda's story "represents . . . an internalization of the carnivalesque. The transformational energy of the masquerade . . . moves into the private world of the bourgeois household, into the realm of individual psychology." (326). I see a similar "internalization" occurring in Elmwood's version of honor and in the authority he would claim.

37. In her own life Inchbald had affiliations with Jacobinism and with Wollstonecraft's circle about which she kept quiet but which she greatly valued. Her first biographer, James Boaden, sees this need for secrecy about her political and social affiliations as one of the great themes of Inchbald's life. See his *Memoirs of Mrs. Inchbald*, 2 vols. (London: Richard Bentley, 1833), 1:140–41.

38. Boaden, 1:274–77.

Conclusion

1. *Le Rouge et le Noir, Romans et Nouvelles de Stendhal*, ed. Henri Martineau (Paris: *Editions Gallimard*, 1952), 1:639. Brooks (1985), 67, cites this passage, translating it, "My novel is finished."

2. *Imagining A Self: Autobiography and Novel in Eighteenth-Century England* (Cambridge, Mass.: Harvard University Press, 1976).

3. *Masquerade and Civilization* (1986), 343.

4. Ibid., 344.

5. Robert Lovelace, of course, is an eighteenth-century character who invents selves. But he tends to impose his inventions upon others, and his inventiveness is associated with his villainy.

6. *Imagining a Self* (1976), 63.

7. In all the recent contests about Freudian psychology, one point has become clear. Although Freud designed his study of the psyche to be universal and timeless, he was shaped in basic ways by his cultural milieu—nineteenth-century Vienna. His discovery of the "family romance," I believe, probably had much to do with its fictional adumbrations in Stendhal and Dickens. Brooks rightly links nineteenth-century novels and Freud's case histories under the rubric "narrative."

8. Gothic fiction, from *The Castle of Otranto* to *The Monk*, also provides a fine example of this "divided impulse." These novels turn upon the revelation of a birth mystery, but the anagnorisis brings only loss and horror. Walpole reveals the government of the principality of Otranto to be illegitimate; Lewis reveals that Ambrosio has murdered his mother and raped and then murdered his sister. The narrative technique that, as used by Fielding, rightly places virtuous servants and foundlings brings closure to these Gothic tales, but closure that leaves characters—witness Theodore in *Otranto* and Lorenzo in *The Monk*—deracinated and broken. The conventionality of Gothic plots accompanies a powerful subversion

of both the literary and the social status quo. The Gothic setting, in a foreign land at a remote time, allows British authors to raise basic questions about religious and political legitimacy without appearing overtly seditious or inflammatory. Gothic fiction, then, is an anamnestic response to the issue of status inconsistency. See Elizabeth R. Napier, *The Failure of the Gothic: Problems of Disjunction in an Eighteenth-Century Literary Form* (Oxford: Clarendon Press, 1987), for a convincing argument that Gothic "conventions . . . speak directly to English anxieties about the war [with France]," even as they pretend to "escape from the political frenzy of the moment" (45). In writing about *Otranto*, Napier finds Walpole "boasting of his connection to a world of public responsibility while pretending to eschew all association with it" (74).

9. See Laslett (1949), 13.

10. Tristram Shandy is an instructive character in this regard. Sterne suggests that Tristram may not be Walter's son and also indicates that the Shandy estate, while in disrepair, has extent and value. But these topics go undeveloped. Tristram's problems are "personal" and, apparently, not to be solved by a discovery about his paternity or by his engendering a child.

Bibliography

Abrams, M. H. "The Deconstructive Angel." *Critical Inquiry* 3 (1976): 425–38.

Allen, John J. *Don Quixote: Hero or Fool?* Gainesville: University of Florida Press, 1971.

——. *Don Quixote: Hero or Fool? Part II.* Gainesville; University of Florida Press, 1979.

Alter, Robert. *Fielding and the Nature of the Novel.* Cambridge, Mass.: Harvard University Press, 1968.

Anonymous. *The Orphan Heiress of Sir Gregory: An Historical Fragment of the Last Century.* London: Sampson Low, 1799.

Armstrong, Nancy. *Desire and Domestic Fiction: A Political History of the Novel.* New York and Oxford: Oxford University Press, 1987.

Austen, Jane. *Emma.* Edited by David Lodge and James Kinsely. London: Oxford University Press, 1971.

Backscheider, Paula R. *Daniel Defoe: Ambition and Innovation.* Lexington: University of Kentucky Press, 1986.

——. *Daniel Defoe: His Life.* Baltimore and London: The Johns Hopkins University Press, 1989.

Bakhtin, M. M. *The Dialogic Imagination: Four Essays.* Edited by Michael Holquist. Translated by Caryl Emerson and Michael Holquist. Austin: University of Texas Press, 1981.

——. *Problems of Dostoevsky's Poetics.* Edited and translated by Caryl Emerson. Minneapolis: University of Minnesota Press, 1984.

Barth, John. Afterword to *Roderick Random* by Tobias Smollett, 469–79. New York: New American Library, 1964.

Basker, James G. *Tobias Smollett: Critic and Journalist.* Newark: University of Delaware Press, 1988.

Battestin, Martin C. "The Authorsip of Smollett's *Don Quixote.*" *Studies in Bibliography* 50 (1997): 295–321.

——. "Fielding's Definition of Wisdom: Some Functions of Ambiguity and Emblem in *Tom Jones.*" *ELH* 35 (1968): 188–217.

——. "Henry Fielding, Sarah Fielding, and the 'dreadful Sin of Incest.'" *Novel: A Forum on Fiction* 13 (1979): 6–18.

——. *The Moral Basis of Fielding's Art.* Middletown, Conn.: Wesleyan University Press, 1959.

————. "The Problem of *Amelia*: Hume, Barrow, and the Conversion of Captain Booth." *ELH* 41 (1974): 613–48.

————, with Ruthe R. Battestin. *Henry Fielding: A Life*. London and New York: Routledge, 1989.

Baxter, Richard. *The Life of Faith*. London: R. W. for Nevil Simmons, 1670.

Beasley, Jerry C. *Novels of the 1740s*. Athens: University of Georgia Press, 1982.

Blanchard, Frederick, T. *Fielding the Novelist*. New Haven, Conn.: Yale University Press, 1927.

Blewett, David. *Defoe's Art of Fiction*. Toronto: University of Toronto Press, 1979.

Bloch, Tuvia. "Smollett's Quest for Form." *Modern Philology* 65 (1967): 103–13.

Bloom, Harold. *The Anxiety of Influence*. New York: Oxford University Press, 1973.

Boaden, James. *Memoirs of Mrs. Inchbald*. 2 vols. London: Richard Bentley, 1833.

Boethius. *The Consolation of Philosophy*. Translated by R. H. Green. Indianapolis: Bobbs-Merrill, 1962.

Bonfield, Lloyd. "Marriage Settlements and the 'Rise of Great Estates': The Demographic Aspect." *Economic History Review*, 2d ser., 32 (1979): 483–93.

————. *Marriage Settlements, 1601–1740: The Adoption of the Strict Settlememt*. Cambridge: Cambridge University Press, 1983.

Booth, Wayne C. *The Rhetoric of Fiction*. Chicago and London: University of Chicago Press, 1961.

Boucé, Paul-Gabriel. *The Novels of Tobias Smollett*. Translated by Antonia White. London and New York: Longman, 1976.

Brooks, Peter. *Reading for the Plot: Design and Intention in Narrative*. New York: Albert A. Knopf, Inc., 1984.

Buck, Howard Swayze. *A Study in Smollett: Chiefly of "Peregrine Pickle."* 1925. Rpt. Mamaroneck, N. Y.: Paul P. Appel, Publisher, 1973.

Burney, Frances. *Cecelia*. Edited by Peter Sabor and Margaret Anne Doody. Oxford and New York: Oxford University Press, 1990.

————. *Evelina*. Edited by Edward A. and Lillian D. Bloom. Oxford and New York: Oxford University Press, 1968.

Butler, Judith. *Gender Trouble: Feminism and the Subversion of Identity*. New York: Routledge, 1990.

Byron, William. *Cervantes: A Biography*. Garden City, N.Y.: Doubleday, 1978.

Campbell, Gina. "Bringing Belmont to Justice: Burney's Quest for Paternal Recognition in *Evelina*." *Eighteenth-Century Fiction* 3 (1991): 321–40.

Campbell, Jill. *Natural Masques: Gender and Identity in Fielding's Plays and Novels*. Stanford: Stanford University Press, 1995.

Castle, Terry. *Clarissa's Ciphers: Meaning and Disruption in Richardson's "Clarissa."* Ithaca and London: Cornell University Press, 1982.

————. *Masquerade and Civilization: The Carnivalesque in Eighteenth-Century English Culture and Fiction*. Stanford: Stanford University Press, 1986.

Cervantes de Saavedra, Miguel. *Don Quixote*, the Ormsby translation revised. Edited by Joseph R. Jones and Kenneth Douglas. New York: W. W. Norton, 1981.

Craft-Fairchild, Catherine. *Masquerade and Gender: Disguise and Female Identity in Eighteenth-Century Fictions by Women*. University Park: The Pennsylvania State University Press, 1993.

Cross, Wilbur L. *The History of Henry Fielding*. 3 vols. New Haven, Conn.: Yale University Press, 1918.

Damrosch, Leopold Jr. *God's Plot and Man's Stories: Studies in the Fictional Imagination from Milton to Fielding*. Chicago and London: University of Chicago Press, 1985.

Davies, R. Trevor. *The Golden Century of Spain, 1501–1621*. London: Macmillan and Co., 1958.

de Beauvoir, Simone. *The Second Sex*. Translated by H. M. Parshley. New York: Alfred A. Knopf, 1952.

de Bruyn, Frans. "Latitudinarianism and Its Importance as a Precursor of Sensibility." *Journal of English and Germanic Philology* 80 (1981): 349–68.

Defoe, Daniel. *An Essay on Projects*. 1697. Rpt. Menston, England: Scolar Press, 1969.

———. *A Journal of the Plague Year*. Edited by Paula R. Backscheider. New York: W. W. Norton, 1992.

———. *The Letters of Daniel Defoe*. Edited by George H. Healey. Oxford: Clarendon Press, 1969.

———. *Moll Flanders*. Edited by Edward Kelly. New York: W. W. Norton, 1973.

———. *Robinson Crusoe*. Edited by Angus Ross. Harmondsworth, England: Penguin Books, 1965.

———. *Roxana*. Edited by David Blewett. Harmondsworth, England: Penguin Books, 1982.

———. *Tour thro' the Whole Island of Great Britain*. 1724–27. Introduction by G. D. H. Cole. 2 vols. New York: Kelley, 1968.

Derrida, Jacques. *Of Grammatology*. Edited by Gayatri Chakravorty Spivak. Baltimore and London: The Johns Hopkins University Press, 1976.

Dobson, Austen. *Fanny Burney (Madame D'Arblay)*. London: Macmillan and Co., 1903.

Doody, Margaret Anne. "Beyond *Evelina*: The Individual Novel and rhe Community of Literature." *Eighteenth-Century Fiction* 3 (1991): 359–71.

———. *Frances Burney: The Life in the Works*. New Brunswick, N.J.: Rutgers University Press, 1988.

———. Introduction to *The Female Quixote* by Charlotte Lennox, edited by Margaret Dalziel. Oxford and New York: Oxford University Press, 1989: xi–xxxii.

Douglas, Aileen. *Uneasy Sensations: Smollett and the Body*. Chicago and London: University of Chicago Press, 1995.

Duckworth, Alistair. "Michael McKeon and Some Recent Studies of Eighteenth-Century Fiction." *Eighteenth-Century Fiction* 1 (1988): 53–66.

Eagleton, Terry. *The Rape of Clarissa*. Minneapolis: University of Minnesota Press, 1982.

Efron, Arthur. *Don Quixote and the Dulcineated World*. Austin: University of Texas Press, 1971.

Emerson, Caryl, ed. and trans. *Problems of Dostoevsky's Poetics*. Minneapolis: University of Minnesota Press, 1984,

Epstein, Julia. "Burney Criticism: Family Romance, Psychobiography, and Social History." *Eighteenth-Century Fiction* 3 (1991): 277–82.

———. *The Iron Pen: Frances Burney and the Politics of Women's Writing*. Madison: The University of Wisconsin Press, 1989.

Erickson, Robert A. "'Written in the Heart': *Clarissa* and Scripture." *Eighteenth-Century Fiction* 2 (1989): 17–52.

Feyerabend, Paul. *Against Method: Outline of an Anarchistic Theory of Knowledge*. London: Verso, 1975.

Fielding, Henry. *Amelia*. Edited by Martin C. Battestin and Fredson Bowers. Middletown, Conn.: Wesleyan University Press, 1983.

———. *An Enquiry into the Causes of the Late Increase of Robbers and Related Writings*. Edited by Malvin R. Zirker. Middletown, Conn.: Wesleyan University Press, 1988.

———. *Joseph Andrews*. Edited by Martin C. Battestin. Middletown, Conn.: Wesleyan University Press, 1967.

———. *The Journal of a Voyage to Lisbon*. Vol. 16 of *Complete Works*, edited by W. E. Henley. London: Heineman, 1903.

———. *Tom Jones*. Edited by Martin C. Battestin and Fredson Bowers. Middletown, Conn.: Wesleyan University Press, 1975.

———. *The True Patriot*. Edited by Miriam Austin Locke. University: University of Alabama Press, 1964.

Forster, E. M. *Aspects of the Novel*. New York: Harcourt Brace, 1927.

Foucault, Michel. *Discipline and Punish: The Birthplace of the Prison*. Translated by Alan Sheridan. New York: Pantheon Books, 1979.

———. *Madness and Civilization: A History of Insanity in the Age of Reason*. Translated by Richard Howard. New York: Random House, 1965.

Francome, Colin. *Abortion Practice in Britain and the United States*. London: Allen and Unwin, 1986.

Freud, Sigmund. "Family Romances" [*Der Familien Roman der Neurotiker*]. 1908. Rpt. in *The Standard Edition of the Complete Psychological Works of Sigmund Freud*, edited and translated by James Strachey, 9:237–41. London: Hogarth Press, 1953–74.

Frye, Northrop. *Anatomy of Criticism: Four Essays*. Princeton, N.J.: Princeton University Press, 1957.

Gallagher, Catherine. *Nobody's Story: The Vanishing Acts of Women Writers in the Marketplace, 1670–1720*. Berkeley and Los Angeles: University of California Press, 1994.

Genette, Gerard. *Narrative Discourse: An Essay on Method*. Translated by Jane E. Lewin. Ithaca, N.Y.: Cornell University Press, 1980.

Gibbs, Vicary, ed. *The Complete Peerage*. London: St. Catharine Press, 1916.

Gilbert, Sandra M., and Susan Gubar. *The Madwoman in the Attic: The Woman Writer and the Nineteenth-Century Literary Imagination*. New Haven and London: Yale University Press, 1979.

Golden, Morris. "Public Context and the Imagining Self in *Amelia*." *University of Toronto Quarterly* 56 (1987): 377–91.

Goody, Jack. "A Comparative Approach to Incest and Adultery." *British Journal of Sociology* 7 (1956): 286–305.

Grant, Damian. *Tobias Smollett: A Study in Style*. Manchester: Manchester University Press, 1977.

Green, Otis. "El 'Ingenioso' Hidalgo." *Hispanic Review* 25 (1957): 175–93.

Greene, Donald J. *The Politics of Samuel Johnson*. New Haven, Conn.: Yale University Press, 1960.

Greenfield, Susan. "'O Dear Resemblance of Thy Murdered Mother': Female Authorships in *Evelina*." *Eighteenth-Century Fiction* 3 (1991): 301–20.

Gwillym, Tassie. *Samuel Richardson's Fictions of Gender*. Stanford: Stanford University Press, 1993.

Habakkuk, Sir John. "English Landownership, 1680–1740." *Economic History Review* o.s. 10 (1940): 2–17.

———. "Marriage Settlements in the Eighteenth Century." *Transactions of the Royal Historical Society*, 4th ser., 32 (1950): 15–30.

———. "The Rise and Fall of English Landed Families, 1600–1800." *Transactions of the Royal Historical Society*, 5th ser., 29 (1979): 187–207; 30 (1980): 199–221; 31 (1981): 195–217.

Hale, Matthew. *The History and Analysis of the Common Law in England*. Edited by Charles M. Gray. Chicago and London: The University of Chicago Press, 1971.

———. *De Successionibus apud Anglos: The Law of Hereditary Descents Shewing The Rise, Progress and Successive Alterations thereof: Also the Law of Descents as Now in Use*. London: S. S., 1700.

Harraway, Donna J. *Simians, Cyborgs, and Women: The Reinvention of Nature*. New York: Routledge, 1991.

Harth, Phillip. *Swift and Anglican Rationalism: The Religious Background of A Tale of A Tub*. Chicago: University of Chicago Press, 1961.

Havens, Raymond Dexter. *The Influence of Milton on English Poetry*. Cambridge, Mass.: Harvard University Press, 1922.

Hill, Christopher. "Clarissa Harlowe and Her Times." *Essays in Criticism* 5 (1955): 315–40.

Hilles, Frederick W. "Art and Artifice in *Tom Jones*." In *Imagined Worlds: Essays on Some English Novels and Novelists in Honour of John Butt*, edited by Maynard Mack and Ian Gregor. London: Methuen, 1968.

Holderness, B. A. "Widows in pre-industrial society: an essay upon their economic functions." In *Land, Kinship, and Life-Cycle*, edited by Richard M. Smith, 423–42. Cambridge: Cambridge University Press, 1984.

Hollingsworth, T. H. "Demography of the British Peerage." *Population Studies* 18 (1964): iv–108.

Huarte de San Juan, Juan. *The Examination of Men's Wits*. Translated by Richard Carew. 1594. Rpt. New York: Da Capo Press, 1969.

Hunter, J. Paul. *Before Novels: The Cultural Contexts of Eighteenth-Century English Fiction*. New York: W. W. Norton, 1990.

———. "The Lesson of *Amelia.*" In *Quick Springs of Sense: Studies in the Eighteenth Century*, edited by Larry S. Champion, 157–82. Athens: University of Georgia Press, 1974.

———. *Occasional Form: Henry Fielding and the Chains of Circumstance.* Baltimore and London: The Johns Hopkins University Press, 1975.

———. *The Reluctant Pilgrim: Defoe's Emblematic Method and the Quest for Form in Robinson Crusoe.* Baltimore: The Johns Hopkins University Press, 1966.

Hurston, Zora Neale. "Sweat." In *I Love Myself When I Am Laughing*, edited by Alice Walker. Old Westbury, N. Y.: The Feminist Press, 1979.

Inchbald, Elizabeth. *A Simple Story.* Edited by J. M. S. Tompkins. Oxford and New York: Oxford University Press, 1988.

Irigaray, Luce. *Ce Sexe qui n'est pas un.* Paris: Editions de Minuit, 1977.

Irwin, Michael. *Henry Fielding: The Tentative Realist.* Oxford: The Clarendon Press, 1967.

Isles, Duncan. Appendix to *The Female Quixote* by Charlotte Lennox, edited by Margaret Dalziel, 419–28. Oxford and New York: Oxford University Press, 1989.

James, Henry. *The Art of the Novel.* Edited by R. P. Blackmur. New York: Charles Scribner's Sons, 1934.

Johnson, Carroll B. "A Gallery of Decadents: Society in *Don Quijote*, Part II." *Indiana Journal of Hispanic Literature* 5 (1994): 195–211.

———. *Madness and Lust: A Psychological Approach to "Don Quijote."* Berkeley and Los Angeles: University of California Press, 1983.

Kauffman, Linda S. *Discourses of Desire: Gender, Genre, and Epistolary Fictions.* Ithaca and London: Cornell University Press, 1986.

Kiernan, V. G. *The Duel in European History: Honour and the Reign of Aristocracy.* Oxford: Oxford University Press, 1988.

Knapp, Lewis M. *Tobias Smollett: Doctor of Men and Manners.* Princeton, N.J.: Princeton University Press, 1949.

Ladurie, E. Leroy. "Un Concept: L'Unification Microbienne Du Monde (xive–xvlle siecles)." In *Le Territoire De l'Historien*, 2:43–71. Paris: Editions Gallimard, 1978.

Laslett, Peter, ed. *Patriarcha and Other Political Works of Sir Robert Filmer.* Oxford: Basil Blackwell, 1949.

Lee, Sidney. "John Phillps." In *Dictionary of Natonal Biography*, edited by Sir Leslie Stephen and Sir Sidney Lee, 5:1091–93. London: Humphrey Milford, 1917.

———. "Thomas Shelton." In *Dictionary of Natonal Biography*, edited by Sir Leslie Stephen and Sir Sidney Lee, 28:44–45. London: Humphrey Milford, 1917.

Lennox, Charlotte. *The Female Quixote.* Edited by Margaret Dalziel. Oxford and New York: Oxford University Press, 1989.

Lewis, C. S. *The Allegory of Love: A Study in Medieval Tradition.* London: Oxford University Press, 1936.

Ley, James, Earl of Marlborough. *A Learned Treatise Concerning Wards and Liveries.* London: G. Bishop and R. White for Henry Shephern and Henry Twyford, 1642.

Locke, John. *An Essay Concerning Human Understanding*. Edited by Peter Nidditch. Oxford: Clarendon Press, 1975.

———. *Two Treatises of Government*. Edited by Peter Laslett. Cambridge: Cambridge University Pres, 1966.

Lomas, Mrs. S. C., ed. *Manuscripts of the Earl of Denbigh*. London: Historical Manuscripts Commission, 1911.

Lynch, James J. "Romance and Realism in Charlotte Lennox's *Female Quixote*." *Essays on Literature* 14 (1987): 51–63.

Macfarlane, Alan, ed. *The Diary of Ralph Josselin 1616–1683*. Records of Social and Economic History, New Series. Vol. 3. London: The Oxford University Press, 1976.

———. *The Family Life of Ralph Josselin: A Seventeenth-Century Clergyman*. Cambridge: Cambridge University Press, 1970.

Mancing, Howard. *The Chivalric World of "Don Quixote": Style, Structure, and Narrative Technique*. Columbia: University of Missouri Press, 1982.

McCrea, Brian. "'Had not Joseph Withheld Him': The Portrayal of the Social Elite in *Joseph Andrews*." In *Man, God, and Nature in the Enlightenment*, edited by Donald C. Mell Jr., Theodore E. D. Braun, and Lucia D. Palmer, 123–28. East Lansing, Mich.: Colleagues Press, 1988.

———. *Henry Fielding and the Politics of Mid-Eighteenth-Century England*. Athens: University of Georgia Press, 1981.

———. "Politics and Narrative Technique in Fielding's *Amelia*." *Journal of Narrative Technique* 13 (1983): 131–40.

———. "Rewriting *Pamela*: Social Change and Religious Faith in *Joseph Andrews*. *Studies in the Novel* 16 (1984): 137–49.

McKeon, Michael. *The Origins of the English Novel, 1600–1740*. Baltimore: The Johns Hopkins University Press, 1987.

Middendorf, John. "Scholarly Texts: An Unapologetic Defense." In *Theory and Tradition in Eighteenth-Century Studies*, edited by Richard B. Schwartz, 143–61. Carbondale: Southern Illinois University Press, 1990.

Milton, John. *Complete Poems and Major Prose*. Edited by Merrit Y. Hughes. Indianapolis and New York: Bobbs Merrill, 1957.

Mitchell, Juliet, and Jacqueline Rose, eds. *Feminine Sexuality: Jacques Lacan and the école freudienne*. Translated by Jacqueline Rose. New York: W. W. Norton, 1982.

Montrelay, Michele. *L'Ombre et le nom sur la femininité*. Paris: Editions de Minuit, 1977.

Moore, Norman. "Matthew Hale." In *Dictionary of National Biography*, edited by Sir Leslie Stephen and Sir Sidney Lee, 902–9. Oxford: Humphrey Milford, 1917.

Napier, Elizabeth R. *The Failure of the Gothic: Problems of Disjunction in an Eighteenth-Century Literary Form*. Oxford: Clarendon Press, 1987.

Noye, William. *The Compleat Lawyer*. London: John Amery, 1674.

Parr, James A. *Don Quixote: An Anatomy of Subversive Discourse*. Newark, Del.: Juan de la Cuesta, 1988.

Paulson, Ronald. "The Pilgrimage and the Family: Structure in the Novels of Fielding and Smollett." In *Tobias Smollett: Bicentenary Essays to Lewis Knapp*, edited by G. S. Rousseau and P.-G. Boucé, 57–78. New York: Oxford University Press, 1971.

———. *Satire and the Novel in Eighteenth-Century England*. New Haven and London: Yale University Press, 1967.

Pawl, Amy J. "'And What Other Name May I Claim?': Names and Their Owners in Frances Burney's *Evelina*." *Eighteenth-Century Fiction* 3 (1991): 283–99.

Peacham, Henry. *The Garden of Eloquence*. London: R. F. and H. Jackson, 1593.

Plato. *Euthyphro, Apology, Crito, Phaedo, Phaedrus*. (Loeb Classical Library, 36.) Translated by Harold N. Fowler. Cambridge, Mass.: Harvard University Press, 1914.

———. *Laches, Protagoras, Meno, Euthydemus*. (Loeb Classical Library, 165.) Translated by W. R. M. Lamb. Cambridge, Mass.: Harvard University Press, 1924.

Poovey, Mary. "Journeys From This World to the Next: The Providential Promise in *Clarissa* and *Tom Jones*." *ELH* 43 (1976): 300–315.

Putney, Rufus D. "The Plan of *Peregrine Pickle*." *PMLA* 60 (1945): 1051–65.

Quay, Eugene R. "Justifiable Abortion—Medical and Legal Foundations—Part II." *The Georgetown Law Journal* 49 (1961): 395–538.

Radcliffe, Ann. *The Mysteries of Udolpho*. Edited by Bonamy Dobrée. London: Oxford University Press, 1966.

Ragland-Sullivan, Ellie. *Jacques Lacan and the Philosophy of Psychoanalysis*. Urbana and Chicago: University of Illinois Press, 1987.

Rawson, C. J. *Henry Fielding and the Augustan Ideal Under Stress*. London: Routledge and Kegan Paul, 1972.

Read, Malcom K. *Juan Huarte de San Juan*. Boston: G. K Hall, 1981.

Richardson, Samuel. *Clarissa or The History of a Young Lady*. Edited by Angus Ross. Harmondsworth, England: Penguin Books, 1985.

———. *Pamela or Virtue Rewarded*. Edited by Peter Sabor. New York: Penguin Books, 1980.

Richetti, John. "The Old Order and New Novel of the Mid-Eighteenth Century." *Eighteenth-Century Fiction* 2 (1990): 183–96.

———. "Reply to David Richter: Ideology and Literary Form in Fielding's *Tom Jones*." *The Eighteenth Century: Theory and Interpretation* 37 (1996): 205–17.

Richter, David. "The Closing of Masterpiece Theatre: Henry Fielding and the Valorization of Incoherence. *Eighteenth Century Theory and Interpretation* 37 (1996): 195–204.

Sauer, R. "Infanticide and Abortion in Nineteenth-Century Britain." *Population Studies* 32 (1978): 81–93.

Schroeder, Maurice Z. "The Novel as Genre." *Massachusetts Review* 4 (1963): 291–308.

Scott, Joan Wallach. *Gender and the Politics of History*. New York: Columbia University Press, 1988.

Seccombe, Thomas. "John Ozell." In *Dictionary of National Biography*, edited by Sir Leslie Stephen and Sir Sidney Lee, 15:19–20. London: Humphrey Milford, 1917.

Shawcross, John. *Milton and Influence: Presence in Literature, History, and Culture.* Pittsburgh: Duquesne University Press, 1991.

Sheridan, Frances. *The Memoirs of Miss Sidney Biddulph.* Edited by Patricia Koster and Jean Coates Cleary. Oxford and New York: Oxford University Press, 1995.

Smith, Richard M. "Some issues concerning families and property in rural England, 1250–1800." In *Land, Kinship, and Life-Cycle,* edited by Richard M. Smith, 1–86. Cambridge: Cambridge University Press, 1984.

Smollett, Tobias. *Humphry Clinker.* Edited by Thomas R. Preston. Athens: University of Georgia Press, 1990.

———. *The Life and Adventures of Sir Launcelot Greaves.* Edited by Peter Wagner. London: Penguin Books, 1988.

———. *Roderick Randon.* Edited by Paul-Gabriel Boucé. Oxford: Oxford University Press, 1979.

Smollett, Tobias et. al. *The Critical Review.* Vol. 7. London: A. Hamilton, 1759; Vol. 9. London: A. Hamilton, 1761.

Soufas, Teresa Scott. *Melancholy and the Secular Mind in Spanish Golden Age Literature.* Columbia: University of Missouri Press, 1990.

South, Robert. *Sermons Preached Upon Several Occasions.* Oxford: The Clarendon Press, 1823.

Spacks, Patricia Meyer. *Desire and Truth: Functions of Plot in Eighteenth-Century Novels.* Chicago and London: University of Chicago Press, 1990.

———. *Imagining a Self: Autobiography and Novel in Eighteenth-Century England.* Cambridge, Mass.: Harvard University Press, 1976.

Spencer, Jane. Introduction to *A Simple Story* by Elizabeth Inchbald, edited by J. M. S. Tompkins, vi–xx. Oxford and New York: Oxford University Press, 1988.

Spilka, Mark. "Comic Resolution in Fielding's *Joseph Andrews.*" *College English* 15 (1953): 11–19.

Starr, George A. *Defoe and Casuistry.* Princeton, N.J.: Princeton University Press, 1971.

———. *Defoe and Spiritual Autobiography.* Princeton, N.J.: Princeton University Press, 1965.

Staves, Susan. *Married Women's Separate Property in England, 1660–1833.* Cambridge and London: Harvard University Press, 1990.

Stendhal (Marie-Henri Beyle). *Le Rouge et le Noir.* Vol. 1 of *Romans et Nouvelles de Stendhal,* edited by Henri Martineau. Paris: Editions Gallimard, 1952.

Sterne, Laurence. *The Life and Opinions of Tristram Shandy, Gentleman.* 3 vols. Gainesville: University of Florida Press, 1978.

Stone, Lawrence. *The Family, Sex and Marriage in England, 1500–1800.* (Abridged Edition.) New York: Harper and Row, 1979.

——— and Jeanne C. Fawtier. *An Open Elite? England 1540–1880.* Oxford: Clarendon Press, 1984.

Stuber, Florian. "Introduction." In *Clarissa,* 1:1–43. New York: AMS Press, 1990.

Thornbury, Ethel Margaret. *Henry Fielding's Theory of the Comic Prose Epic.* Madison: University of Wisconsin Press, 1931.

Townsend, Peter, ed. *Burke's Peerage.* 99th ed. London: D. Guinness, 1950.

Trilling, Lionel. *The Liberal Imagination*. Garden City, N.Y.: Doubleday, 1957.

Twitchell, James B. *Forbidden Partners: The Incest Taboo in Modern Culture*. New York: Columbia University Press, 1987.

Ty, Eleanor. *Unsex'd Revolutionaries: Five Women Novelists of the 1790s*. Toronto: University of Toronto Press, 1993.

Van Boheemen, Christine. *The Novel as Family Romance: Language, Gender, and Authority from Fielding to Joyce*. Ithaca and London: Cornell University Press, 1987.

Van Marter, Shirley. "Richardson's Revisions of *Clarissa* in the second Edition." *Studies in Bibliography* 26 (1973): 107–32.

———. "Richardson's Revisions of *Clarissa* in the third and fourth Editions." *Studies in Bibliography* 28 (1975): 119–52.

Warner, William Beatty. *Reading "Clarissa": The Struggles of Interpretation*. New Haven: Yale University Press, 1979.

Watt, Ian. *The Rise of the Novel*. Berkeley and Los Angeles: University of California Press, 1957.

Wilt, Judith. "'He Could Go No Farther': A Modest Proposal About Lovelace and Clarissa." *PMLA* 92 (1977): 19–32.

Woolf, Virginia. "Defoe." In *The Common Reader*. 1st sers. New York: Harcourt, Brace and World, 1925.

Wrigley, E. A., and Paul Schofield. *The Population History of England, 1541–1981: A Reconstruction*. Cambridge, Mass.: Harvard Univerity Press, 1981.

Yoder, Paul. "Clarissa Regained: Richardson's Redemption of Eve." *Eighteenth-Century Life* 13 (1989): 87–99.

Zirker, Malvin R. General introduction to *An Enquiry into the Causes of the Late Increase of Robbers and Related Writings* by Henry Fielding, edited by Malvin R. Zirker. Middletown, Conn.: Wesleyan University Press, 1988: ix–cxiv.

Zomchick, John P. *Family and the law in eighteenth-century fiction: The public conscience in the private sphere*. Cambridge: Cambridge University Press, 1993.

Index